Christmas, 1981

Dear Carol, Gerry, Gre[...]
    To a friendship [...]es
to grow; and memories we shall
always cherish - May the Peace and
Joy of Christmas be with you
throughout the years

All our love -

Tom, Miriam
Jennie & Jon -
& Snowflake

THE
GREEN THUMB
COOKBOOK

THE GREEN THUMB COOKBOOK

by the editors of Organic Gardening and Farming®

edited by Anne Moyer

Book and jacket design by Terri Lepley
Photographs by the Rodale Press Photo Department
Illustrations by H. Bruce Halpin

® **Rodale Press,** Emmaus PA

Printed on recycled paper

Library of Congress Cataloging in Publication Data
Main entry under title:
The Green thumb cookbook.
   Includes index.
   1.   Cookery (Vegetables)   I.   Moyer, Anne.
II.   Organic gardening and farming.
TX801.G72   641.6'5   77-1745

ISBN 0-87857-168-X   hardcover

6   8   10   9   7   5   hardcover

Contents

CONTENTS

CONTENTS

Acknowledgments

My thanks to all the many people who gave of their time and talents to test and submit recipes, and special thanks to the following:

—*Organic Gardening and Farming*® contributors Bonnie Fisher, Lynn Jankowiak, Carole Shoemaker and Ruth Tirrell, and also Sara Bell, Anna Gordon and Page Cullen for their many recipes;
—Faye Martin and Yvonne Molloy for their tireless testing, suggesting and creating;
—Carole Turko for her editorial help;
—the Rodale Press Photo Department: T. L. Gettings, Robert Griffith, John Hamel, Margaret Smyser, Laura Hendry and Dennis Gillette;
—Cinruss of Allentown and the Colonial Gift Shoppe of Emmaus for supplying the props used in the photos.

—A.M.

Preface

The family garden has again become an American institution. During the warm summer months, almost everybody, it seems, is spending some of their spare time outdoors; planting, mulching, weeding, watering, and at last, harvesting their own fresh vegetables. For the small town or country dweller the garden can mean digging up a corner of the backyard, or even tilling an acre or two for a truck patch. For the urbanite, the summer garden might consist of just a couple of tomato plants growing in pots on the terrace. But no matter how large or how small, there's something about working the earth, nurturing a food-producing plant and eating food grown with your own hands that instills a deep sense of well-being and satisfaction. When the first young peas are picked or the first juicy red tomato is brought in from the vine, the gardener experiences a feeling of accomplishment that is too often denied to us in this fast-paced, mass-produced world of ours. Perhaps this is the reason for the resurgence of family gardening.

Of course the quality of homegrown, fresh-picked vegetables is beyond comparison. Firm, crisp snap beans and succulent young beets fresh from the garden bear little resemblance to the limp, pale beans and large, thick-skinned beets displayed in supermarket bins.

This book was written especially for all the backyard gardeners who appreciate the very special goodness of vegetables lovingly grown and picked at their peak. Vegetables you've taken the time to grow yourself deserve the same care after you bring them into the house that they had in the garden. The recipes and suggestions in this book will help you to treat your home-grown vegetables with respect, to preserve their special quality at every step of the way from garden to table.

We've collected these recipes and tips from the kitchens of gardeners far and wide. Since American gardeners are becoming more sophisticated these days, we've included many unusual vegetables that are ignored by most cookbooks, but are found in gardens nonetheless, because of their special flavors and ease of cultivation and storage. All of the recipes use natural ingredients, because we believe it would be a crime to hide your fresh, organically grown vegetables under a blanket of artificial flavors and colors, manufactured foods, and chemical preservatives. You'll find a variety of dishes for each vegetable—salads, soups, side dishes, main dishes, and even desserts. There are also many different approaches—homespun family favorites, ethnic and regional specialties, simple, straightforward treatments, and elegant gourmet classics. Many of the recipes were created especially for this book, and we hope that reading and using them will inspire your creativity, too.

Introduction

These opening pages are devoted to a general discussion of the best ways to harvest, store, and cook your fresh vegetables. More detailed suggestions which apply to the harvesting, handling and preparation of specific vegetables, as well as nutritional information, appear in the beginning of each section of recipes.

HARVESTING YOUR FRESH VEGETABLES

The vegetables found in supermarkets are harvested for ease of shipping and storage rather than for optimum quality. Some varieties, such as tomatoes, are picked green and ripened artificially. Others, such as beets and turnips, are harvested when they attain their largest size. This kind of produce just can't compare in quality with vegetables harvested in their prime. As a rule, vegetables reach their peak flavor and nutritional value when they are still young and tender. As vegetables grow older, and larger, their quality begins to deteriorate. Of course, there are exceptions to every rule. Winter squash is one vegetable which must be allowed to fully mature—if picked too early, winter squash bears an uncanny resemblance to cardboard. But generally speaking, biggest does not always mean best in terms of vegetables. Young peas and corn, for example, contain natural sugars that lend a touch of sweetness to their flavor. However, as these vegetables age, their sugars gradually turn to starch, and the taste suffers accordingly. Snap beans are at their best when the pods are tender and fleshy; when the beans inside the pods mature and turn plump, the pods become stringy and tough. Summer squash are tenderest when they are still small and their skins are soft. Leafy vegetables are crisp when young, but grow fibrous and tough with age. Root crops, too, are generally of better quality if harvested when they are still rather small. Large beets and turnips tend to toughen and lose flavor; carrots and parsnips sometimes develop woody cores. Watch your vegetables carefully as the season progresses to be sure and catch them at their peak harvesttime. You can peek and estimate the size of root vegetables by pushing away some soil from around their tops.

One way to make it easier to keep up with your vegetable harvest is to take advantage of succession planting techniques. This approach will give you two or three smaller, more manageable crops of perishable vegetables like tomatoes, peas, and beans, instead of one larger crop. Smaller harvests won't overwhelm you with canning and preserving chores, and will enable you to pick all your vegetables as they reach their prime, and to serve more of them fresh. Staggered planting also means you can plan for vegetables such as cabbage and Brussels sprouts, which are best when harvested late in the season, to be just the right size for picking when summer comes to a close.

STORING THE HARVEST

Veteran gardeners all seem to agree that in most cases, the best time to pick vegetables is early in the morning, while the dew is still on them. Harvesting in the morning is supposed to catch the vegetables at their very freshest, with an extra crispness imparted by cool nighttime temperatures. This does not mean rising at the crack of dawn to pick a basketful of broccoli or tomatoes, only to leave it on the porch while you go off to work. Whether or not you harvest your vegetables in the morning, the important thing to remember is to eat or store them right away. Allowing fresh vegetables to sit around neglected for more than a few minutes wreaks havoc with moisture and vitamin content—greens start to wilt, beans go limp, carrots dry out, and peppers lose their crunch. More important, vitamin depletion begins with exposure to air. So, as soon as the vegetables are off the vine, you've got to decide what to do with them.

As a rule, it pays to set aside your finest quality produce for storage—it will "keep" lots better than damaged vegetables. Eat during the season or can for future use anything that is marked or blemished. Perishable vegetables, such as beans, tomatoes, peppers, greens, broccoli, and cauliflower should go right into the refrigerator, unwashed. For the most part, it's best to keep them in airtight containers until you are ready to use them.

Vegetables that are considered "good keepers"—root crops, cabbages, celery, onions, pumpkins, and winter squashes—can often be kept fresh for several weeks or even all through the winter if they are properly stored. Some vegetables, such as parsnips, leeks, salsify, and Jerusalem artichokes, can be left right in the ground in areas where the winters aren't too severe. A good layer of mulch makes it easier to dig them out of frozen ground.

Although a variety of vegetables will hold up well during long-term storage, they won't all thrive under the same conditions. Basically, sweet potatoes, pumpkins, and winter squash keep best in a warm, but not hot (about 50° to 60°F.) and dry environment, such as an unheated basement or an attic. Onions and garlic prefer a cold (about 35°F.), dry climate. Root crops like turnips and beets, the cabbage family, and celery all need to be stored where it's cold, but not freezing (about 35° to 40°F.), and moist. A root cellar, of course, is ideal for this kind of storage. Few people have root cellars these days, but there are several other ways to produce the right conditions for storing root crops.

One method is to place the vegetables in a two-foot-deep hole in the ground, which has been provided with drainage and lined with leaves and straw. The hole is covered with several inches of soil and a thick layer of mulch. You can also use a cold frame to cover a storage mound. The cold frame is filled with root vegetables packed in leaves or straw. The sides and top of the frame protect the stored vegetables from both wandering animals and harsh winter weather.

Ordinary wooden barrels also make good storage containers for root crops. The barrels can be kept in the garage, a cold spot in the basement, or on the back porch.

HANDLING AND PREPARING VEGETABLES

Becoming an expert vegetable cook does not necessarily mean having a repertoire of elaborate dishes. But it does mean knowing how to prepare vegetables that taste good, look good and are high in nutritional value as well. In other words, you'll want to preserve each vegetable's garden-fresh quality to the highest degree possible. Proper cooking techniques are important, as we'll see shortly, but expert vegetable preparation begins before cooking.

First of all, it is helpful to be aware of the nutritional value of vegetables, and of the kinds of handling techniques that preserve the most nutrients intact. The chief contribution vegetables make to our diets, in addition to providing fiber, is supplying assorted vitamins and minerals. These nutrients are substantially reduced by the wrong handling techniques. Vitamin depletion begins with exposure to light and air (vitamin C is lost this way), so it is best to store vegetables in a dark place. Remember, too, that the more cut surfaces there are, the greater is the chance for vitamin depletion. When you do chop or slice your vegetables for cooking, do so when you're ready to cook them, not an hour ahead of time. In addition, it is important to cut vegetables all the same size so they cook evenly. And why not try different shapes as well? The way vegetables are cut can add greatly to their appeal, especially where children are concerned. Vegetables can be sliced diagonally as for stir-fry dishes, diced, cut in cubes, or sliced in long, thin julienne strips.

Nutrient losses from cut vegetables increase with exposure to water, and become even more severe in the presence of heat. Vitamin C and the B vitamins are water-soluble, and leach out into soaking or cooking water, along with important minerals. For this reason, vegetables should not be soaked before cooking, except in a few special cases, and should be cooked in the smallest amount of water possible. Vegetables containing a great deal of moisture of their own, such as greens, tomatoes, cucumbers, zucchini, chard, spinach, celery, and cabbage, can be cooked in just the water that clings to them after washing. Since heat also increases nutrient loss, vegetables should be cooked for as short a time as possible, until they are just tender—still firm and at their brightest color. It only takes a few minutes to cook most vegetables to the right stage of tenderness. Overcooking results in drastic vitamin and mineral depletion, as well as in a mushy, unappealing dish. Perhaps the best way to avoid the problems of overcooking is simply to eat more raw vegetables. Be creative with salads, and for a tempting *hors d'oeuvre,* try serving assorted raw vegetables with a tangy dip to whet the family's appetite before dinner.

In many vegetables, nutrients are concentrated in the skin or just below the skin. Peeling strips away this rich layer of nutrients, so by all means leave vegetables unpeeled when you can. If you grow your own produce organically, you can eat the skins without fear of ingesting pesticide residues. Peels are a good source of fiber, too. Many times, peeling vegetables is more a matter of habit than necessity, especially when you're working with young, tender produce. A tough skin is many times characteristic of an older vegetable. Carrots, cucumbers, tomatoes, summer squash, and eggplant can all be cooked and eaten with skins intact if picked before they get too large. Potatoes, too, can be cooked and served in their jackets for most recipes.

The best cooking methods for vegetables are those which have a high initial heat, prevent contact with oxygen, are of a short duration, and conserve cooking liquid.

Vegetables contain enzymes whose activity in the presence of light and air is the agent responsible for the destruction of vitamin C we discussed earlier. Chilling inactivates these enzymes and rapid heating destroys them, so vegetables should go quickly from the refrigerator to a waiting hot pan or oven for maximum vitamin conservation.

If vegetables are kept in contact with oxygen during cooking, vitamin C loss is quite rapid. This can be avoided by coating the cut surfaces with oil (sautéing), replacing the oxygen in the pan with steam (steaming), or by leaving the vegetables unpeeled.

The liquid in which vegetables are cooked contains part of the vitamins and minerals, and should never be thrown out. Even the water from steaming vegetables is valuable. If you aren't serving it with the vegetables or as the liquid in a sauce that accompanies the meal, be sure to save the liquid for later use in soups and sauces. Besides adding nutrients, this vegetable stock will impart a mellowness to the seasoning of any dish.

The most desirable methods of vegetable cookery, then, are steaming, sautéing and stir-frying. Baking and broiling are also good techniques if properly employed.

Steaming, as we said before, is desirable because the air in the pan is replaced by steam, thus reducing vitamin loss. Also, steam is hotter than boiling water due to the energy expended to turn the water into vapor, so food cooks more quickly, another plus. Because vegetables contain a great deal of water, they can be placed in a covered pan with only the water that clings to them after washing, or in the case of denser vegetables, with just a few additional tablespoons of water to create steam, and then cooked in their own juices. Or, the vegetables can be put in a bamboo or metal steaming basket and steamed over boiling water in a covered pot. For added flavor, a sliver of garlic or a slice of onion may be put into the water, and its essence will gently permeate the vegetables.

When vegetables are sautéed, the coating of oil does double duty, sealing in flavor and natural juices, and sealing out air to preserve vitamin content. Only a small amount of oil is needed to sauté—a tablespoon or two is enough for four and sometimes five servings of vegetables. Choosing among the more strongly flavored kinds of oil, such as corn, peanut, soy, and sesame, for sautéing vegetables, will lend a more distinctive taste to the dish.

The stir-fry technique is based on the same principle as sautéing, but is done over higher heat for a shorter period of time. In a *wok* or a large, heavy skillet, vegetables are tossed quickly about in a small amount of oil. Because a fairly high heat is used, the vegetables cook quickly, often in two to three minutes. Usually a combination of vegetables is stir-fried, with the various vegetables being added to the pan at one-minute intervals, beginning with the hardest, such as onions, and ending with those which cook fastest, such as greens or sprouts.

Baking and broiling are other good ways to save nutrients if the vegetables are put into a preheated oven. You can bake vegetables in their skins, like potatoes, in broths or sauces, or in their own juices in a covered casserole. Squashes, eggplant, and tomatoes are especially good broiled. Brushing the cut surfaces with oil preserves nutrients and keeps the vegetables firm and moist. Grated cheese, wheat germ or bread crumbs become a crunchy topping when broiled with vegetables.

To conclude this section, here are just a few miscellaneous suggestions for cooking better vegetables. First of all, plan your vegetable preparation so the vegetables are ready right at serving time. Never cook your vegetables ahead of time and then reheat them. Reheating is a good way to turn beautiful crisp vegetables into grey mush. Instead of reheating leftover vegetables, serve them cold in a salad or use them in soup.

Adding baking soda to the cooking water to keep green vegetables green is an old restaurant trick. Don't fall for it—baking soda makes vegetables mushy and destroys vitamin A, B vitamins, and minerals.

When cooking home-frozen vegetables, cook them while they are still frozen. If you let them thaw first, they lose nutrients and tend to turn watery.

Finally, if you wish to salt your vegetables, do so after cooking rather than before, as salt draws out natural juices. Now, on to the vegetables.

Artichoke Bottoms Florentine, Page 6

Asparagus, Carrots, and Pineapple, Page 16

Swiss Green Beans,
Page 27

Beets in Savory Yogurt Sauce,
Page 38

Vegetables Normandy,
Page 46

Beef-Vegetable Borsch,
Page 60

Danish Sweet and Sour Cabbage,
Page 64

French-Style Carrots,
Page 70

Red, White, and Green Salad,
Page 78

Cool Summer Salad, Page 108

Mushroom and Watercress Salad,
Page 131

hef Salad Deluxe,
ge 122

Kohlrabi Salad,
Page 135

Okra Pilaf, Page 153

French Leeks,
Page 162

Onions Au Gratin,
Page 161

Parsnip Fiesta Salad,
Page 170

Salad-Stuffed Peppers,
Page 183

Potato-Scallion Soup,
Page 193

Potatoes in Pepper Boats,
Page 189

Cranberry Candied Sweet Potatoes,
Page 198

Rhubarb Bread,
Page 208

Soybean Salad, Page 219

Curried Turkey and Sprouts, Page 230

Summer Squash with Tomatoes and Corn, Page 244

Yellow Squash in Sour Cream Sauce, Page 241

Orange-Baked Squash,
Page 258

Baked Spinach-Topped Tomatoes,
Page 270

Artichokes

These members of the thistle family have been popular in European kitchens since the days of the ancient Romans, and were first cultivated along the shores of the Mediterranean, in Italy. Today, one of the prime artichoke-producing areas in the world is found in northern California's coastal region.

Artichokes are actually flower buds, and must be picked while the heads are still compact and tightly closed, and bright green in color. If allowed to open fully, artichokes turn into large, striking-looking purple thistles. One thing to remember about harvesting artichokes is that they won't all be the same size. Some will be ready to pick when still fairly small; others will grow much larger before they are fully mature.

The best way to harvest artichokes is to cut the stem about an inch and a half below the base of the head, leaving a bit of stem attached. Artichokes can be cut as they mature throughout the season, until you notice that the stem looks like it is beginning to fold up. This signals the end of the harvest season. If you cut off the stem at its base, new shoots will grow from the base next season. Given this kind of care, artichokes will usually produce for about four years.

Don't wash your artichokes until you are ready to use them. After picking, you can store them in a plastic bag in the refrigerator for up to four

days. For long-term storage, artichoke hearts (which have had their leaves and fuzzy centers removed) are sometimes frozen or canned in a brine solution.

HOW TO PREPARE ARTICHOKES FOR COOKING

For best results, artichokes should be prepared for cooking in the following manner. Place the artichoke on its side on a cutting board. Slice off the stem to make the bottom surface flat. Next, cut off about an inch of the top leaves. Cut off the tips of the remaining outer leaves with kitchen shears, and rub all the cut places, including the bottom, with a piece of lemon so they don't turn brown (artichokes discolor very quickly). As the artichokes are prepared, put them into a large bowl filled with water to which a few table-spoons of vinegar or the juice of half a lemon have been added.

Open the center of each artichoke with your fingers, pushing the leaves apart. To push it further open, turn it upside down on the counter or cutting board and press on the bottom with both hands. Remove the fuzzy "choke" from the center with a spoon or melon ball cutter. When all the artichokes have been prepared in this manner, take them out of the water and drain them thoroughly. They are now ready for stuffing or cooking.

The part of the artichoke that remains after all the leaves and the choke have been removed is called the artichoke heart, or bottom, and is often served by itself. It has a cavity that handily holds various stuffings or sauces. To prepare artichoke hearts, cook artichokes until tender (about 20 minutes, although cooking time varies with size), pull off all the leaves and remove the chokes. Trim the bottoms to make them smooth and neat. They are now ready to be stuffed.

HOW TO EAT AN ARTICHOKE

When whole artichokes are served, begin by pulling off the leaves with your fingers one at a time, and eat only the light green bit at the base of each leaf. This is best accomplished by simply pulling the leaf through your teeth. The rest of the leaf is discarded. When all the leaves are gone, cut the heart into pieces and eat it with a fork. Artichokes are usually served with a sauce

for dipping. Lemon butter, mayonnaise, and hollandaise and vinaigrette sauces are all popular dips for artichokes. See the Accompaniments chapter for recipes.

Artichokes are noted for being low in calories, and they also contain modest amounts of vitamins A, B and C, and assorted minerals. Plan one average- to large-sized artichoke for each serving.

STUFFED ARTICHOKES

Preheat oven to 350°F.

4 artichokes

STUFFING:
 3 to 4 mushrooms, chopped
 3 tablespoons olive oil
 ¾ cup whole wheat bread crumbs
 ¼ cup wheat germ
 4 green olives, minced
 3 tablespoons chopped parsley
  salt and pepper to taste

1. Prepare the artichokes for stuffing as directed on page 2.
2. Next, prepare the stuffing:
   Sauté mushrooms in oil until just tender. Add bread crumbs, wheat germ, olives and seasonings; mix thoroughly.
3. Gently spread open the leaves of each artichoke, spoon stuffing into the center, and push back the leaves.
4. Set artichokes upright in an oiled casserole, brush with a little more oil, and cover.
5. Bake at 350°F. for 20 minutes. Remove cover and bake for another 15 to 20 minutes, or until artichokes are tender.

Makes 4 servings

ARTICHOKES WITH SAVORY SAUCE

4 large artichokes
4 to 6 cups stock or seasoned water

SAUCE:
½ cup butter
2 tablespoons olive oil
2 tablespoons lemon juice
2 teaspoons tarragon leaves

1. Prepare artichokes as directed on page 2. Wash them thoroughly and set upright in a large saucepan which has a tight-fitting lid. Add enough stock or water to reach halfway up the sides of the artichokes. Cover, bring to a boil, and simmer for about 20 minutes, or until the artichoke bases are tender.
2. Meanwhile, prepare sauce:
Melt butter and oil. Add lemon juice and tarragon and heat thoroughly.
3. Place one artichoke and a small dish of sauce on each plate. Serve immediately.

Makes 4 servings

● *When you are preparing artichoke hearts, save the young, inner leaves that you cut off, and use them in salads.*

ARTICHOKE TEMPURA

8 artichoke hearts (prepared as directed on page 2)
water, enough to make batter the consistency of heavy cream
peanut oil
½ to 1 cup whole wheat pastry flour
¼ teaspoon salt

1. Cut artichoke hearts into 12 pieces (pie-wedge fashion).
2. Combine flour, salt and water to make a thin batter.
3. Dip artichoke pieces into batter and fry in oil at 350°F. until nicely browned. Drain and serve immediately.

Makes 4 servings

ARTICHOKE SAUCE

4 artichokes
   oil for sautéing
1 small onion, chopped
1 clove garlic, minced
1 cup chopped fresh tomatoes
1 tablespoon chopped fresh parsley
1 teaspoon chopped fresh basil
   salt and pepper to taste

1. Prepare artichokes for cooking; remove leaves and chokes to leave hearts. Slice hearts.
2. Heat oil in a saucepan, add onion and garlic, and cook until clear. Add sliced artichoke hearts and toss lightly.
3. Add tomatoes and seasonings, cover and simmer slowly for about 45 minutes, until artichokes are tender and flavors are blended.
4. Serve over a bed of brown rice or noodles. This sauce is also good served over veal slices.

Makes 4 servings

Note: If you prefer a smoother texture, puree the sauce in a blender before serving.

ARTICHOKE BOTTOMS FLORENTINE

Preheat oven to 400°F.

6 artichokes
1 pound fresh spinach
1 tablespoon oil or butter
   salt and pepper to taste
⅛ teaspoon nutmeg

CREAM SAUCE:
   1 tablespoon butter
   1 tablespoon whole wheat flour
   ⅔ cup milk
     salt and pepper to taste
   pinch of nutmeg
   yolk of one small egg
   6 teaspoons grated cheese

1. Prepare artichoke bottoms, or hearts, as directed on page 2.
2. Wash and drain the spinach, discarding tough stems. Steam briefly, just until wilted and tender. Drain and chop the spinach.
3. Heat oil in a skillet and add the spinach, salt, pepper, and nutmeg. Stir constantly until heated through. Spoon the spinach into the artichoke bottoms.
4. Prepare sauce:
   Melt butter in a saucepan, then blend in flour to make a *roux*. Add the milk, seasonings, and egg yolk, and cook over low heat, stirring, until thickened.
5. Pour sauce over the filled artichoke bottoms and sprinkle each with a teaspoon of grated cheese. Bake about 10 minutes, until cheese is melted.

Makes 6 servings

ARTICHOKE HEARTS MORNAY

Preheat oven to 375°F.

4 large fresh artichokes

MORNAY SAUCE:
>   2 tablespoons butter
>   2 tablespoons whole wheat flour
>   ½ cup chicken broth
>   ½ cup milk
>   ½ cup Swiss cheese, grated
>   1 tablespoon sherry, optional
>   ¼ teaspoon salt
>   dash of freshly ground pepper

1. Cook artichokes in boiling water to cover, about 30 minutes or until tender. Drain and prepare artichoke hearts as directed on page 2.
2. Arrange artichoke hearts in bottom of an oiled, shallow casserole.
3. Meanwhile, prepare Mornay sauce:
   Melt butter in a saucepan and blend in flour to make a *roux*. Gradually stir in chicken broth and milk, and cook until thickened.
4. Add ¼ cup of the cheese, sherry if desired, and seasonings, and stir until smooth. Pour sauce over artichoke hearts, and sprinkle with remaining cheese.
5. Bake at 375°F., 15 to 20 minutes, or until cheese is melted and brown.

Makes 4 servings

● *To be sure artichokes will cook evenly, stand them upright in the pan of water. This is easy to do if you trim the stem ends to make them flat.*

Jerusalem Artichokes

Despite their name, these large, potato-like tubers are not related to the globe artichoke. The Jerusalem artichoke is actually a member of the sunflower family; its appellation is a corruption of the Italian word *girasol,* which means "turning to the sun."

Over 300 years ago, French explorers found the Indians in America growing and eating an odd kind of root that looked rather like a large, reddish peanut. The explorers took the strange root back to France, and from there it spread to England and other countries. Constant propagation and crossbreeding have improved it into the Jerusalem artichoke we know today. In Europe, this humble tuber has long served farmers as a practical, easy-to-grow stock and poultry food.

A very desirable feature of the Jerusalem artichoke is that it stores its carbohydrates in the form of inulin rather than starch, and its sugar as levulose, like many fruits do. Consequently, Jerusalem artichokes have very few calories, and are sometimes recommended as a substitute for other carbohydrates in the menus of diabetics. In addition to being low in calories, Jerusalem artichokes contain various vitamins and minerals, particularly thiamin (vitamin B_1) and potassium.

These hardy tubers offer another bonus to the gardener in that they don't need to be harvested. They may be left in the ground all winter, and dug as

needed any time after the first frost, and throughout the winter season. Actually, since their tender skin makes Jerusalem artichokes fairly perishable when stored indoors, it's really best to keep them outside. If you do bring them indoors, keep them moist until you use them, as they dry out quickly. In northern areas, the tubers need to be protected from alternate freezes and thaws with a thick layer of mulch.

After digging as many artichokes as you're ready to use, toss them into a bucket of water to loosen the dirt, then scrub them with a vegetable brush. The American strain doesn't have as many tiny cracks as the French variety, and thus is easier to clean. Peeling is usually unnecessary. If you are determined to peel your 'chokes, place them immediately in a pan of cold water to which small amounts of salt and lemon juice or vinegar have been added, to prevent them from turning dark.

This versatile vegetable has a multitude of uses in the kitchen. You can do practically anything to Jerusalem artichokes that you do to potatoes—try them baked, broiled, mashed, juiced, or sautéed. Or, grind them to a pulp and add them to meat loaf or vegetable loaves. One pound of Jerusalem artichokes will make four servings.

SAUCY ARTICHOKES

2 to 3 pounds Jerusalem artichokes, scrubbed
3 tablespoons butter, melted
1 tablespoon chopped parsley
1 tablespoon chopped rosemary
¼ teaspoon cayenne
   salt and pepper to taste
   Parmesan cheese, grated

1. Steam artichokes until tender, 15 to 20 minutes. Slice or cut into cubes.
2. Combine next five ingredients and pour over artichokes. Sprinkle with grated Parmesan and serve.

Makes 8 servings

HERBED JERUSALEM ARTICHOKE SALAD

12 to 15 Jerusalem artichokes, thinly sliced
1 cup oil
½ cup cider vinegar
1 onion, sliced thinly in half-circles
1 clove garlic, crushed
   dill, thyme and marjoram, to taste
   salt and pepper to taste

Combine all ingredients and mix well. Chill overnight to blend flavors.

Makes 12 servings

● *Don't overcook Jerusalem artichokes or they will become tough. If you cook them unpeeled, you can rub off the skin afterwards if you prefer a finer-textured vegetable.*

JERUSALEM ARTICHOKE COMBO

1 cup Jerusalem artichokes, scrubbed and cubed
½ cup broccoli, cut in cubes
½ cup carrots, diced
¼ cup chopped red onion
¼ cup diced green pepper

DRESSING:
   1 egg
   2 cloves garlic, slivered
   1 tablespoon fresh dill
   1 teaspoon salt
   ½ cup olive oil

1. Steam vegetables until tender. Drain and chill.
2. Prepare dressing:
   Allow egg to come to room temperature. Place egg, garlic and seasonings in blender; blend briefly on high speed. Reduce speed and gradually add olive oil while blender is running. Continue adding oil until mixture is thick.
3. Toss dressing with vegetables and serve on a bed of shredded lettuce.

Makes 4 servings

COUNTRY-STYLE 'CHOKES

1 pound Jerusalem artichokes, scrubbed
2 tablespoons butter
   thyme and rosemary to taste
   salt and pepper to taste
2 tablespoons chopped fresh parsley
3 green onions, sliced

1. Drop whole artichokes into boiling water and cook for 10 minutes, until not quite tender.
2. Drain and slice artichokes, then fry like potatoes in butter that has been seasoned with thyme, rosemary, salt and pepper.
3. When slices are just tender, garnish with parsley and green onions and serve.

Makes 4 servings

Note: This dish makes an excellent accompaniment to roast chicken. For a different presentation, pour the partially cooked artichoke mixture over the chicken during the last half hour of roasting.

GIRASOL SALAD

2 pounds Jerusalem artichokes, cleaned
2 hard-boiled eggs, chopped
½ cup thinly sliced green onions
    salt and pepper to taste
1 tablespoon chopped parsley
½ teaspoon paprika

1. Drop whole artichokes into boiling water and cook until just tender (15 minutes or less). Drain, cool, and slice them.
2. Add chopped eggs, sliced onions, salt and pepper, and mix with your favorite salad dressing. Chill; garnish with chopped parsley and paprika, and serve.

Makes 6 servings

Note: Some recipes for making your own fresh salad dressings appear in the Accompaniments chapter.

PICKLED JERUSALEM ARTICHOKES

2 quarts apple cider vinegar
¼ cup honey
2 tablespoons celery seed
1 tablespoon chopped fresh dill
¼ cup mustard seed (white is preferred)
2 tablespoons dry mustard
¼ cup salt
2 whole peppercorns
4 to 6 pieces of ginger root (according to taste)
4 pounds Jerusalem artichokes

1. Bring vinegar to a boil, remove from stove, and add remaining ingredients, except for artichokes.
2. While pickling mixture cools, scrub artichokes and slice them into thin rounds. Pack the slices into clean, sterilized pint jars, fill with cooled pickling mixture and seal.
3. Allow to ripen at least 3 weeks before using.

Makes 8 pints

GIRASOL SKILLET MEDLEY

½ pound Jerusalem artichokes, peeled and thinly sliced
1 onion, peeled and chopped
2 cloves garlic, minced
2 tablespoons oil
¼ pound mushrooms, sliced
2½ teaspoons lemon juice
½ pound spinach, washed and coarsely torn
tamari soy sauce to taste

1. Sauté artichokes, onion and garlic in oil until barely tender, about 5 to 8 minutes. Add mushrooms and sauté until almost tender.
2. Stir in lemon juice. Add spinach and continue to cook until spinach is wilted, 3 to 5 minutes. Season with soy sauce and serve at once.

Makes 6 servings

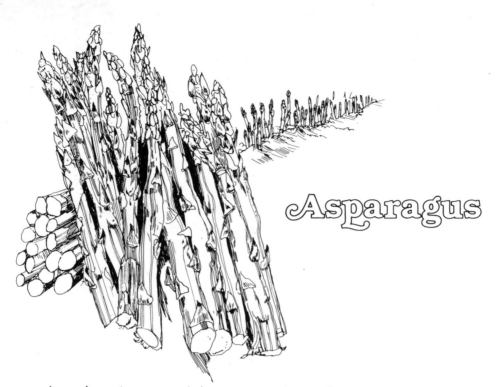

Asparagus

In early spring, one of the greatest pleasures for the home gardener is the harvest of the first tender spears of asparagus. These delicate shoots have been the herald of spring since ancient times, when the Persians gave it the name of *asparag,* meaning sprout. Until modern times, asparagus was grown primarily as a medicinal plant. But like many other medicinal plants, it has turned into a garden favorite.

Among the most economical of vegetables from the gardener's point of view (but not necessarily the shopper's), asparagus is a perennial which comes up year after year. It can be harvested in the third year after planting, when the spears are six to eight inches above the ground, and the tips are still compact. Although asparagus is often cut, it's better to snap off the stalks at ground level to avoid injuring the other shoots below. Nicely rounded stalks are generally of better quality than flatter ones, which tend to be stringy and tough.

After harvesting, asparagus may be kept in the refrigerator in an airtight container (such as a plastic bag) or vegetable crisper for up to four days. But by all means, try to use it as soon as possible.

Asparagus is a rather perishable food, and cannot be stored for extended periods. The best method of preserving is to freeze it.

To prepare asparagus for cooking, break the stalks as far down as they snap easily and discard the tough ends. Wash thoroughly, taking care to rinse away any silt that may be trapped in the heads.

Because the tips cook more quickly than the stalks, asparagus should be cooked standing upright so that the spears cook evenly. Tie the spears in a bunch, just tightly enough to keep them from falling over. If you tie them too tightly, the string will cut into the spears as they cook. There are special tall, narrow pots made for steaming asparagus, but a double boiler will work just fine. Stand the asparagus in the bottom half, along with a small amount of water, and invert the top half over it. The asparagus will cook in 8 to 12 minutes, depending on how large it is. When you're working with spears that are especially large and tough, some cooks recommend putting enough water in the pot to cover the stems but not the tips, so that the stalks boil while the tips steam.

Asparagus is rich in vitamins A and C, calcium, phosphorus, and potassium, and contains appreciable amounts of iron. You'll need about 2 pounds of asparagus for four servings.

CREAM OF ASPARAGUS SOUP

2 pounds fresh asparagus
3 tablespoons butter
3 tablespoons whole wheat flour
3 cups nonfat milk
   salt to taste

1. Since the asparagus is blended, only the very end need be cut off. Cut asparagus into 2-inch pieces and cook in boiling water to cover until tender. Do not drain asparagus. Instead, place in blender and puree.
2. Melt butter in saucepan, then stir in flour to make a *roux*. Gradually add milk to prepare a white sauce. Cook, stirring, until slightly thickened.
3. Add asparagus puree and simmer 5 minutes, stirring occasionally. Add salt before serving.

Makes 6 servings

ASPARAGUS LOAF

Preheat oven to 375° F.

1 cup whole grain bread cubes
4 tablespoons butter
1 tablespoon chopped parsley
1 teaspoon finely grated onion
½ teaspoon salt
2 eggs
2 cups hot nonfat milk
4 cups asparagus, cut into 1-inch lengths

1. Sauté bread cubes in butter with parsley, onion and salt for 5 minutes.
2. Beat eggs slightly; add a small amount of hot milk to the eggs, stirring constantly. Then blend slowly into remaining hot milk.
3. Combine with asparagus and bread cubes.
4. Bake in a buttered loaf pan approximately 5½ x 9 at 375°F. for about 30 minutes, or until set.

Makes 6 servings

● *If you ever harvest just a few stalks of asparagus on a given day at the beginning or end of the harvest season, slice them raw into a salad.*

ASPARAGUS, CARROTS AND PINEAPPLE

1 13½-ounce can pineapple chucks, packed in juice
2 cups sliced carrots
  salt and pepper to taste
½ pound asparagus, sliced into 1-inch lengths
  nutmeg for garnish

1. Drain pineapple juice into measuring cup, reserving pineapple chunks. Add enough water to juice to make 1 cup liquid; pour into medium saucepan.

2. Add carrots, salt and pepper.
3. Cook until almost tender (10 to 15 minutes). Add asparagus and cook until tender, about 5 more minutes.
4. Stir in reserved pineapple chunks and heat through. Just before serving, sprinkle with nutmeg.

Makes 8 servings

● *The French esteem asparagus so highly that they serve it as a separate course.*

MALAYSIAN ASPARAGUS

1 tablespoon tamari soy sauce
1½ teaspoons ginger, finely chopped
1 clove garlic, crushed
1 pound asparagus
2 tablespoons vegetable oil

SAUCE:
   ½ cup half-and-half or light cream
   2 teaspoons cornstarch
   ¼ teaspoon salt

1. Combine soy sauce, ginger and garlic. Mix well and let stand 30 minutes.
2. Slant-cut the asparagus into 2-inch pieces.
3. In a skillet or *wok,* heat the oil over high heat. Add the sauce and the asparagus. Stir-fry about 2 minutes, then cover and steam until asparagus is just tender.
4. Meanwhile, prepare cream sauce:
In a small bowl or cup, blend together the cream, cornstarch and salt. Heat until sauce thickens.
5. When asparagus is done, pour cream sauce over it. Serve immediately.

Makes 4 servings

BAKED ASPARAGUS

Preheat oven to 350°F.

1 pound asparagus spears
¼ cup butter, melted
1 small onion, diced
¼ cup cheddar cheese, grated
¼ cup wheat germ
1 teaspoon thyme
   salt to taste

1. Place asparagus in an oiled baking dish.
2. Pour melted butter over asparagus.
3. Combine remaining ingredients and pour over asparagus.
4. Bake at 350°F. for 45 minutes.

Makes 4 to 6 servings

● *Instead of throwing out the tough ends of asparagus which are snapped off before cooking, save them for soup.*

CHEESY BAKED ASPARAGUS AND MUSHROOMS

Preheat oven to 375°F.

2 pounds fresh asparagus
½ pound fresh mushrooms

SAUCE:
   ½ cup butter
   ½ cup flour
   1 teaspoon salt
   2 cups milk
   ¼ pound cheddar cheese, grated

1. Wash and trim fresh asparagus; arrange in 9 x 11 baking pan.
2. Wash and slice mushrooms and arrange over asparagus.
3. Prepare white sauce:
   Melt butter in small saucepan. Blend in flour, add salt, then gradually stir in milk. Cook until thickened. Pour sauce over asparagus and mushrooms.
4. Cover and bake at 375°F. for 30 minutes.
5. Uncover and sprinkle cheese over pan. Leave uncovered and bake 15 more minutes, or until cheese is brown and bubbly.

Makes 8 servings

ASPARAGUS CASSEROLE

Preheat oven to 350°F.

1½ teaspoons butter
1½ teaspoons flour
½ cup milk
   few drops hot sauce, or small amount of minced hot
     pepper
2 hard-boiled eggs, sliced
1 small onion, minced
1 cup cooked asparagus, cut in 1-inch pieces
¼ cup whole wheat bread crumbs
¼ cup wheat germ

1. Melt butter in a small, heavy skillet. Stir in flour until well blended. Add milk and hot sauce, and cook over medium heat, stirring, until thickened.
2. Fold in eggs, onion and asparagus.
3. Pour into a small buttered baking dish. Sprinkle with bread crumbs and wheat germ, which have been mixed together.
4. Bake at 350°F. for 15 minutes, or until crumbs are browned.

Makes 3 to 4 servings

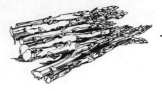

ASPARAGUS SOUFFLÉ

Preheat oven to 375°F.

3 tablespoons whole wheat flour
1 cup milk
4 eggs, separated
1 cup cooked asparagus, mashed or finely chopped
    salt and freshly ground pepper to taste
    dash of nutmeg or pinch of tarragon

1. Butter a 2-quart casserole.
2. In a medium-size saucepan, blend flour with small amount of milk until smooth. Add remaining milk. Bring to a boil and cook, stirring constantly, until thickened. Continue stirring and add egg yolks, one at a time. Bring mixture to a boil again, and stir in asparagus and seasonings. Set aside to cool.
3. Beat the egg whites until stiff and fold into the asparagus mixture. Pour into prepared casserole. Bake at 375°F. on lowest rack in oven for 30 to 40 minutes.

Makes 6 servings

Note: This recipe can be adapted to use almost any cooked vegetable. The important thing to remember is to choose seasonings that will enhance the vegetable you are substituting; anise or thyme on carrots, for instance; marjoram on mushrooms, zucchini or peas; basil with eggplant or tomatoes. Grated Parmesan or Romano cheese may be sprinkled on top.

ASPARAGUS AND EGG SALAD

1 head lettuce
2 cups asparagus, cooked and cut in pieces
3 hard-boiled eggs

DRESSING:
    ½ cup sour cream or yogurt
    2 tablespoons fresh lemon juice
    2 tablespoons chopped fresh chives
    2 tablespoons drained capers
       several olives, sliced

    parsley for garnish

1. Use the outer leaves of the lettuce to line a large salad bowl. Shred the rest of head, add the asparagus and hard-boiled eggs.
2. Prepare dressing:
   Blend sour cream or yogurt and lemon juice; add chives and capers, and mix well.
3. Pour the dressing over asparagus mixture, toss lightly, then place in lettuce-lined bowl.
4. Sprinkle with sliced olives and chopped fresh parsley and serve.

Makes 6 servings

● *If you fall behind in your asparagus harvest and allow the spears to grow quite large and old, you may find they have taken on a bitter taste. Some of this bitterness can be removed by peeling the stalks. Take a knife, and starting just below the head, slice off the outer layer, cutting slightly deeper as you go farther down the stalk. The asparagus is then cooked as usual, but it is best to serve it with a sauce or in a well-seasoned dish.*

Beans

SNAP BEANS

Beans are among the most valuable (and popular) foods we grow, because they are not only a prolific, easy-to-grow crop, but because they enrich the soil as well, by adding nitrogen to it, which other plants need in order to grow. Snap beans, one of the most familiar bean varieties to home gardeners, come in green, yellow and purple-podded varieties (the purple beans turn green when cooked). All three are very much alike and can be used in most of the same ways.

About two or three weeks after the first blossoms appear, snap beans will be ready to harvest. For best quality, pick them while they are young (three to four inches long), when the tips are soft and the beans are still small inside the pods. Watch your bean plants carefully, for a bean's peak harvesttime lasts only a few days. Snap pole beans just below the stem end, and you'll be able to pick another bean from the same spot later in the season. As long as the beans are picked, pole beans will continue producing for several weeks. Production will stop if the beans are left to mature on the plants. Bush beans yield only one harvest, so it doesn't matter where you snap the pod from the bush. If you are planning to dry your string beans to make "leather britches," allow them to dry on the stems before you pick them.

Snap beans are one vegetable whose quality noticeably suffers when they are stored. Most of the snap beans found in supermarkets were picked too old and kept too long, and as a result they are limp, tough and dry in comparison to young, freshly picked beans.

When handling string beans, remember to watch out for the brownish discoloration called rust, which the beans will develop with prolonged exposure to moisture. For this reason, it's better to pick them on a dry day than just after a heavy rain, and more desirable to refrigerate them unwashed. Although they are best when used as quickly as possible, string beans will "keep" refrigerated in a nonporous container up to five days. Beyond that point, their quality will rapidly deteriorate to the level of the limp, tough supermarket bean.

There's no snap bean like a fresh snap bean. No matter how carefully you preserve them, frozen or canned beans just don't have the crispness of fresh-picked beans. But when you have beans in abundance, blanching and freezing is the most desirable way to preserve them, although they may also be canned or dried.

To prepare string beans for cooking, just wash them and snap off the ends. In the old days, cooks used to have to pull off the tough string that ran along each bean's outer edge, but luckily for us, newer varieties of snap beans have made this time-consuming process unnecessary today. The beans may be left whole, cut in diagonal or French-style lengthwise slices, or broken into one-inch pieces. It's better to snap them by hand when possible, instead of using a knife—keeps them crisper. Plan on using 1 to 1½ pounds of beans for four servings. They need only brief steaming (three to five minutes) before they're ready to serve. Overcooking results in that bane of children—dried-out, tough to chew, thoroughly *un*-tasty string beans that can be the beginning of a lifetime of vegetable hating. For variety, a quarter cup of sliced mushrooms, slivered almonds or sliced water chestnuts can be added to the beans before serving.

String beans contain calcium, phosphorus, vitamin A and vitamin C.

LIMA BEANS

Like snap beans, lima beans also come in pole and bush varieties. Bush limas will yield several pickings; pole limas will produce until frost. Harvest

your lima beans when the seeds are green and tender in the pods, just before they attain their full size and plumpness. If limas are allowed to get too big they become tough. If you're planning to dry lima beans, let them mature on the plants and pick them when they're dry.

To prepare lima beans for cooking, pop the shells open along their seams and remove the beans. Rinse them and pick out any bad or discolored beans. Lima beans require about 12 to 15 minutes of cooking until they are tender.

One quart (4 cups) of shelled beans will usually serve six people, but figure on a half pound of unshelled beans for each serving. Limas combine especially well with sautéed onions or mushrooms. They contain protein, iron and other minerals, vitamin A and B vitamins.

Fava, broad and butter beans are closely related to the more familiar green lima, and may be prepared in much the same way. Many of the recipes in this section which call for lima beans will work equally well with these related beans.

CHILLED GREEN BEANS

> 1 pound fresh green beans
> ½ medium onion
> 1 small clove garlic
> 6 tablespoons olive oil
> 2 tablespoons wine vinegar
> ½ teaspoon salt
>   freshly ground black pepper
>   grated Parmesan cheese

1. Wash the beans, snap off the ends and cut them into 1-inch lengths. Drop them into a small amount of boiling water, and let them steam until just tender. Drain.
2. Mince onion and garlic. Combine the beans with the other ingredients, except for the Parmesan cheese. Chill. Top with the grated cheese immediately before serving.

Makes 4 to 6 servings

ITALIAN-STYLE SNAP BEANS

> 1 pound snap beans
> 2 to 3 tablespoons oil
> 1 clove garlic, sliced
> ½ teaspoon salt
> ⅓ to ½ cup grated Parmesan or mozzarella cheese
> ¼ cup parsley, chopped

1. Wash the beans, snap off the ends and break into 1-inch pieces. Steam the beans until *almost* tender, about 5 minutes. Drain well.
2. Heat oil in a skillet, and lightly sauté the garlic for a few minutes. Add the beans and cook until tender, about 5 to 10 minutes, stirring often.
3. Season with salt, grated cheese and chopped parsley. Mix together well and serve piping hot.

Makes 4 to 6 servings

LIMA BEANS AND MUSHROOMS

> 2 cups shelled lima beans
> 2 tablespoons butter
> 2 teaspoons minced shallots
> 6 large mushrooms, sliced
>   herb-seasoned salt, to taste
> ⅛ teaspoon white pepper

1. Steam limas until almost tender. Drain and set aside.
2. While limas are cooking, melt butter in a skillet or saucepan. Sauté shallots for 2 to 3 minutes, then add mushrooms and sauté until tender.
3. Add cooked beans and seasonings, cover and let simmer 5 to 10 minutes more.

Makes 3 to 4 servings

ROSEMARY MINESTRONE

½ cup dried kidney or black beans
1 pint water or stock
1 medium onion, chopped
1 sliced clove garlic or 1 clove green garlic, chopped
1 4-inch rosemary branch tip
1 tablespoon olive oil
2 peeled ripe tomatoes
2 or 3 celery leaves, chopped
1 small carrot, cut up
1 scant cup cut-up cabbage
   freshly ground pepper to taste
½ teaspoon salt
1 cup fresh green beans, broken into 1-inch pieces
1 tablespoon whole wheat macaroni
   grated Parmesan or Romano cheese

1. Simmer the washed, soaked kidney or black beans in a pint of water or stock, covered, for 20 minutes. Turn off heat while you sauté the onion, garlic, and rosemary gently in oil in a 3- or 4-quart saucepan for about 5 minutes.
2. Add cut-up tomatoes, celery leaves, carrot, cabbage and some of the liquid from the beans. Bring to a gentle boil, add the pepper and the salt, and the hot beans.
3. Simmer 15 minutes, add green beans, and simmer 15 minutes more. Remove the rosemary—unless it's so tender you can't find it. Add hot water if needed.
4. Five minutes before serving, add macaroni. Serve topped with grated Romano or Parmesan, with a green salad alongside.

Makes 4 servings

SWISS GREEN BEANS

Preheat oven to 400°F.

1½ pounds green beans
2 tablespoons butter
2 tablespoons whole wheat flour
¼ teaspoon pepper
½ teaspoon grated onion
1 cup yogurt
½ pound Swiss cheese, grated

CRUMBLE TOP:
   1 cup whole wheat flour
   ½ cup rolled oats
     salt, pepper and herbs to taste
   3 tablespoons butter, softened

1. Wash beans, snap off ends and break into 1-inch pieces. Steam beans until just tender; drain well.
2. Melt butter in saucepan. Stir in flour, pepper and onion and cook 2 minutes.
3. Reduce heat, add yogurt and stir until smooth. Fold in beans and heat gently.
4. Fold into a buttered casserole, sprinkle with cheese.
5. Mix crumble top:
   Combine the flour, oats and seasonings. Work in the soft butter until evenly blended.
6. Scatter crumble top over cheese. Bake at 400°F. for 20 minutes, or until bubbly and crumbs are nicely browned.

Makes 8 servings

GOURMET SAUCE FOR BEANS

¾ cup milk
8 ounces cream cheese, softened
½ teaspoon salt
½ teaspoon garlic salt
½ cup Parmesan cheese
  hot cooked beans, 6 to 8 servings (lima, broad, butter or fava)

1. Add milk to softened cream cheese in a small saucepan, blending until smooth.
2. Heat milk and cream cheese, and add seasonings and ¼ cup Parmesan cheese.
3. Pour over beans and toss lightly.
4. Place in serving dish and top with remaining Parmesan cheese.

Makes 6 to 8 servings

Note: The delicate sweetness of wilted Chinese cabbage would be enhanced by this dressing, too.

GREEN BEANS WITH SUNFLOWER SEED KERNELS

¼ cup butter
½ teaspoon marjoram
½ teaspoon basil
½ teaspoon chervil
  pinch of savory
  pinch of thyme
1 pound green beans
1 tablespoon chopped parsley
1 tablespoon chopped chives
1 clove garlic, minced
¼ cup sunflower seed kernels
  salt, and freshly ground pepper to taste

1. Melt butter in a small saucepan and add marjoram, basil, chervil, savory and thyme.
2. Wash beans, remove ends, and break into 1-inch pieces.
3. In a large frying pan, add just enough water to cover the bottom of the pan, and bring to a boil. Add parsley, chives, garlic and beans and cook until beans are just crisp-tender.
4. Pour off excess water, add herb butter and sunflower kernels. Stir to coat beans, add salt and pepper to taste. Toss over medium heat a few minutes, until well mixed.

Makes 6 servings

FAVA BEAN CASSEROLE

Preheat oven to 375°F.

2 cups fresh or dried fava beans
1 teaspoon salt
4 small onions, chopped
1 teaspoon rosemary
¼ cup butter
3 tomatoes, sliced
¾ cup grated cheese
3 tablespoons chopped parsley

1. Cook the favas in salted broth or water until tender, then drain, saving the cooking liquid for soup.
2. Sauté the onions and rosemary in melted butter, and mix with the drained favas.
3. In a 2-quart casserole, place a layer a fava mixture, a layer of tomato slices, and a layer of cheese. Repeat, topping with tomato and cheese and parsley.
4. Bake at 375°F. for 20 minutes, or until heated through.

Makes 4 servings

FAVA VEGETABLE DISH

2 cups fresh fava beans
3 tablespoons butter or olive oil
4 green onions
2 cloves garlic, thinly sliced
2 tablespoons chopped parsley
   almond slices

1. Steam favas until tender.
2. Melt butter and very lightly sauté onion, garlic, and parsley. Pour over favas.
3. Serve garnished with almond slices.

Makes 4 servings

LIMA BEAN-TOMATO RAREBIT

4 tablespoons butter or oil
3 tablespoons whole wheat or rye flour
½ teaspoon salt
   dash of cayenne
   dash of black pepper
1 teaspoon paprika
½ teaspoon Worcestershire sauce
2½ cups cooked limas (drained, liquid reserved)
1 can tomatoes, or 1 pint home-canned tomatoes, drained and chopped
1 cup shredded, medium-sharp cheddar cheese

1. In a heavy skillet, melt butter or heat oil. Stir in flour, salt, cayenne, black pepper, paprika and Worcestershire sauce.
2. Add liquid from beans and tomatoes. Cook, stirring constantly, until thickened. Stir in cheese and heat until smooth.
3. Add beans and tomatoes; heat thoroughly. Serve over whole grain toast.

Makes 6 servings

STRING BEAN SALAD

1 egg
1 clove garlic
6 small scallions or green onion tops, cut up
¼ cup chopped parsley
1 tablespoon lemon juice
½ cup sour cream or yogurt, optional
¾ pound string beans, cooked and chilled

1. Place egg, garlic, scallions, parsley and lemon juice in a blender or mixing bowl. Blend or mix at low speed until well mixed.
2. If you like sour cream or yogurt, add it to the dressing just before serving. Serve over chilled string beans.

Makes 4 servings

FAVA BEAN SOUP

3 quarts broth
2 cups fresh fava beans
1 bay leaf
3 tablespoons olive oil or butter
8 cups total of chopped vegetables
    (onions, squash, tomatoes, peas, corn, carrots, snap
    beans, mild California peppers, etc.)
1 cup cooked brown rice

1. Heat broth and add favas and bay leaf.
2. Sauté any crisp vegetables in oil and add to pot, simmering until they are all tender. Then add softer vegetables.
3. Add cooked rice and simmer ½ hour.
4. Serve with grated cheese and homemade bread.

Makes 10 servings

Note: This hearty and colorful soup will be welcomed by the whole family.

FRESH LIMA SALAD

1¼ cups freshly shelled limas
1 red onion, peeled, thinly sliced and separated into
    rings
½ cup fresh parsley, coarsely chopped

DRESSING:
    ½ cup oil
    ½ cup vinegar
    ½ teaspoon honey
    ½ teaspoon salt
    ¼ teaspoon pepper

1. Cook lima beans until tender, about 15 minutes. Drain thoroughly.
2. Combine beans, onion and parsley in a bowl.
3. Place remaining ingredients in blender and blend until well mixed. Pour dressing over vegetables, cover, and chill 12 hours or overnight.
4. To serve salad, drain the vegetables and serve on a bed of lettuce, garnished with a few onion rings and additional chopped parsley.

Makes 4 servings

● *When hulling fresh limas, press on the seam with your thumb and fingers—the pods will pop right open.*

HERBED GREEN BEANS

1 pound green beans, broken into 1-inch pieces (about
    3 cups)
1 to 2 tablespoons butter
1 cup onion, peeled and finely chopped
1 cup celery, finely chopped
2 small cloves garlic, peeled and crushed
¼ teaspoon basil leaves

¼ teaspoon rosemary leaves
⅛ teaspoon dried thyme leaves
¼ to ½ teaspoon salt
    pepper to taste
2 tablespoons finely chopped parsley

1. Parboil beans about 7 minutes; drain well.
2. In a medium-sized pan, melt butter over moderate heat. Add onion, celery and garlic and cook until celery is tender, about 10 to 12 minutes.
3. Stir in beans and remaining ingredients. Cover tightly and cook 5 minutes more, or until beans are just tender.

Makes 6 to 8 servings

● *Lima and fava beans should not be eaten raw, because they contain a toxic substance that is destroyed by cooking.*

LIMA BEAN BAKE

Preheat oven to 350°F.

½ pound green baby lima beans, cooked until tender
1 tablespoon honey
1 tablespoon prepared mustard
½ pint sour cream or yogurt
    salt, to taste

Combine all ingredients in a casserole and bake at 350°F. for 30 minutes, until bubbly.

Makes 4 to 6 servings

Note: The tangy sauce makes this dish a good way to get lima bean haters to eat limas and like them.

CREATIVE CASSEROLE

2 cups water
½ cup lentils
½ cup millet
1 teaspoon salt
3 medium or small broccoli stems, sliced
4 carrots, sliced
2 stalks celery, sliced
1 small onion, sliced
½ pound fresh green beans, sliced in half lengthwise
   oil as needed
   tamari soy sauce to taste (approximately ⅓ cup)
¼ cup parsley, chopped
   salt and/or *Herb-a-mar* to taste

SAUCE:
   2 celery stalks, sliced
   4 medium parsnips, sliced
   ½ cup parsley, chopped

1. Bring 2 cups of water to a boil, add the lentils, millet and salt, and simmer for 15 minutes or until all the water has been absorbed. Set aside.
2. In a cast-iron skillet or *wok* sauté the broccoli stems, carrots, celery, onion, and green beans in oil and soy sauce until the vegetables just begin to soften. Add parsley. Flavor with salt and/or *Herb-a-mar*. set aside.
3. Prepare the sauce:
   Sauté the celery and parsnips in a small amount of oil until tender. Put the sautéed vegetables and the parsley in the blender with a small amount of water and salt to taste. Puree and heat through.
4. Combine lentils and millet mixture with the sautéed vegetables and top with sauce, and additional fresh parsley if desired.

Makes 6 servings

LIMA BEAN AND PEANUT ROAST

Preheat oven to 350°F.

2½ cups cooked baby limas
1 cup shelled, roasted peanuts
2 cups mashed potatoes
½ cup milk
1 egg, beaten
1 teaspoon salt
½ teaspoon paprika
⅛ teaspoon pepper
1 tablespoon finely chopped onion
    butter as needed

1. Drain beans; chop peanuts finely, reserving 1 tablespoon.
2. Spread a layer of potatoes in the bottom of a greased baking dish. Add a layer of peanuts, then a layer of beans.
3. Repeat until all potatoes, peanuts, and beans are used, ending with a layer of beans.
4. Combine milk, egg, seasonings, and onion, and pour over layered mixture. Dot with butter.
5. Bake uncovered at 350°F. for 30 minutes. Serve with tomato or cheese sauce, garnished with reserved peanuts.

Makes 6 servings

● *With lima beans, the rule is the smaller, the better. Large, fully mature beans which make big bumps in the pods have probably already turned starchy, and won't be as good as smaller beans.*

Beets

Red beets and the less common golden beets can be grown all over the United States, but really thrive in northern areas. They can withstand cold weather and light frost in late spring or early autumn, but cannot be left outside all winter. Beets almost always have to be thinned after planting because the "seed" is really a small fruit containing from two to six seeds, each of which can produce a plant. Unless beets are thinned when quite young, the thinnings will have developed small beets which can be eaten whole.

It's good practice to pull all your beets when they are only a few inches in diameter—not very much bigger than walnuts. These small beets are tender, sweet and juicy. As beets grow larger, they become coarse and woody. Good quality beets are smooth and firm. Soft, wet spots indicate decay, and a rough, shriveled feel means the beet will be tough.

Because of their thick skins, beets store well. They can be refrigerated in a nonporous container or vegetable crisper up to two weeks after harvest. When storing beets, remove the leafy tops, but leave an inch or two of stem and root to preserve nutrients and tenderness. Save the tops to use as greens.

Beets are most often canned or pickled for long-term storage, but can be frozen as well.

To prepare beets, scrub them thoroughly and drop into boiling water to cover. Leave the root and stem ends still attached, to prevent the beets

from "bleeding." As the term implies, bleeding occurs when the red juices seep out of the vegetable and into the cooking water. Any time the inside of the beet is pierced, such as by peeling or by cutting off the root and stem, bleeding will occur during cooking. This means that testing beets with a fork for "doneness" will also cause bleeding. Beets will continue to bleed for as long as they are cooked, until eventually you will be left with a pale pinkish, tasteless and rather tough vegetable.

It is important, then, to keep an eye on cooking time in order to avoid unnecessarily testing your beets. Unless they are quite large, most beets will be tender in 15 to 20 minutes. Take care not to overcook, and gauge the amount of cooking needed by what you're going to use them for. Beets for salad will need longer cooking than beets to be used in another cooked dish. When beets are done, remove them from the water and slip off the skins as soon as they can be handled.

Beets contain calcium, phosphorus, sodium, potassium, and vitamins A and C. Six medium-sized or a dozen small beets will make three to four servings.

GREENS AND BEETS PIQUANT

1 pound greens
¼ cup butter or vegetable oil
3 green onions, minced
1 cup minced cooked beets
2 tablespoons vinegar
1 or 2 hard-boiled eggs, chopped
½ teaspoon salt
   dash of pepper

1. Clean and cook greens until barely tender; drain and chop coarsely.
2. Melt butter or oil in a saucepan. Gently sauté green onion until tender. Add beets and heat. Add remaining ingredients and cooked greens, toss until heated through. Serve hot.

Makes 4 servings

Note: If you prefer, use the eggs as a garnish, rather than including them in the cooking.

37

BEETS IN ORANGE SAUCE

6 medium-sized beets

SAUCE:
  1 tablespoon cornstarch
  2 tablespoons cold water
  2 tablespoons honey
  1 tablespoon lemon juice
  ½ cup orange juice
  2 teaspoons grated orange peel

1. Cook beets until tender, then peel and slice.
2. Meanwhile, prepare sauce:
    Mix cornstarch and water; set aside.
3. Blend honey, lemon juice, orange juice and grated orange peel in a saucepan. Stir in cornstarch and water mixture, and cook, stirring, over medium heat until sauce thickens.
4. Stir in beets and heat through; serve immediately.

Makes 4 servings

BEETS IN SAVORY YOGURT SAUCE

6 medium-sized beets
⅔ cup yogurt
2 teaspoons parsley, finely chopped
1 teaspoon chives, finely chopped

1. Scrub beets and cut off all but an inch or two of tops and roots.
2. Cook until tender, about 25 minutes.
3. Peel and slice beets, and mix with yogurt and herbs. Heat briefly to warm sauce, or refrigerate and serve chilled.

Makes 3 to 4 servings

Note: This sauce is also good with carrots.

DAIRY BORSCHT

1 large bunch beets
2 teaspoons salt
   juice of 1 lemon
⅓ to ½ cup honey, to taste
2 cups water or beet juice
   sour cream and parsley for garnish

1. Boil beets in water to cover until tender, 15 to 25 minutes, depending on size of beets. Skin and mash.
2. Combine beets, salt, lemon juice, honey and water. Check seasonings. Add more liquid if desired.
3. Serve cold, topping each serving with a tablespoon of sour cream and a few sprigs of fresh parsley. Or heat and serve.

Makes 4 cups

SWEET 'N SOUR BAKED BEETS

Preheat oven to 350°F.

6 medium beets, well scrubbed
1 tablespoon prepared horseradish
2 tablespoons honey
¼ cup cider vinegar
   salt and pepper to taste
1 tablespoon butter

1. Cook beets until almost tender, then peel and dice. Reserve ½ cup of the cooking liquid. Put beets in a 1½-quart casserole that has a cover.
2. Mix beet liquid, horseradish, honey, and vinegar. Add salt and pepper to taste. Pour over beets, dot with butter.
3. Bake in covered casserole at 350°F. for 30 minutes.

Makes 6 servings

HARVARD BEETS

½ cup vinegar
¼ cup honey
1 tablespoon cornstarch
½ teaspoon salt
2 whole cloves
3 cups cooked, sliced beets

1. Combine all ingredients except beets in a saucepan, and cook until sauce is smooth and clear.
2. Add beets and cook until heated. Serve immediately.

Makes 6 servings

TANGY BEETS (WITH HORSERADISH)

6 medium-sized beets (2 cups, grated)
5 teaspoons lemon juice
4½ teaspoons prepared horseradish
1 teaspoon brown sugar (optional)

1. Scrub beets and cook until almost tender. Beets should be slightly under-cooked, or they'll be mushy when grated.
2. When beets are cool enough to handle, slip off skins and grate them.
3. Add remaining ingredients and mix together well. Reheat briefly and serve.

Makes 3 to 4 servings

Broccoli

This hardy member of the cabbage family is becoming an increasingly common sight in backyard gardens. As it reaches maturity, watch it carefully so you can harvest the heads at their peak. Broccoli is harvested when the heads are firm and dark green or purplish green in color. If you don't pick it in time, the tiny green buds shoot up into bright yellow flowers and the broccoli is no longer edible. Although a few blooms won't hurt if the rest of the head is still firm, broccoli is better before it reaches this stage, because the stems start to become tough and stringy when the blossoms appear.

After the main head has been cut, smaller side shoots will continue to produce heads up until frost. When cutting the heads, leave a fairly long portion of stem attached. The tougher lower parts of the stalk are tasty and nutritious, and fine for soup. They shouldn't be wasted.

Broccoli must be refrigerated immediately after picking, or it will begin to lose its crispness. In an airtight container, it can be refrigerated up to a week without serious loss of quality. For long-term storage, broccoli should be frozen.

To prepare broccoli for cooking, trim off the leaves and tough stem ends to use in soup. If the stems are thick, you may wish to slit them up the middle to reduce cooking time. Although not too desirable from a nutritional stand-

41

point, it may be necessary to soak the heads in cold salted water for about 15 minutes before cooking to release any tiny bugs that sometimes hide in the buds. Don't let your broccoli soak for longer than 30 minutes, though, or it will begin to ferment, and its flavor will be ruined.

Broccoli contains large amounts of calcium, iron, vitamin A and vitamin C, and provides B vitamins as well. Plan about 2 pounds of broccoli for four servings.

ITALIAN BROCCOLI CASSEROLE

Preheat oven to 350°F.

1½ pounds broccoli, cut in bite-sized pieces

CHEESE SAUCE:
   2 tablespoons butter
   2 tablespoons whole wheat flour
   scant 1 cup milk
   ½ teaspoon salt
   ½ cup grated cheddar cheese
   2 eggs, beaten
   1 teaspoon oregano
   2 medium tomatoes, cut up
   ¼ cup Parmesan cheese

1. Steam broccoli until barely tender, 5 to 7 minutes; drain well.
2. Meanwhile, prepare cheese sauce:
   Melt butter and stir in flour to make a *roux*. Add milk and salt; cook, stirring until thickened. Stir in cheese.
3. Combine eggs, cheese sauce and oregano, and stir in broccoli and tomatoes.
4. Pour into baking dish and sprinkle with grated Parmesan cheese.
5. Bake, uncovered, in 350°F. oven for 30 minutes, or until heated all the way through.

Makes 4 to 6 servings as a side dish

BROCCOLI POLONAISE

1 large bunch broccoli
2 tablespoons onion, finely chopped
4 tablespoons oil
1 clove garlic, finely minced
2 tablespoons butter
1 tablespoon chopped fresh parsley
¼ teaspoon salt
2 tablespoons whole wheat bread crumbs
1 hard-boiled egg, finely chopped

1. Divide broccoli into florets, and chop stems. Steam until just tender.
2. Sauté onion in oil for 2 minutes. Add garlic and cook another minute or two, until onion is soft.
3. Add butter, parsley, salt, bread crumbs and egg, and mix thoroughly.
4. Blend in broccoli and serve immediately.

Makes 4 to 6 servings

Note: This recipe is also a delicious way to serve cauliflower.

● *Broccoli leaves have more vitamin A than either the stalks or the heads, and can be cooked and served as greens.*

SAVORY BROCCOLI

1 large bunch broccoli
2 tablespoons butter
¼ teaspoon rubbed sage
   seasoned salt, to taste

1. Steam broccoli until just tender and still bright green.
2. Melt the butter, add seasonings, and stir together. Add the broccoli, stir to coat pieces and serve.

Makes 5 to 6 servings

BROCCOLI WITH CHEESE SAUCE

2 pounds broccoli

SAUCE:
    2 tablespoons butter
    2 tablespoons arrowroot flour
    2 cups milk
    1 teaspoon salt
    ¼ teaspoon pepper
    ¼ teaspoon nutmeg
    2 cups grated cheese

1. Wash broccoli and trim tough stem ends. Place vegetable on an adjustable vegetable steamer and cook over simmering water in a covered pot 15 minutes, until barely tender.
2. Meanwhile, prepare sauce:
   Melt butter over medium heat. Blend in arrowroot, then milk and seasonings. Cook until thickened. Stir in cheese and keep stirring until smooth.
3. When broccoli is done, drain well and serve with sauce.

Makes 4 to 6 servings

Note: This dish is simple to prepare and quite filling. Serve it with a fresh tomato salad and whole grain bread for a satisfying summer meal.

● *The flower heads of broccoli cook more quickly than the thick stalks. If you prefer the stalks very tender and still wish to avoid overcooking the buds, cook it upright in bundles, as some cooks treat asparagus.*

SPRING CASSEROLE

Preheat oven to 350°F.

6 hard-boiled eggs
½ cup chopped ham
1 tablespoon finely chopped onion
½ teaspoon dry mustard
    salt and pepper to taste
½ teaspoon Worcestershire sauce
1 pound broccoli, cooked until barely tender

SAUCE:
    3 tablespoons butter
    3 tablespoons whole wheat flour
    1½ cups milk
    1 cup grated cheese
    ½ teaspoon salt
    ⅛ teaspoon paprika

1. Slice the eggs in half lengthwise. Remove the yolks and mash them. Add to them the chopped ham and onion, seasonings and Worcestershire sauce. Mix together thoroughly and stuff back into the eggs.
2. Arrange the cooked broccoli in the bottom of an oiled casserole dish. Place the deviled eggs on top.
3. Make a sauce by melting butter in a saucepan and blending in flour. Add milk, stir and cook until thickened. Stir in cheese and seasonings; keep stirring until cheese is melted and smooth.
4. Pour sauce over the eggs and broccoli, and bake at 350°F. for 20 minutes.

Makes 6 servings

Note: The deviled eggs give this colorful dish a delightful new twist.

BROCCOLI WITH LEMON BUTTER

    1 large bunch broccoli
    ¼ cup butter
    2 tablespoons fresh lemon juice
    1 tablespoon sliced almonds, optional

1. Divide broccoli into spears, steam until bright green and just tender. Drain.
2. Meanwhile, melt butter in small saucepan. Add lemon juice and beat with a wire whisk until smooth and creamy.
3. When broccoli is done, pour lemon butter over it, sprinkle with sliced almonds if desired and serve immediately.

Makes 4 servings

VEGETABLES NORMANDY

2 cups coarsely cut broccoli, carrots, and cauliflower

SAUCE:
¼ cup butter
2 tablespoons milk
½ teaspoon dry mustard
½ teaspoon salt
6 tablespoons water
1 tablespoon whole wheat flour
¼ teaspoon paprika
¼ cup grated cheddar cheese
    dash tabasco sauce
1 teaspoon lemon juice

1. Cook vegetables in a small amount of salted water, until just tender.
2. Meanwhile, prepare sauce:
   Melt butter. Combine all remaining ingredients in a small bowl and blend thoroughly; slowly add melted butter while continuing to blend.
3. Pour into pan used to melt butter and heat, stirring, until thickened. Pour over cooked vegetables.

Makes 4 servings

CHILLED BROCCOLI IN LEMON DRESSING

1 large bunch broccoli, separated into spears or
    chopped into bite-size pieces
¼ cup lemon juice
¼ cup vegetable oil
¼ teaspoon paprika
½ teaspoon honey
1 clove garlic, finely minced
1 tablespoon onion, finely chopped
1 hard-boiled egg, chopped

1. Steam broccoli until just tender; drain well.
2. Combine all remaining ingredients except egg. Pour over broccoli and chill 3 to 4 hours to blend flavors.
3. Serve garnished with chopped egg.

Makes 4 servings

SUMMER SOUP

2 small onions, thinly sliced
2 tablespoons oil
broccoli trimmings (stems, leaves and leftover buds)
2 carrots, grated
tops of 4 stalks celery
1 bay leaf
1 teaspoon salt
¼ teaspoon pepper
5 to 6 cups cold water
2 to 3 cups yogurt

1. Sauté onions in oil until transparent. Add broccoli trimmings and any other leftover vegetables and vegetable trimmings on hand; cook 1 minute.
2. Add all remaining ingredients except yogurt, bring to a boil, cover, reduce heat, and simmer gently 1 hour. The amount of water you will need depends on your supply of vegetable trimmings; use enough water to just cover the vegetables in the pot.
3. When cooking is completed, puree the soup in a blender until almost smooth. At serving time, warm the soup slightly and stir in yogurt, figuring ½ cup of yogurt per cup of soup.

Makes about 2 quarts

Note: This cool, creamy soup is a great way to use up garden leftovers on a hot day. For cooler days, add cooked grains and serve the soup hot, as is, or with strands of cooked egg, in the manner of Chinese egg drop soup.

STIR-FRIED BROCCOLI

6 dried black mushrooms
1 cup fresh daylily buds, or ¼ cup dried lily buds
2 pounds broccoli
2 tablespoons peanut oil
1 teaspoon salt
¼ teaspoon honey
¼ cup halved almonds
1 teaspoon cornstarch dissolved in 1 tablespoon
    chicken or vegetable stock

1. Cover mushrooms with ½ cup warm water and soak 30 minutes. If using dried lily buds, soak separately in warm water to cover 15 to 30 minutes. Then drain, reserving ¼ cup mushroom liquid. Cut mushrooms in quarters.
2. Meanwhile, wash broccoli and cut flowers from stems in clusters. Slice stems diagonally into 1-inch pieces.
3. In a *wok* or large skillet, heat the oil. Add broccoli stalks and stir-fry over medium heat for 1 minute. Add broccoli buds and stir-fry for a minute longer.
4. Add salt, honey, the reserved mushroom liquid, mushrooms, lily buds and almonds. Stir briefly, cover, and cook over moderate heat 2 to 3 minutes.
5. Stir cornstarch mixture and pour into pan. Stir until vegetables are coated with a light, clear glaze. Serve immediately.

Makes 6 servings

Note: This dish tastes like it came from an authentic Chinese kitchen, and may be accompanied by whole wheat or buckwheat spaghetti in a *miso* or soy sauce broth.

● *If overcooked, broccoli is awful. The heads get mushy, the color becomes grayish, and its flavor is ruined.*

Brussels Sprouts

Unfairly regarded as a commoner in the vegetable kingdom, Brussels sprouts can be quite elegant when prepared with a little flair. Brussels sprouts look like miniature cabbages, and their taste is similar to that of cabbage, only more delicate and refined. The edible buds grow in spirals around the plant's thick stem, and mature from the bottom up. Harvesting can begin when the sprouts are one to two inches in diameter, compact, firm, and bright green—the large sprouts sold in supermarkets are tougher and more strongly flavored than these small ones. Remove the leaf below each sprout when you pick it, but always allow a crown of leaves to remain at the top to provide food for the plant. Twist off the bud to remove it from the plant.

This plant likes cold weather, and will continue to bear when the temperature dips below the freezing mark. The flavor of Brussels sprouts is actually improved by a few light frosts; however, if you live in a northern area which has extended periods of weather well below freezing, you can extend the harvest season by carefully uprooting the plant with some soil still attached and transplanting it to a moist greenhouse, cold frame, or basement. If the soil is kept damp, the buds will continue to mature for another two months or so.

Although they taste best when prepared soon after picking, Brussels sprouts can be stored in an airtight container in the refrigerator for up to

four days. Freeze them for longer storage.

To prepare Brussels sprouts for cooking, cut off the stem ends and remove any loose or discolored leaves. Wash them well in cold water. Steam or sauté the sprouts, and serve them simply with butter or lemon, or go creative and top them with one of your favorite sauces. Brussels sprouts are rich in vitamin C, and also contain substantial amounts of vitamin A and iron. Plan about 1 pound (or 1 quart) of sprouts for four servings.

BRUSSELS SPROUTS WITH GARLIC AND SUNFLOWER SEEDS

½ pound Brussels sprouts (about 2 cups)
1 clove garlic, minced
1 tablespoon olive oil
2 tablespoons hulled sunflower seeds
¼ teaspoon salt

1. Steam Brussels sprouts for 15 minutes, or until barely tender.
2. Sauté garlic in oil for 2 minutes. Add sunflower seeds and continue to sauté for another 5 minutes, shaking or stirring occasionally.
3. Add steamed sprouts and salt, and toss or stir for about 1 minute until piping hot.

Makes 3 servings

● *Slashing the stem ends of Brussels sprouts before cooking will allow the steam to penetrate better, and the sprouts will cook more quickly and evenly.*

BRUSSELS SPROUTS IN NUTTY CHEESE SAUCE

1 quart Brussels sprouts

CHEESE SAUCE:
1 tablespoon butter or oil
1 tablespoon whole wheat flour
½ cup grated medium cheddar cheese
¼ teaspoon honey
dash black pepper

scant ⅛ teaspoon seasoned salt
¼ teaspoon paprika
   dash dry mustard
½ teaspoon Worcestershire
½ cup milk
3 tablespoons coarsely chopped walnuts

chopped chives

1. Trim the stems off close to the sprouts and remove any discolored leaves.
2. Steam sprouts, tightly covered, in colander or sieve over boiling water, just until tender when pierced with a fork, about 15 minutes.
3. Meanwhile prepare sauce:
   Heat butter or oil in small, heavy saucepan, over low heat, until melted. Sprinkle in the flour and blend well. Add the cheese, honey, and seasonings, and stir together well until the cheese is melted, being careful not to scorch. Gradually pour in the milk, continuing to stir constantly until the sauce is thickened. Add the walnuts and mix to blend.
4. Pour sauce over steamed sprouts in serving dish and garnish with chopped chives.

Makes 4 servings

SESAME SPROUTS

1 pound Brussels sprouts
2 tablespoons butter
½ cup fresh rye crumbs
2 tablespoons sesame seeds
2 tablespoons grated Parmesan cheese

1. Steam sprouts until tender.
2. Melt butter in a small pan, add crumbs and sesame seeds, and toast until golden brown. Add cheese, and toss for a few minutes.
3. When ready to serve, pour crumbs over hot sprouts.

Makes 4 servings

BRUSSELS SPROUTS WITH RAISIN ALMOND SAUCE

1 pound Brussels sprouts

SAUCE:
  1 tablespoon butter
  1 tablespoon whole wheat flour
  1½ cups chicken stock
  ½ cup raisins
  2 tablespoons slivered almonds

1. Steam Brussels sprouts until tender.
2. Meanwhile, prepare sauce:
   Melt butter in skillet or saucepan. Add flour and blend into a *roux*. When well blended, add stock slowly, stirring until smooth.
3. Add raisins and allow sauce to simmer for about 8 minutes.
4. When ready to serve, pour sauce over sprouts and top with almonds.

Makes 4 servings

CREAMED BRUSSELS SPROUTS

1 to 1½ pounds Brussels sprouts
¼ cup butter
2 tablespoons dry white wine
½ cup half-and-half or light cream
1 teaspoon salt
  dash of nutmeg

1. Wash Brussels sprouts carefully; steam until just barely tender and drain well.
2. Melt butter in a skillet, then stir in wine and heat for a few minutes. Add Brussels sprouts and cook in the wine and butter mixture until sprouts are tender.
3. Stir in remaining ingredients and heat until piping hot. Serve immediately.

Makes 4 to 6 servings

BRUSSELS SPROUTS WITH SCALLIONS

1 pound Brussels sprouts
4 tablespoons butter
4 scallions, thinly sliced
¼ teaspoon lemon juice
   salt and pepper to taste

1. Steam Brussels sprouts until tender. Drain well.
2. Meanwhile, melt butter in a skillet and sauté scallions until tender.
3. Add the cooked, drained sprouts to the pan and stir to blend vegetables. Add lemon juice and salt and pepper to taste.

Makes 4 servings

Note: For an unusual variation on this dish, sauté ½ cup of sliced mushrooms along with the scallions.

● *When winter sets in and harvest season is over, pick off the small sprouts from the top of the plant, those that never got a chance to develop, and drop them in broth or stock to cook. They'll cook very quickly, and will be quite tasty.*

Cabbage

Cabbage has been cultivated by man longer than any other vegetable—at least 4,000 years, and we can assume that it's been mistreated by cooks for nearly as long. All too frequently cabbage is allowed to grow beyond its prime and then boiled for hours. It's no wonder the poor vegetable has long had an unsavory reputation for offensive odors and mushy texture. Recent research, however, has shown that the two secrets to improving cabbage flavor —early harvest and quick cooking in a small amount of water—also help to maintain its high vitamin C content. Overcooking cabbage in too much water, or at too high a temperature, causes a breakdown of sulfur compounds and produces the strong taste so many people consider objectionable.

If you've planted early cabbage, you can begin harvesting when the heads are firm and hard and feel heavy for their size. They should be picked before they mature fully, while their color, whether red or green, is still good. Try to catch them before they split, and if one splits before you notice, use it as soon as possible. Splitting can be prevented by cutting or breaking off the roots on one side with a spade after a rain. To harvest cabbage, cut through the plant's stem at the base of the head. If you see evidence of worm or insect damage, drive out any remaining intruders by soaking the head in cold, salted water for ten minutes. Early cabbage is usually cooked or used raw in cole-

slaw. If you can't use it immediately, you can store undamaged, unwashed heads in a plastic bag in the refrigerator for up to two weeks.

Late cabbage, planned for storage as sauerkraut or in outdoor pits, is improved by a light frost or two; repeated thawing and freezing, however, will mar its keeping qualities. Since they tend to send out strong odors, stored cabbages are usually not kept in the house, although root cellar conditions would preserve them very well. The easiest storage technique is to uproot the plants, and stack them, roots and all, upside down in a protected corner of the yard or garage on a bed of straw or leaves. Cover the pile with at least 12 inches of additional straw or leaves, and you should have perfectly good cabbage available for consumption anytime during the following winter or early spring.

You can also store late cabbage in a metal drum buried outdoors. For this kind of storage, first cut off the roots and peel away any damaged leaves. Insulate the drum with a layer of dry leaves, and then lay down a thick layer of moist sand. Space the heads so they're not touching one another on the sand, and then cover them with more sand, filling in the spaces between the heads so that they're completely buried. Top with more leaves, then more sand. Replace the drum's lid, and cover the whole drum with more leaves.

Do not cut or shred cabbage until just before you're ready to cook it. Wash it thoroughly, discarding any damaged leaves. It can be cooked whole, quartered, cut in wedges, stuffed or shredded, and can, of course, be eaten raw as well. If you'll be serving cabbage in wedges, remove most of the core, leaving only enough to hold the leaves together. If shredding it, use a knife, not a vegetable chopper, to preserve more vitamin C. (Using a vegetable chopper shreds the cabbage into smaller pieces, thus leaving more cut surfaces exposed to air and water.) A head weighing 1 to 1½ pounds will usually serve four people.

Cabbage, whether red, green, or a curly-leafed Savoy variety, is a good, inexpensive source of vitamin C. However, the vitamin content varies with the head's maturity and with the length of time it has been stored. Immature, early varieties with green leaves have the largest quantity. When made into sauerkraut, cabbage loses much of its nutritional value.

CHINESE CABBAGE OR CELERY CABBAGE

This sweetly flavored, leafy, lettuce-like member of the mustard family is frequently found in Chinese dishes and is delicious either raw or cooked. 55

Seed should be planted early, about three months before the first expected frost, since hot weather will cause the plants to bolt and produce an undesirably strong cabbage flavor. Chinese cabbage grows best during cool, moist weather.

The plants can be harvested as needed during the growing season; even immature thinnings can be stir-fried, added to soups, or used in salads. The plants are considered mature when the stalk has thickened into a compact cylindrical head. When harvesting, pull the plant from the ground with its roots still attached. Celery cabbage can be stored for a few days in a plastic bag in the refrigerator after the roots and any damaged outer leaves have been removed.

At the first light frost, any remaining heads should be pulled. They can be stored for up to two months in a cool cellar, cold frame, or outdoor storage pit. The plants should not be washed. Carefully place the roots in moist sand or soil, keeping them as upright as possible. Water the covered roots occasionally, but do not wet the leaves.

About 1 pound of celery cabbage will serve four people. Mature cabbage can be served raw, cooked as greens, or sliced and stir-fried. If added to soups shortly before serving, its tender crunchiness will provide an attractive contrast with other vegetables more thoroughly cooked. Celery cabbage contains appreciable quantities of vitamin A and potassium.

SPICY RED CABBAGE

1 large, or 2 medium red cabbages, coarsely shredded
¼ pound butter
1 cup water
2 tablespoons honey
¾ cup apple cider vinegar
⅛ teaspoon ground cloves
1 teaspoon salt

Combine ingredients in large saucepan and simmer gently for 1 to 1½ hours. Serve hot.

Makes 6 to 8 servings

CELERY CABBAGE WITH SOUR CREAM DRESSING

1 head celery or Chinese cabbage (about 1 pound)
½ cup sliced red onion
1 teaspoon chopped chives

DRESSING:
¾ cup sour cream
2 tablespoons lemon juice
1 teaspoon prepared mustard
1 teaspoon dillweed
salt and pepper to taste

1. Cut celery cabbage into ½-inch slices across the rib. Add onion and chives.
2. Prepare dressing:
   Combine sour cream, lemon juice, mustard and dill.
3. Add dressing to cabbage and toss until thoroughly coated. Add salt and pepper to taste.

Makes 4 servings

Note: A pungently delicious new way to serve celery cabbage.

CHINESE CABBAGE SOUP

2 cups cooked chicken, shredded
7 cups chicken broth
6 cups sliced Chinese cabbage
tamari soy sauce to taste
freshly ground pepper to taste
¼ cup slivered almonds, browned in butter (optional)

1. Heat chicken in broth in a large saucepan. Add Chinese cabbage; cook 4 to 5 minutes or until cabbage is just tender. Do not overcook.
2. Stir in the soy sauce and pepper. Serve sprinkled with almonds.

Makes 6 to 8 servings

SIMMERED RED CABBAGE AND APPLES

1 medium-sized head red cabbage (about 6 cups shredded)
6 strips nitrite-free bacon
1 medium onion, chopped
½ teaspoon salt
⅛ teaspoon pepper
½ cup water
2 cups baking apples, cored and thinly sliced
½ cup vinegar
2 tablespoons honey

1. Quarter and core the cabbage, then shred it. Meanwhile, fry the bacon in a skillet until it is crisp and brown.
2. Remove bacon from pan and drain. Pour off all but a tablespoon or two of the fat. Sauté the onion in the remaining bacon fat until it is somewhat tender, 2 to 3 minutes.
3. Add the cabbage, salt, pepper and water; cover and simmer over low heat 5 to 7 minutes.
4. Then add the apples, vinegar and honey, and gently cook uncovered 5 to 10 minutes more, or until apples are tender and liquid is absorbed.
5. Crumble the bacon over the cabbage and serve.

Makes 6 to 8 servings

SAUTÉED RED CABBAGE AND SPROUTS

2 tablespoons olive oil
3 cups grated red cabbage
1 cup mung bean sprouts
1 tablespoon caraway seeds, optional
  tamari soy sauce to taste
1 tablespoon vinegar
  salt and pepper to taste

1. Heat olive oil in a cast-iron skillet.
2. Sauté the red cabbage for 3 to 5 minutes.
3. Add mung bean sprouts and sauté for 2 more minutes.
4. Add caraway seeds, soy sauce, vinegar, salt and pepper, and allow to cook gently as you toss together for a few more minutes. Serve piping hot.

Makes 6 servings

● *When planning to serve shredded or chopped cabbage, figure that one pound of raw cabbage will make two cups when cooked.*

ACORN CABBAGE BAKE

Preheat oven to 400°F.

2 large acorn squashes
½ pound ground beef
2 tablespoons butter
1 medium onion, chopped
1 small apple, pared and chopped
2 cups shredded green cabbage
2 tablespoons sunflower seeds
¾ teaspoon salt
¼ teaspoon pepper
¼ teaspoon dried leaf thyme
½ teaspoon dried leaf sage, crumbled

1. Cut acorn squash in half lengthwise and scoop out seeds and fibers. Place in baking pan, cut side down, and add ½ inch of water. Bake in 400°F. oven for 20 minutes.
2. Meanwhile, cook ground beef in skillet until browned. Drain off excess fat. Add butter, onion, apple, cabbage and sunflower seeds, cook until vegetables are tender. Add seasonings and mix well.
3. Turn squash halves cut side up and fill centers with cabbage mixture. Return to baking pan and bake in 400°F. oven 30 minutes longer.

Makes 4 servings

COOL COLESLAW

2 cups shredded cabbage
2 or 3 stalks fresh celery, diced (about 1 cup) or 1 tea-
    spoon celery seed
1 carrot, shredded
1 or 2 young stalks of fresh dill, chopped
    leaves from one stem of fresh basil, chopped
1 teaspoon poppy seed
3 tablespoons mayonnaise
1 to 2 tablespoons wine vinegar, to taste
    salt and pepper to taste

Combine all ingredients in a large bowl and chill for at least an hour before serving to blend flavors.

Makes 4 servings

BEEF-VEGETABLE BORSCH

1 pound stew beef
8 cups beef or vegetable broth
    salt and pepper to taste
1 bay leaf
2 tablespoons butter
1 medium onion, chopped
2 carrots, sliced
4 raw beets, sliced
    small head cabbage, shredded
1 pound potatoes, cubed
1 cup tomato puree
1 tablespoon vinegar
    lemon slices
1 cup yogurt
    chopped dill or parsley, optional

1. Put beef and broth in kettle. Add salt and pepper to taste and the bay leaf. Bring to a boil and skim. Simmer, covered, about 30 minutes.
2. Melt butter in Dutch oven. Add vegetables and sauté, stirring, for 5 minutes. Add tomato puree and vinegar and simmer an additional 10 minutes.
3. Pour meat and broth over vegetables in Dutch oven and simmer, covered, for 1 hour, or until meat is tender. Add salt and pepper to taste.
4. Serve each bowl of borsch with a lemon slice and a tablespoon of yogurt. Sprinkle with chopped dill or parsley, if desired.

Makes 12 servings

Note: This is a hearty and delicious soup that uses many of the season's vegetables.

● *Red cabbage must be cooked with some kind of acid to keep its rich, red hue. If acid is neglected, the cabbage will turn a grayish purple shade.*

HOT RED CABBAGE SLAW

3 slices nitrite-free bacon, diced
2 cups finely shredded red cabbage
1 egg
1 tablespoon vinegar
½ teaspoon salt
1 tablespoon honey

1. Slowly brown diced bacon in skillet. Pour off excess grease.
2. Add shredded cabbage. Cover skillet and steam 3 minutes over medium heat, until cabbage is tender but crisp, and retains its bright color.
3. Mix together remaining ingredients. Add to cabbage and bacon and toss lightly until egg is cooked—about 2 minutes. Serve immediately.

Makes 4 servings

Note: Mustard greens would work nicely in place of the red cabbage.

SIMPLE COUSCOUS

1½ pounds beef or lamb, cut into pieces
1 onion, minced
3 ounces tomato paste
1 quart water
1 cup tomatoes, peeled and chopped

BOUQUET GARNI:
1 teaspoon basil
2 teaspoons sage
2 teaspoons parsley
1 teaspoon tarragon
1 teaspoon oregano
1¾ cups cabbage
1¼ cups diced turnips
1¼ cups cubed winter squash
½ cup sliced green onions
1¼ cups diced sweet potatoes
1 cup diced pumpkin
   salt to taste
   pepper to taste
1 cup millet (uncooked)

1. Brown the meat with the onion. Add tomato paste diluted with the water, the tomatoes and the *bouquet garni* and simmer, covered, for 30 minutes.
2. Peel and chop the vegetables, add to the meat and tomato mixture, season to taste, and simmer for 1 hour or until the meat is tender. Remove the meat and vegetables from the sauce and keep them warm.
3. Add the uncooked millet to the hot liquid and simmer until it is tender, about 30 minutes. Add meat and vegetables and serve hot.

Makes 6 servings

● *Cooking time varies with the variety of cabbage served, and the way it is cut. Common green cabbage will cook in 15 minutes or less when cut in wedges, and shredded cabbage will be tender in 5 to 7 minutes. Wedges of Savoy cabbage need closer to 20 minutes to cook.*

SAVORY STUFFED CABBAGE ROLLS

Preheat oven to 350°F.

1 large cabbage
1 pound ground beef, browned and drained
3 tablespoons uncooked rice
4 tablespoons grated onion
3 teaspoons salt
½ teaspoon pepper
1 egg
3 tablespoons cold water
1¾ cups tomato sauce
1 tablespoon vegetable oil
1 cup stewed tomatoes
3 tablespoons honey
2 tablespoons lemon juice
¼ cup seedless raisins

1. Pour boiling water over the whole cabbage to cover and let soak for 15 minutes. Carefully remove 12 leaves; if leaves are small use 18.
2. Mix together beef, rice, grated onion, salt and pepper, egg and water. Put about 2 tablespoons of the meat mixture on each cabbage leaf. Tuck in sides and roll up carefully.
3. Place in a deep casserole dish; pour tomato sauce, oil and stewed tomatoes over cabbage rolls, then cover and bake at 350°F. for 1½ hours.
4. Add the honey, lemon juice, and raisins to sauce and cook 30 minutes longer.

Makes 6 servings

Note: This dish makes a good complete meal served with a tossed salad and whole grain bread.

VEGETABLE CURRY

1 cup shredded cabbage
1 cup green peas
1 cup green or yellow snap beans
2 potatoes, diced
3 tablespoons salad oil
2 onions, sliced thin
½ cup green pepper, chopped
1 tablespoon ground coriander
½ teaspoon cumin
½ teaspoon anise seed, crushed
¼ teaspoon ground cardamom
⅛ teaspoon ground cinnamon
⅛ teaspoon ground cloves
¼ teaspoon chili powder
½ teaspoon ginger
2 tablespoons coriander leaves, chopped
   salt, to taste
1½ cups coconut milk (not sweetened coconut juice)
1 tablespoon lemon juice

1. Bring 1 cup of water to boil in large saucepan. Add cabbage, peas, beans and potatoes. Simmer 5 minutes. Drain.
2. Heat oil in frying pan and sauté onions until golden. Add green pepper and spices; mix well to coat with oil.
3. Add mixed vegetables and salt to frying pan, mixing well. Cook 3 to 5 minutes, stirring frequently. Add coconut milk and lemon juice and simmer gently until vegetables are tender.

Makes 8 servings

DANISH SWEET AND SOUR CABBAGE

4 tablespoons butter
1 medium head red cabbage, shredded
½ cup water
3 tablespoons cider vinegar

3 tablespoons red currant jelly
½ teaspoon caraway seed, optional
    salt to taste

1. Melt butter in a large saucepan. Stir in the remaining ingredients.
2. Bring to a boil, cover, and simmer gently for 1½ hours. Stir the mixture occasionally and add more water if the cabbage gets dry.
3. Salt to taste and serve hot.

Makes 6 servings

LION'S HEAD

1 pound ground lean pork
½ pound mushrooms, minced
1 large onion, minced
12 water chestnuts, minced
1 egg
¼ teaspoon ginger
2 tablespoons sherry
4 tablespoons tamari soy sauce
½ teaspoon salt
1 teaspoon honey
2 teaspoons cornstarch
1 tablespoon salad oil
1 head Chinese cabbage or celery cabbage, sliced
1½ cups boiling water

1. Mix and shape meatballs using the pork, mushrooms, onion, water chestnuts, egg, ginger, sherry, soy sauce, salt, honey, cornstarch and oil. Brown in frying pan, and drain off fat.
2. Arrange sliced cabbage in a Dutch oven, and put the drained meatballs on top. Add boiling water and simmer ½ hour, covered. Do not stir.

Makes 6 servings

Note: If you wet your hands while making meatballs, the mixture will not stick to you. To reduce the odor of cabbage, place a slice of bread on top of the meatballs and remove before serving.

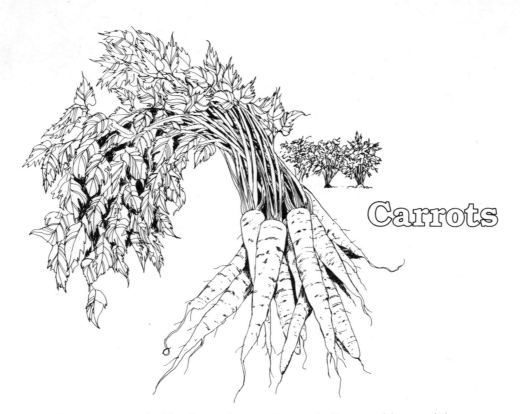

Carrots

Carrots are probably the easiest to grow of all vegetables, and few vegetable gardens would be considered complete without them. In the Middle Ages, carrots were esteemed for the beauty of their delicate foliage, but today carrots are popular primarily because of their high vitamin A content. Actually, carrots contain not vitamin A, but carotene, a substance which our bodies use to manufacture vitamin A. Varieties with a bright golden orange color have the largest amounts of carotene. Paler carrots contain less.

Carrots should be thinned to stand about two inches apart in the row, when the seedlings are two to three inches high. Wise gardeners begin harvesting their young carrots when they have grown to slightly less than half an inch in diameter. These baby carrots, served whole and unpeeled, are a gourmet's delight—tender, sweet, and altogether delicious whether served raw or cooked. For peak flavor and tenderness, try not to let your carrots get much bigger than four inches in length and an inch in diameter.

Carrots can be grown for immediate use or, as they are a root crop, may be left in the ground in fall until after the first frost. But unlike the hardier roots, such as parsnips and salsify, carrots have to be dug and stored before they are hit by heavier frosts.

There are several ways to store carrots, depending on the size of your crop. When properly stored, carrots keep well and retain their flavor. Cool,

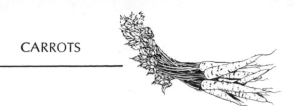

moist surroundings, with the temperature from 32° to 42°F., and the humidity around 90 to 95 percent, provide the best environment for long-term storage of carrots. The storage barrel and pit methods described on page xiii are probably the handiest ways to keep your carrots for extended storage.

Please take note that unlike beets, the tops and stems of carrots must be removed before storage since they drain the moisture from the root. If you leave the tops attached, your carrots will be limp and dry within a day or two. Carrots for immediate use can be refrigerated in a plastic bag or vegetable crisper for one to two weeks. They are usually preserved by freezing, but may also be canned.

To prepare your organically grown carrots for cooking, all you need to do is trim the ends and give them a good scrubbing with a vegetable brush. Carrots should only be peeled if they are old and their skins are tough, because peeling destroys the nutrients that lie just beneath the skins of carrots. Many of the newer varieties have been specially bred to have thin skins that are easily eaten. In addition to carotene, carrots also supply B vitamins and minerals. Plan on using 1 to 1½ pounds for four servings.

CINNAMON CARROT STICKS

> 12 medium-large carrots (enough carrot sticks to fill a
>   1-quart container)
> 2½ cups water
> ½ cup cider vinegar
> ½ cup honey
> 1 stick cinnamon

1. Scrub the carrots well, scrape if necessary, and cut into sticks. Place in a saucepan and add the water. Bring to a boil, covered, until the carrots are just tender, about 5 minutes. Drain them and reserve the liquid.
2. Put the carrots into a refrigerator bowl, with cover, and add the spices to the carrot liquid. Bring to a boil, and pour over the carrots. Refrigerate overnight before serving. These will keep about two weeks and are very good on an antipasto plate.

Makes about 1 quart

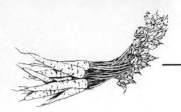

CARROT COCONUT BREAD

Preheat oven to 350°F.

3 eggs
¾ cup oil
1 teaspoon vanilla
2 cups shredded carrots
1 cup shredded coconut
1 cup chopped walnuts
½ cup honey
1 cup raisins
1½ cups whole wheat flour
½ cup oat flour
1 teaspoon baking powder
1 teaspoon baking soda
1 teaspoon cinnamon
½ teaspoon salt

1. Beat eggs until light. Stir in oil, vanilla, carrots, coconut, walnuts, honey and raisins.
2. Mix flours, baking powder, baking soda, cinnamon and salt. Add to first mixture. Do not overmix.
3. Spread in oiled 9 x 5 x 3 loaf pan and bake at 350°F. for 70 minutes or until done. Let stand 10 minutes and turn out of pan, right side up. Cool thoroughly.

Makes 1 loaf

CARROT CASSEROLE

Preheat oven to 350°F.

1 cup whole wheat bread crumbs
2 cups grated carrots
2 eggs, slightly beaten
1½ cups milk

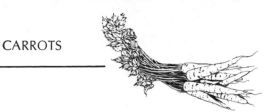

1¼ teaspoons salt
⅛ teaspoon pepper
¼ cup butter, melted
½ cup granola

1. Mix all ingredients except granola in a bowl. After mixing, place in buttered 1½-quart casserole.
2. Sprinkle with granola. Bake in a preheated oven at 350°F. for 45 minutes.

Makes 6 servings

CARROT RELISH

2 cups diced carrots
½ cup diced celery
½ small green pepper, finely diced
1 cup mung bean sprouts, chopped
1 onion, diced
¼ cup water
½ teaspoon salt
3 tablespoons apple cider vinegar
1 tablespoon safflower oil
1½ teaspoons honey
1 teaspoon mustard seed
½ teaspoon dry mustard
⅛ teaspoon pepper

1. Place carrots in small amount of boiling water and cook until tender-crisp.
2. Drain and put into a bowl with celery, pepper, mung bean sprouts and onion.
3. Put ¼ cup water into saucepan and add remaining ingredients. Bring to a boil and pour over vegetables.
4. Mix well, cover and chill overnight, stirring once or twice. Add a little more salt, if necessary.

Makes 6 to 8 servings

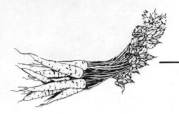

JOYCE'S CARROT CAKE

Preheat oven to 350°F.

1 cup oil
4 eggs
1 cup honey
2 cups unbleached flour
2 teaspoons baking powder
½ teaspoon baking soda
½ teaspoon salt
1 teaspoon vanilla
1 cup grated carrots (4 or 5)
1 cup raisins
1 cup chopped walnuts

1. Blend oil, eggs and honey in a large mixing bowl.
2. Gradually add dry ingredients, and beat well.
3. Add vanilla, carrots, raisins and nuts and mix thoroughly.
4. Bake in oiled and floured tube pan at 350°F. for 1 hour. Serve with softened cream cheese, if desired.

Makes 8 to 10 servings

FRENCH-STYLE CARROTS

½ cup water
6 medium carrots, cut into julienne strips
2 tablespoons butter
2 teaspoons honey
¼ teaspoon salt
1 teaspoon lemon juice
½ teaspoon chopped fresh chives
½ teaspoon chopped fresh parsley

1. Bring water to a boil in a saucepan.
2. Add all ingredients except chives and parsley, cover, and cook over medium-high heat until water evaporates, about 5 to 10 minutes.
3. Remove pot from heat, and stir carrots until all are coated with remaining sauce. Sprinkle with chives and parsley, and serve immediately.

Makes 3 to 4 servings

Note: Try making the sauce and serving it with raw carrots for an interesting texture contrast.

CARROT PINEAPPLE MOLD

1 cup cold orange juice
2 envelopes unflavored gelatin
½ lemon, seeded and peeled
1½ tablespoons honey
¼ teaspoon salt
1½ cups carrot pieces
1½ cups canned crushed pineapple, packed in juice
salad greens

1. Put half the cold orange juice into blender with gelatin. Whirl at low speed to soften gelatin.
2. Bring remaining orange juice to boil, add to blender and whirl at low speed to dissolve. (If gelatin granules cling to container, push down with rubber spatula.)
3. When gelatin is dissolved, add lemon, honey and salt and whirl at high speed until smooth. Add carrot pieces, cover and chop a second or two. Add pineapple and chop again for a second.
4. Turn into mold and chill until firm. Unmold on greens.

Makes 6 servings

CURRIED CARROT SOUP

1 medium onion, chopped
2 tablespoons butter
4 carrots, thinly sliced
4 cups chicken broth
¼ teaspoon lemon juice
1 teaspoon curry powder
    salt and pepper to taste
¼ cup sprouts, chopped

1. Sauté onion in the butter in a saucepan until golden.
2. Add carrots, broth, lemon juice and curry powder. Bring to a boil, cover, and simmer 20 minutes or until carrots are tender.
3. Add salt and pepper to taste.
4. Put half the mixture into blender and blend until smooth.
5. Stir blended soup back into remaining soup, add chopped sprouts and heat until hot.

Makes 3 to 4 servings

● *Late thinnings produce the succulent baby carrots that are so delectable when served whole, with just a whisper of butter and a sprinkling of fresh parsley.*

CARROT TZIMMES

3 tablespoons fine barley
5 cups grated raw carrots
1 cup grated apple
1½ teaspoons salt
1 tablespoon honey (more if desired)
½ cup water
5 tablespoons butter
½ teaspoon powdered ginger

1. Wash the barley, cover with water in a saucepan, and bring to a boil. Turn heat off, let soak 1 hour; drain.
2. Add the remaining ingredients to the saucepan. Cover and cook over low heat 1½ hours, or until barley is tender. Stir frequently, and add a little water if mixture becomes too dry.

Makes 6 servings

● *If you have large carrots, you may find that you prefer their taste when they are cut in julienne strips rather than when they are sliced in rounds.*

ZESTY CARROTS

Preheat oven to 375°F.

1 dozen medium-sized carrots
3 tablespoons grated onion
2 tablespoons horseradish
½ cup mayonnaise
1 teaspoon salt
½ teaspoon freshly ground pepper
½ cup buttered whole grain bread crumbs

1. Slice carrots lengthwise and arrange in buttered baking dish.
2. Combine remaining ingredients, except bread crumbs, and spread over carrots.
3. Top with buttered crumbs and bake 20 to 30 minutes at 375°F.

Makes 6 servings

Note: This is a tasty recipe to try when your carrots are perhaps past their prime. If yours are quite large, six or eight carrots would do it.

73

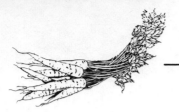

SUMMERY CARROT BAKE

Preheat oven to 375°F.

4 cups sliced carrots
½ teaspoon salt
2 tablespoons molasses
3 tablespoons butter
2 tablespoons fresh mint leaves, chopped

1. Place carrots in an oiled casserole that has a cover.
2. Sprinkle with salt and molasses; dot with butter. Top with chopped mint.
3. Cover and bake at 375°F. for 30 to 45 minutes.

Makes 4 servings

Note: Honey may be substituted for molasses if you prefer a lighter flavor.

Cauliflower

This oddball member of the cabbage family is grown for its flowers rather than its leaves. Cauliflower can pose a challenge to the gardener, for it does not tolerate as much cold as the other cabbages and will not head up properly in hot summer weather. Despite its sensitivity to frosts, cauliflower grows best in a cool, humid climate.

Very fertile soil with a high moisture content facilitates the cultivation of large, leafy cauliflowers. Just before maturity, a small flower appears at the heart of the plant. When the flower head of the cauliflower becomes egg-sized, the large, inner leaves should be drawn together and tied loosely to shield the head from the sun. The covered head must be watched closely because when a solid flower develops, the cauliflower must be harvested immediately, while the curds are compact and firm, or they will quickly become dried out and ricey-looking. It is better to cut this crop a bit too early than too late.

The weather determines how long it takes the head to mature. In warm weather, the cauliflower will be ready to harvest three to five days after the leaves are tied. However, when the weather is cool, it may take as long as two weeks until the head is ready to be cut. When harvesting the cauliflower, cut the stem well below the head. The plant may also be pulled up by the

roots and stored in a cool cellar, where it will keep about one month.

Cauliflower can be refrigerated in a plastic bag or other airtight container up to five days before it begins to deteriorate in quality. Cauliflower freezes well, and is also a popular ingredient in mixed pickles. To prepare cauliflower for cooking, remove the outer leaves and cut off the stem at the base of the head. Although it damages the nutrient content of the vegetable, you may find it necessary to soak your cauliflower in cold, salted water for 15 to 20 minutes before cooking to draw out any tiny bugs. Cook the cauliflower whole or separate it into florets first.

Cauliflower contains appreciable amounts of calcium and potassium, and vitamins A and C. One medium-sized head will make four servings.

CAULIFLOWER CASSEROLE

Preheat oven to 350°F.

1 medium cauliflower, separated into florets
1 cup green pepper, diced

SAUCE:
   3 tablespoons oil
   3 tablespoons unbleached or whole wheat flour
   1½ cups milk
   1 cup grated cheddar cheese
   ½ teaspoon salt
   dash pepper

1. Steam cauliflower and diced pepper until barely tender; drain and arrange in 1½-quart casserole.
2. In skillet, blend oil and flour; add milk, stirring constantly. Bring to boil; cook for 1 minute. Stir in half the cheese, the salt and pepper; stir until smooth. Pour sauce over vegetables.
3. Bake at 350°F. for 25 minutes. Sprinkle remaining cheese over top of casserole and bake for 5 minutes more.

Makes 4 to 6 servings

BAKED CAULIFLOWER

Preheat oven to 350°F.

1 head cauliflower
¼ cup butter
1 cup sharp cheese, grated
    salt and pepper to taste
1 teaspoon tarragon

1. Cut cauliflower into pieces and arrange in shallow casserole.
2. Melt butter and pour on top.
3. Sprinkle with cheese, salt and pepper, and garnish with tarragon.
4. Bake at 350°F. for 30 minutes.

Makes 4 to 6 servings

Note: This tangy dish is a simple and sure way to deal with cauliflower.

ENGLISH-STYLE CAULIFLOWER

1 fresh-picked cauliflower
2 tablespoons butter
1 tablespoon chopped fresh chives
1 tablespoon chopped fresh parsley
    salt and pepper to taste

1. Select a mature head of cauliflower from the garden, with fresh green leaves. Clean and wash, leaving two rows of leaves surrounding the head.
2. Steam cauliflower until just tender. Place on a hot serving platter.
3. Melt the butter, blend in the seasonings and pour over the cauliflower. Serve at once.

Makes 4 to 6 servings

Note: This is a most attractive and delicious way to serve fresh-from-the-garden cauliflower. Be sure to eat the leaves—excellent!

RED, WHITE, AND GREEN SALAD

1 small head cauliflower
1 pound spinach
1 medium-sized red onion, sliced and separated into rings

DRESSING:
    6 tablespoons olive oil or vegetable oil
    3 tablespoons white wine vinegar
    1 clove garlic, minced
    ½ teaspoon basil
    ½ teaspoon dry mustard
      salt and freshly ground pepper to taste
      dash of nutmeg

½ cup slivered almonds
1 tablespoon butter

1. Coarsely chop well-rinsed cauliflower. Wash spinach leaves well and pat dry. Tear leaves into a salad bowl with cauliflower and onion rings.
2. In a jar, combine oil, vinegar, garlic, basil, dry mustard, salt, pepper, and nutmeg. Shake to blend well.
3. Brown almonds in butter in a small skillet.
4. Pour dressing over vegetables, add almonds and toss gently. Serve.

Makes 6 servings

Note: The outstanding combination of colors in this tasty salad makes it an especially good dish to serve company.

CAULIFLOWER-LIMA SALAD

1 small cauliflower, separated into florets and cooked until barely tender
2 to 3 cups lima beans, cooked, or 1 cup dry limas, cooked

¼ cup chopped onion
¼ cup chopped green pepper
¼ pound to ½ pound Swiss cheese, cut in chunks
½ teaspoon salt
¼ teaspoon basil
    pepper to taste
3 tablespoons oil
1 tablespoon vinegar

1. Place vegetables, cheese and seasonings in a bowl and toss well.
2. Combine oil and vinegar, pour over salad and mix until coated.

Makes 8 to 10 servings

SWISS CAULIFLOWER

Preheat oven to 350°F.

1 fresh cauliflower
2 to 3 stalks celery, with leaves
2 tablespoons butter
1 clove garlic, minced
    salt and pepper to taste
    pinch of thyme or rosemary
1 tablespoon chopped fresh parsley
¼ pound Swiss cheese, grated

1. Separate cauliflower into florets. Slice celery. Steam both vegetables to-gether until almost tender, 5 to 8 minutes. Drain.
2. Melt butter in a large skillet. Sauté garlic briefly, then add vegetables and sauté lightly for 5 minutes. Stir in seasonings and blend together well.
3. In a small but deep baking dish, layer vegetables and cheese, ending with cheese. Bake at 350°F. 15 to 20 minutes, until cheese is melted.

Makes 4 servings

SUMMERTIME SUPPER

Preheat oven to 375°F.

1 small cauliflower, cut into florets
½ cup green beans, cut into pieces
½ cup shredded red cabbage
    pinch each of rosemary, thyme and summer savory
½ cup onion, finely chopped
1 clove garlic, minced

SAUCE:
   2 tablespoons butter
   2 tablespoons whole wheat flour
   1½ cups milk
   ½ teaspoon salt
   1 teaspoon dry mustard
     dash cayenne
   1 cup grated sharp cheese

6 slices nitrite-free bacon, fried and crumbled (optional)

1. Steam cauliflower, beans and cabbage until barely tender. Add herbs.
2. Stir-fry vegetables with onion and garlic just until vegetables are coated with oil and onion is clear.
3. Prepare sauce:
   Melt butter in a saucepan and stir in flour to make a *roux*. Add milk and seasonings and cook, stirring, until thickened. Stir in cheese until melted and sauce is smooth.
4. Mix vegetables and bacon in a 1½-quart casserole and cover with cheese sauce.
5. Bake at 375°F. for 5 to 7 minutes, or until bubbly. Serve with brown rice and a green salad.

Makes 3 to 4 servings

Variation: A large bunch of broccoli, chopped, may be substituted for the cauliflower.

CAULIFLOWER QUICHE

Preheat oven to 375°F.

3 cups cooked brown rice
1 cauliflower
4 eggs, beaten
2 cups milk
1 cup grated cheese (of your choice)
2 tablespoons whole wheat bread crumbs
   pinch of nutmeg
   salt and pepper to taste

1. First, make *quiche* shells of brown rice. Press half the rice into each of 2 pie plates, to form shells. Bake at 375°F. just until dry, about 5 minutes. Set aside to cool.
2. Steam the cauliflower until barely tender and chop it into half-inch pieces.
3. Combine all the other ingredients, add the cauliflower, and mix well.
4. Pour into brown rice shells and bake at 375°F. for 20 to 30 minutes, until set.

Makes 2 pies

● *The parts of the cauliflower that are usually discarded—the stem and leaves— can both be put to good use in the kitchen. The stem can be peeled and diced and used in soups, and the leaves, if fresh and unblemished, can be cooked and served with butter and seasonings.*

● *When cooking a whole cauliflower, place it stem down in a small amount of water and cover the pot tightly. This method allows the cauliflower to steam evenly, and also preserves its white color.*

● *Many children don't like cauliflower cooked, but will eat it raw, especially when it's served with a tangy dip. Cauliflower has a high content of sulfur, some of which is released during cooking to create the strong flavor kids dislike.*

CAULIFLOWER AND PEAS WITH CURRY CREAM SAUCE

SAUCE:
    2 tablespoons butter
    2 tablespoons whole wheat flour
    1 teaspoon ground cumin
    ¾ teaspoon tumeric
    ½ teaspoon ground cardamom
    1 cup milk

1 head cauliflower, separated into florets, cooked
2 cups cooked, fresh peas
1 tablespoon chopped parsley
    dash of paprika

1. Melt butter in skillet or saucepan. Add flour and seasonings and blend into a *roux*. Gradually add milk and stir until sauce is smooth and thick.
2. Add cauliflower and peas and heat thoroughly. Top with chopped parsley and paprika and serve immediately.

Makes 4 to 6 servings

●   *A head of cauliflower that has developed some brownish, discolored spots doesn't have to be thrown away. If the rest of the head is firm, just cut off the discolored parts and use the rest of the head.*

Celery

In many kitchens, celery is a staple item. Like carrots and onions, it's always available to chop into a green salad or flavor a soup or stew. Raw celery stalks are a standard component on relish trays, and when finely chopped, they can extend chicken or shrimp or tuna in a salad. Celery can also be steamed and served as a vegetable all by itself, and its leaves and seeds are flavorful seasonings for many other dishes.

It's been termed a difficult vegetable for home gardens because it demands lots of moisture, rich soil, and cool nights. Many people also feel that it's necessary to blanch celery, believing that it makes the stalks more tender and less stringy. However, white celery, whether it's a standard variety which has been blanched or a lighter self-blanching type, has less nutritional value than the green. If you'd like to try blanching your celery, cover the plants with paper collars made of thick building paper or with 12-inch boards inverted in a 'V' over the row. Allow a few inches of leaves to protrude above the covers. Bank soil around the bottoms of the plants in order to exclude light from below. Self-blanching celery, which is hereditarily lighter in color than other varieties, must be blanched two to three weeks before harvest in warm weather, three weeks to a month in cool weather.

You can start harvesting your celery as you need it from the time the plants are half-grown. If intended for immediate use, cut the plant's roots right

below the soil surface. Trim, rinse, and shake off excess moisture before storing in a plastic bag in the refrigerator. It will keep for up to two weeks.

Except in the very coldest areas, celery may be left in the garden over the winter covered with a thick layer of straw or leaves. If you find it more convenient, celery may also be stored in an outdoor trench or in a root cellar. For such storage, pull the entire plant with roots and some soil still attached. Do not wash it, and, to avoid odor contamination, do not store celery near cabbage or turnips. For best results, keep the celery as nearly upright as possible, and pack the plants close together to provide more humidity. Push the roots firmly into moist sand or soil, and press the soil around the roots to provide support. Water the roots occasionally during the storage period, but do not water the leaves.

For outdoor storage dig a trench 12 to 18 inches deep and about 24 inches wide. Pack the plants closely together as described above for root cellar storage, and then cover the trench with boards placed in an inverted 'V'. Cover this roof with straw and earth for more protection. Celery will keep under such conditions through the fall and early winter and will blanch itself while being stored.

To prepare celery for eating or cooking, trim off the root end and any discolored or damaged leaves. Scrub the stalks well before using, and don't discard the leaves if you feel it necessary to peel them off. Save them for use in a salad or soup. Two cups of chopped celery will serve four people. Unblanched celery provides more than 10 times the vitamin A of the blanched product and 3 times the amount of vitamin B_2.

CURRIED CELERY

2 cups chopped celery
2 tablespoons butter
2 tablespoons flour
1 cup milk
¼ teaspoon salt
1 teaspoon curry powder

1. Steam celery until just tender, not mushy.
2. Meanwhile, melt butter in a saucepan, blend in flour to make a *roux*. Add milk and seasonings; cook, stirring, until thickened.
3. Stir cooked and drained celery into sauce and serve at once over brown rice or grain burgers.

Makes 4 servings

Note: Chicken fat and stock may be used instead of butter and milk.

CELERY, ITALIAN STYLE

2 cups diced celery
2 tablespoons butter or oil
¼ cup finely chopped onion
½ clove garlic, minced
4 teaspoons finely chopped green pepper
⅔ teaspoon salt
1 cup fresh tomatoes, skinned and cut in wedges
1 tablespoon chopped fresh parsley
¼ teaspoon basil, scant
   dash cayenne
   pinch black pepper

1. Put celery in a saucepan with ½ cup boiling water and cook 10 minutes, or until tender. Drain, and reserve liquid to use in soups.
2. Melt butter in a skillet. Add onion, garlic, green pepper and salt; sauté slowly 5 minutes. Stir in tomatoes, celery and seasonings. Cook 5 to 10 minutes more.

Makes 4 servings

CELERY PUREE (OR SAUCE)

1 bunch celery, including leaves (about 5 cups)
1 cup chicken stock
⅛ teaspoon chopped fresh basil
  dash of dillweed powder
  salt to taste

1. Cut celery into 1-inch pieces and simmer in chicken stock until tender (15 to 20 minutes). Puree in blender.
2. Add basil and dill. Salt to taste (depending on saltiness of stock). Heat until very hot and serve at once.

Makes 4 to 6 servings

Note: This is surprisingly delicious as a side dish or served as sauce on chicken, fish or other vegetables.

MAIN DISH ANTIPASTO

⅔ cup olive oil
1½ cups celery, cut in 1-inch pieces
2 cups onion, cut and separated into rings
1 cup cauliflower, separated into florets
1 cup mushrooms, sliced lengthwise
1 cup green pepper, seeded and cut in strips
5 cloves garlic, minced
½ cup tomato puree or paste
1 cup dry vermouth
½ pound shrimp, cleaned and deveined
½ pound scallops
1 teaspoon basil
1 cup parsley, chopped
½ cup green olives
½ cup black olives
  small can anchovies, halved
4 eggs, hard-boiled and quartered

1. Braise vegetables in oil in a large frying pan, about 5 minutes. Do not burn. Add tomato paste and vermouth. Let mixture simmer.
2. When vegetables begin to soften, add shrimps and scallops, simmer another 5 minutes.
3. Add basil, parsley, olives, and anchovies. Mix well and chill for at least 3 hours.
4. Serve on a large plate on a bed of lettuce. Garnish with quartered eggs.

Makes 8 to 10 servings

Note: If you prefer, eliminate the tomato puree and serve the antipasto with an oil and vinegar dressing.

TANGY BRAISED CELERY

6 tablespoons butter or oil
6 cups celery, sliced (including leaves)
2 medium green peppers, cut in strips
2 tablespoons onion, finely chopped
1 teaspoon salt
¼ teaspoon pepper
¼ teaspoon oregano
½ cup chicken broth
¼ cup yogurt

1. Melt butter or heat oil in a large, heavy skillet. Add celery, green pepper, and onion; sauté briefly to coat vegetables.
2. Add seasonings and broth. Cover and cook 8 minutes, or until celery is almost tender.
3. Uncover and cook another 3 or 4 minutes, until vegetables are tender and liquid is absorbed.
4. Stir in yogurt and heat briefly; do not boil. Serve at once.

Makes 6 servings

VEGETARIAN CHOP SUEY

1 cup onions, sliced
1 cup celery, chopped
1 cup sliced peppers (green or red)
1 cup sliced mushrooms
1 to 2 cups mung bean sprouts
2 tablespoons nutritional yeast
1½ tablespoons tamari soy sauce
½ cup sliced or whole almonds

1. Sauté onions and celery in a small amount of oil for a few minutes, until onions are limp.
2. Add the peppers and mushrooms, cover and heat thoroughly. Add the sprouts, nutritional yeast and soy sauce.
3. Serve on brown rice and garnish with almonds. Pass the soy sauce and more sprouts.

Makes 4 servings

Celeriac

This subtly flavored root crop is an especially valuable vegetable because it is available fresh when the garden offers few choices. Sometimes known as celery root, or turnip-rooted celery, celeriac is indeed closely related to the common celery plant. The chief difference is that celery forms the familiar thick stalks, and celeriac forms an enlarged, bulbous "knob" at the base of its stem. Because the knob forms underground, celeriac is generally considered a root crop, even though it is not actually a root in a strict botanical sense.

Celeriac is planted in spring like parsnips, and harvested in late fall or during the winter. Harvesting can begin when the stem at ground level reaches a thickness of two inches. This hardy vegetable will survive a mild winter in the garden, especially if tucked in with a blanket of mulch. In northern states, however, it is usually better to pull the plants before the temperature dips below 10°F. If the roots are cut off with a few inches of the tops left attached, they can be stored through the rest of the winter in sand or dirt in a cool, dry garage, barn or basement.

Celeriac tastes like a more delicate and refined version of celery. It is sometimes used raw, shredded into salads, but it tastes especially elegant when cooked. Just peel, slice, and steam until tender, and serve with a cream

sauce. Celeriac can also be substituted with good results in recipes calling for cooked celery.

Plan 1½ pounds of celeriac for four servings.

CELERIAC IN BROTH

6 celeriac roots
1 tablespoon oil or chicken fat
3 cups chicken or beef stock
  salt and pepper to taste
  chopped parsley for garnish

1. Scrape or peel the celeriac; cut lengthwise into thin slices.
2. In a heavy-bottomed pot, briefly sauté the slices in the oil. Add the stock, bring to boil, reduce heat. Cook, covered, until the celeriac is tender, about 30 minutes.
3. Season with salt and pepper; serve garnished with chopped parsley. The liquid can be thickened slightly and served as a sauce.

Makes 3 to 4 servings

Note: Young turnips may be substituted for the celeriac in this recipe.

STUFFED CELERIAC

Preheat oven to 350°F.

2 celeriac roots
2 tablespoons butter
1 small onion, chopped
1 carrot, chopped
½ teaspoon salt
⅛ teaspoon pepper
1 tablespoon butter
1 tablespoon grated cheddar cheese

1. Scrape celeriac roots, then cut them into slices about 1½ inches thick (crosswise). Blanch for 5 minutes in salted water, plunge into cold water, drain and dry on paper towels. Scoop a hollow in each slice to about half its depth.
2. Chop the pulp which has been removed. Melt butter and sauté the celeriac pulp, onion and carrot for about 5 minutes. Add salt and pepper.
3. Stuff the celeriac rounds with the vegetable mixture and place in a buttered shallow casserole. Dot with butter and sprinkle with cheese. Bake at 350°F. for about 30 minutes.

Makes 4 servings

CELERIAC LOAF

Preheat oven to 350°F.

2 cups chopped celeriac, or celery with leaves
1 small bunch parsley
¾ cup pecans
1 large onion
½ green pepper, seeded and sliced
2 eggs, beaten
2 tablespoons vegetable oil
1 tablespoon olive oil
1 teaspoon salt
1½ cups milk
1 cup whole wheat bread crumbs

1. Put celeriac, parsley, pecans, onion and pepper through a food mill or grinder.
2. Combine all ingredients. Pour into loaf pan.
3. Bake for 1 hour, or until firm.
4. Slice, and serve with a tomato sauce.

Makes 6 to 8 servings

Note: The tomato sauce provides a pleasing color contrast in this dish.

CELERIAC JULIENNE

2 celeriac roots
1 tablespoon butter
¼ teaspoon salt
1 teaspoon honey
    water to just cover bottom of saucepan

1. Wash and pare celeriac roots, then cut into julienne strips.
2. Heat butter in a saucepan, add celeriac strips, salt, honey and water. Simmer gently for about 25 minutes, or until tender.

Makes 4 to 6 servings

Note: Serve as an accompaniment or garnish for meat or fowl.

● *The knobby bulb of the celeriac is hard to peel. Many cooks find it easier to cut it in slices, and then peel the slices.*

MASHED CELERIAC AND POTATOES

1 pound celeriac, peeled
½ pound potatoes
1 tablespoon butter
  milk
  salt and pepper to taste
2 tablespoons chopped parsley

1. Cook celeriac and potatoes separately until tender; drain.
2. Mash vegetables together with butter, enough milk to make a fluffy consistency, and salt and pepper to taste. Garnish with chopped parsley.

Makes 4 servings

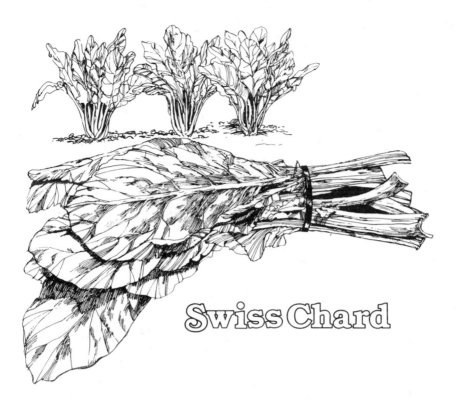

Swiss Chard

Swiss chard is related to the red beet; it has large, thick red or white stems similar to those of rhubarb, but its leaves more closely resemble spinach. Gardeners cultivate this plant primarily for its large, deep green leaves, which are used in much the same way as spinach. In fact, the flavor of chard is not unlike that of spinach, although it is quite a bit milder. Chard is a warm weather plant which thrives in the heat of the summer season. Harvesting begins when the largest outer leaves are seven inches high. These leaves can be removed with a sharp knife. About a week later, the inner leaves will have reached harvest size. Chard usually provides greens for cooking from July until frost. Covering plants with a deep layer of straw or some similar mulch will allow them to keep on producing after the weather has turned cold.

Chard may be refrigerated for a few days, but after that, the leaves will start to wilt and become limp. Freezing is the best method of preservation. To prepare chard for cooking, slice off the thick stems and wash the leaves carefully to remove any dirt or silt. The stems may be saved and cooked separately.

Chard is rich in vitamin A and has substantial amounts of vitamin C and iron, in addition to various other minerals. About 1½ pounds of Swiss chard will make four servings.

BENGALI-STYLE SWISS CHARD

5 tablespoons vegetable oil
3 large yellow onions, thinly sliced
2 cloves garlic, finely minced
1¼ pounds (6 to 8) carrots, sliced
½ pound (medium) eggplant, sliced in 1-inch strips
1¼ teaspoons salt
¼ teaspoon ground turmeric
1 teaspoon ground cumin
¾ pound Swiss chard, washed and drained

1. Heat vegetable oil in a large skillet with a tight-fitting lid. Add onions and garlic and fry for 2 minutes. Add carrots, eggplant, salt, turmeric, and cumin and cook gently, covered, about 20 minutes, or until vegetables are tender.
2. Uncover and, adding a handful of Swiss chard at a time, stir over medium heat for 30 seconds; repeat until all the chard is added.
3. Cook another 5 to 8 minutes, stirring often. Remove from heat and keep covered until ready to serve.

Makes 4 to 6 servings

FRIED SWISS CHARD

2 pounds fresh Swiss chard
6 tablespoons vegetable oil
  pinch of turmeric
¾ teaspoon ground cumin
½ teaspoon ground coriander
½ teaspoon salt
¼ cup chopped peanuts

1. Wash and finely chop Swiss chard. Boil ¼ cup water. Add chopped chard, cover, and cook about 6 minutes or until tender. Drain well.
2. Heat vegetable oil in a skillet and add turmeric, ground cumin, coriander, and salt. Add chard and continue cooking and stirring, over medium-low

heat, about 5 more minutes.
3. Stir in peanuts, and cook slowly for about 2 minutes. Remove from heat and serve.

Makes 4 to 6 servings

BEAN SOUP WITH SWISS CHARD

1 onion, finely minced
1 small clove garlic, minced
3 tablespoons olive or corn oil
¼ cup tomato puree
¼ cup water
2 cups cooked navy or kidney beans
3 cups vegetable stock or water
1 carrot, diced
½ cup celery leaves, chopped
2 cups Swiss chard, shredded
½ teaspoon salt
   dash of pepper
¼ teaspoon basil
1 teaspoon oregano or marjoram
   chopped parsley for garnish

1. In a saucepan, sauté onion and garlic in oil until lightly browned. Add tomato puree and water, and let this basic sauce simmer about 15 minutes, or until it has cooked down and needs water.
2. Add beans, stock, carrot, celery leaves, chard and seasonings. Cover and cook over medium heat until vegetables are soft.
3. Put soup through a food mill or strain through a colander, and put all vegetables in a blender to liquefy. You will have a thick, creamy soup that can be thinned if desired and seasoned to individual taste. Garnish with chopped parsley.

Makes 4 servings

Note: For a hearty supper dish, try this soup thinned down with brown rice or egg noodles cooked in it.

CHARD-EGG LOAF

Preheat oven to 350°F.

2 carrots, grated
1 medium onion, minced
1 tablespoon oil
2 cups cooked chard, chopped (about 6½-7 cups
    chopped)
6 eggs, beaten
½ teaspoon oregano
½ teaspoon thyme
½ teaspoon salt

1. Sauté carrots and onion in oil until tender. Add chard.
2. Stir eggs into vegetables, add seasonings, and mix well.
3. Pour into greased loaf pan, dot with butter and bake at 350°F. 40 to 45 minutes, until eggs are set.

Makes 8 servings

● *A simple rule of thumb to follow in dealing with chard is to cook the stems like asparagus, and the leaves like spinach.*

STIR-FRIED CHARD

1 to 2 tablespoons peanut oil
2 cloves garlic or 1 small onion, minced
2 cups chard, chopped
2 tablespoons tamari soy sauce
1 tablespoon honey
1 teaspoon sherry (optional)
¼ cup water
2 teaspoons cornstarch, mixed with 1 tablespoon water
    pinch of salt

1. Heat peanut oil in *wok* or large skillet. Sauté garlic or onion until tender. Add chard and stir-fry over medium high heat until just wilted.
2. Stir in soy sauce, honey, sherry and water. Then add cornstarch-water mixture and blend evenly.
3. Reduce heat, cover and simmer until chard is barely tender and sauce is thickened. Serve immediately.

Makes 4 servings

Corn

No store-bought corn, even if you buy it from a farm stand, can compare with what you pick from your own backyard. There's just no other way you could rush the ears from stalk to table in less time. And if you delay cooking sweet corn for just one hour, part of its sugar will have turned to starch. You'll miss the tender sweetness only freshly picked corn has.

Sweet corn should be picked at its peak of ripeness, sometimes called the milk stage. When the tassels turn brown, it's your signal to start watching the ears. When the silks are dry-looking, and the tips of the ears are rounded and full, but not hard, make the milk test. Pull back the husk and dent a kernel with your fingernail. If the corn is ready, the kernel will be plump with a milky liquid; if immature, it will exude water. If past its prime, the kernels will be tough, and the milk will be doughy and starchy.

If your corn tests ripe, go back to the house and put on a pot of water to boil. Then, back to the garden, and twist each ripe ear from its stalk. Husk your harvest as fast as possible. Remove the silks, and place the corn in the water ear by ear to keep the water boiling.

Try to cook and serve your corn, or to process it for storage, within an hour, or at the most, two hours, after picking. If the corn must wait, place the unhusked ears in the coldest part of the refrigerator. Freezing is the pre-

ferred method of longer storage, but sweet corn can also be canned and dried.

Boiling on the cob is the most basic method of preparation. It should take from three to ten minutes depending on maturity, and you shouldn't use any salt until after the corn has been cooked. You can still roast the ears in hot coals as the Indians did, and sweet corn can also be creamed, or put into casseroles, puddings, soups, and fritters. Count at least one six-inch ear per serving. Fresh sweet corn provides vitamins A and C and some phosphorus.

ROASTED CORN

6 large ears corn, as fresh from the stalk as possible
water
butter and salt

1. Pull down the cornhusks only far enough to allow you to remove silk. Run water into each ear of corn (as much as it can hold), let it drain out, then close up the husks and twist them shut.
2. Roast ears over hot coals about 20 minutes, or until tender. Turn occasionally.
3. Remove husks and serve corn immediately, with butter and salt as desired.

Makes 6 servings

SUCCOTASH

1½ cups shelled lima beans, cooked until tender
1½ cups corn kernels (about 3 ears), cooked until tender
½ teaspoon salt
¼ teaspoon pepper
3 tablespoons butter
2 to 3 tablespoons cream (optional)

1. Combine cooked limas and corn in a saucepan. Add salt, pepper and butter and heat until vegetables are hot.
2. Add cream, if desired, and heat gently. Serve at once.

Makes 3 to 4 servings

FRESH CORN RELISH

10 ears sweet corn (about 1¼ quarts corn kernels cut
   from cobs)
½ cup chopped green peppers
¼ cup sweet red pepper
½ cup chopped onions
½ cup chopped celery
¼ cup honey
2 teaspoons mustard seed
2 teaspoons salt
½ teaspoon celery seed
¼ teaspoon turmeric
1 cup water
1⅓ cups vinegar

1. Combine all ingredients and simmer for 20 minutes.
2. Pack into clean, hot, pint jars, leaving 1 inch of head space, and making
   sure vinegar covers vegetables. Adjust lids.
3. Process in boiling water bath, 212°F., for 15 minutes.

Makes 3 pints

TOMATO AND CORN BAKE

Preheat oven to 375°F.

3 cups corn kernels
2 cups cherry tomatoes, whole
4 green onions, chopped
1 clove garlic, minced
   basil and oregano to taste
   salt to taste
3 egg yolks
3 egg whites
3 tablespoons wheat germ or bread crumbs

1. Combine the corn, tomatoes, onion, garlic, herbs, salt and egg yolks.
2. Beat egg whites until stiff.
3. Fold into the vegetables.
4. Sprinkle with wheat germ or bread crumbs. Bake at 375°F. for 40 minutes.

Makes 6 servings

Note: If using medium or small eggs, use 4 or 5.

● *Cooking corn in salted water makes the kernels tough.*

CORN 'N SQUASH SCALLOP

Preheat oven to 350°F.

2 cups grated fresh corn
¼ cup milk
1 egg, beaten
½ teaspoon salt
⅛ teaspoon black pepper
2 cups sliced summer squash
½ cup wheat germ
½ cup whole grain bread crumbs
2 tablespoons butter

1. Combine corn, milk, egg, salt and pepper. Mix thoroughly.
2. In a buttered casserole, arrange half the squash, then a layer of the corn mixture, then another layer of squash, and the remaining corn mixture.
3. Top with the wheat germ and crumbs, then dot with butter. Bake at 350°F. for 30 to 40 minutes.

Makes 6 servings

SCALLOPED CORN AND CHICKEN

Preheat oven to 375°F.

2 cups fresh corn kernels (about 4 ears)
3 cups cubed, cooked chicken
2 tablespoons minced green peppers
2 tablespoons finely minced onion
1½ cups soft whole grain bread crumbs
2 eggs, beaten
1 cup milk
2 tablespoons butter

1. Combine the corn, chicken, green pepper, onion, and 1 cup of the bread crumbs.
2. Add the eggs and milk and put into a greased 1½-quart casserole.
3. Top with remaining bread crumbs, dot with butter and bake at 375°F. for about 25 minutes.

Makes 6 servings

CORN CHOWDER

1½ cups milk
1 cup tomato juice
1 large potato, diced
1 small onion, chopped
¼ cup Swiss cheese, grated
1 teaspoon oregano
1½ cups cut corn

1. Combine milk and tomato juice in saucepan.
2. Add potato and onion; cook for 30 minutes.
3. Add cheese, oregano, and corn. Cook for 5 minutes.

Makes 2 to 3 servings

CORN FRITTERS

4 ears corn
2 eggs, separated
  pinch of salt
  dash of pepper

1. With a sharp knife, cut down the middle of each row of kernels on the ears of corn. Turn the knife over and (using the dull side) press out the pulp, leaving the kernel husks on the cob.
2. Stir in the egg yolks, salt, and pepper to taste.
3. Beat the egg whites until barely stiff and stir them in. Add a tiny bit of flour if necessary.
4. Drop the batter by tablespoonfuls onto a well-oiled skillet. Cook until nicely browned on both sides. Serve immediately.

Makes 4 servings

MEXI-CORN

½ cup chopped green pepper
½ cup chopped sweet, red pepper
2 tablespoons chopped onion
3 tablespoons oil, butter or chicken fat
3 cups fresh corn kernels (about 6 ears)
2 tablespoons chopped parsley
½ teaspoon salt
⅛ teaspoon black pepper
  dash of red pepper (optional)
1 medium tomato, skinned and chopped

1. In a large skillet, sauté green pepper, red pepper and onions in the oil or butter for 5 minutes.
2. Add corn and continue sautéing for 12 minutes.
3. Add parsley, seasonings and tomato and cook for another 5 minutes.

Makes 6 servings

FRESH CORN PUDDING

Preheat oven to 350°F.

3 ears corn
4 eggs, lightly beaten
2 cups milk
2 tablespoons melted butter
1 teaspoon salt
¼ teaspoon pepper
1 tablespoon honey

1. Scrape corn kernels from cobs, reserving both the corn and the milk. Combine all ingredients and mix well.
2. Oil 4 individual 1½-cup casseroles or a 4-cup baking dish. Pour corn mixture into oiled casseroles and place in a pan with boiling water ¼ inch deep.
3. Bake at 350°F. for 50 minutes, until set. Cool 5 minutes before serving.

Makes 4 to 6 servings

Cucumbers

When you describe eating cucumbers it's the crisp texture and the cool crunch they make in your mouth that you recall. Cucumbers, like their cousins summer squash and watermelon, get their crispness from a high water content; and perhaps it's this water content that makes them such a refreshing addition to summer salad meals. In addition to being served raw or pickled, cucumbers can be sautéed, fried, or made into soup with delectable results.

Though seed catalogs list pickling and slicing varieties of cucumbers, either type can be used for both purposes. The major difference between the two is size. Catch a slicing cuke when it's finger-sized, and you've got a preliminary pickle. And if a pickling variety reaches the five- or six-inch stage, go ahead and slice it into a salad.

Six to seven weeks after planting, small cucumbers will start to form on the vines. They have to be watched closely, for they seem to burgeon overnight into full-grown cucumbers. Start picking as soon as two or three are found in a clump of vines. Harvest frequently—check the plants daily once production gets started, and pick the cukes before they yellow and mature. Besides providing the crispest cucumbers with the smallest seed cavities, such practices encourage the plants to continue producing. A single mature fruit can signal the end of production.

An eating cucumber tastes best at five inches, is slender, firm, bright green and lustrous (though your homegrown cukes will never be as shiny as the waxed ones you find in supermarkets). Pick cucumbers when the leaves are dry in order to avoid spreading disease, and be careful not to injure the vines by stepping on them or tearing off the fruit. Take along a small kitchen knife and cut the cucumber from the vine, leaving a small piece of stem attached.

Wrapped in plastic, cucumbers will remain fresh in the refrigerator crisper drawer for about a week. The best—in fact the only—method for longer storage is pickling. When eaten fresh, young tender cukes need not be peeled. Fruits with unusually tough skins may be scored or peeled before serving. If you have a mature cucumber, you'll also want to scrape out and discard the seeds. Two medium-sized cucumbers should serve four. Though they're more than 95 percent water, they do provide some vitamin A and C and are low in calories.

MARINATED CUCUMBERS

⅓ cup oil
3 tablespoons vinegar
¼ teaspoon honey
½ teaspoon fresh dillweed
½ teaspoon salt
⅛ teaspoon pepper
1 large cucumber
 yogurt

1. Blend oil, vinegar, honey and seasonings in a medium-sized bowl.
2. Wash cucumber and peel if desired. Slice as thinly as possible into a shallow dish. Add marinade and toss until slices are coated.
3. Chill at least 6 hours. Serve on lettuce leaves, topped with a dollop of yogurt.

Makes 3 servings

CREOLE CUCUMBER BAKE

Preheat oven to 375°F.

CREOLE SAUCE:
   1 small onion, diced
   1 small clove garlic, minced
   1 stalk celery (with leaves), diced
   ½ green pepper, diced
   1 small carrot, diced
   2 tablespoons oil
   1 cup chopped tomatoes
     salt to taste
     pepper to taste
   1 small bay leaf

¼ cup whole grain bread crumbs
¼ cup wheat germ
3 large cucumbers, sliced (about 3½ cups)
2 tablespoons chopped parsley
½ cup grated cheddar cheese

1. First, prepare the sauce:
   In a heavy pot, sauté onion, garlic, celery, green peppers and carrot in oil for 5 to 10 minutes, until tender. Add tomatoes, salt to taste, pepper and bay leaf, cover and simmer 10 minutes more.
2. While sauce simmers, combine bread crumbs and wheat germ, and spread mixture over bottom of an oiled casserole. Put the cucumbers on top, adding just a pinch of salt to each layer.
3. When sauce is done, remove the bay leaf, stir in the parsley and pour over the cucumbers.
4. Top with cheese and bake at 375°F. 30 to 35 minutes, until cucumbers are tender.

Makes 4 servings

PAT'S BREAD AND BUTTER PICKLES

5 quarts sliced cucumbers
¾ cup salt
1 pint vinegar
1 quart sliced onions
1¼ cups honey
3 tablespoons white mustard seed
1 tablespoon celery seed
1 tablespoon turmeric

1. Salt cucumbers and let stand overnight.
2. Rinse thoroughly and drain well.
3. Put cucumbers in cooking pot and add remaining ingredients.
4. Cook slowly for ½ hour.
5. Can and process in hot water for 10 minutes at simmer (180°F.).

Makes 6 pints

● *Cucumbers can be cooked in many of the same ways you cook summer squash.*

COOL SUMMER SALAD

1 cucumber, diced
2 scallions, finely chopped
3 radishes, thinly sliced
½ cup cottage cheese
¼ cup sour cream
1 tablespoon chopped fresh chives
    salt and pepper to taste

1. Combine vegetables in a small bowl.
2. Mix cottage cheese, sour cream, and seasonings. Pour over vegetables and toss well. Serve on a bed of lettuce, accompanied by fresh tomato wedges.

Makes 4 servings

CUCUMBER AND TOMATO SALAD

1 large cucumber
3 tomatoes
1 cup yogurt
1 tablespoon chopped fresh chives
1 teaspoon chopped fresh dill
¾ teaspoon salt
⅛ teaspoon white pepper

1. Wash cucumber and slice thinly. Cut tomatoes into chunks.
2. Combine yogurt and seasonings; pour over cucumber and tomatoes and toss until well mixed.
3. Chill thoroughly. Serve garnished with paprika and minced yolk of a hard-boiled egg.

Makes 3 to 4 servings

CUCUMBER DIP FOR VEGETABLES

1 large cucumber
8 ounces cream cheese, softened
2 tablespoons lemon juice
4 green onions, finely chopped
    salt to taste, if desired

1. Coarsely grate the cucumber, reserving the liquid.
2. Soften the cream cheese with the lemon juice; add cucumber, onion and salt, if desired.
3. Thin to proper dipping consistency with cucumber liquid. Serve with fresh, raw vegetables.

Note: Even some of the most dedicated gardeners have children who don't like vegetables. Introduce raw vegetables with a dip like this before dinner—call it a party—and salad and vegetables become a "treat."

PEPPERED PICKLES

1 large green pepper
4 large cucumbers, thinly sliced
6 tiny white onions, thinly sliced
1 large or 2 small cloves garlic, peeled
¼ cup salt
2 quarts cold water
   one tray ice cubes
1¾ cups honey
1½ cups white vinegar
1 tablespoon mustard seed
1 teaspoon celery seed
1 teaspoon ground turmeric

1. Remove core and seeds from pepper. Chop or put it through coarse blade of food chopper.
2. In a large bowl, combine chopped pepper, cucumbers, onions and garlic. Sprinkle with salt, add the cold water and ice cubes; let stand for 2 hours.
3. Remove garlic cloves and drain vegetables.
4. In a large pot, mix the honey, vinegar, mustard seed, celery seed, and turmeric. Heat to boiling, then add the drained vegetables and bring quickly to a boil again.
5. Remove from heat and pack into sterile jars. Press down contents with a spoon to get rid of any air bubbles. Seal jars.

Makes 3 pints

Eggplant

Compared to other vegetables, eggplant is a real anomaly. Like winter squash, it has a substantial, filling texture and is never served raw. But instead of a hard shell it possesses a thin skin and bruises as easily as the most delicate fruit. It soaks up oil and butter like the pale mushroom, but it could never grow in the dark; eggplant needs warm, sunny days to mature into its regal purple beauty.

The aubergine, as it's known in Europe, is a tropical vegetable that requires a long stable summer of hot days and warm nights. The fruits are best when harvested no larger than four inches in diameter and six inches long, although when allowed to mature they will reach 10 inches in length. Encourage the plants to keep producing by picking the fruits before they fully mature, and you should be able to have fresh eggplant until frost. An eggplant is ripe when its skin has attained a high gloss; if you press on it with your thumb, it should not bounce back. Harvested at this stage, the eggplant will have small seeds which are hardly noticeable, and a tender skin which won't need to be pared off. Eggplant stems are tough and should be cut with a knife to avoid tearing the branches when picking.

Eggplant can be stored for about a week in a cool room (50°F.) or in the refrigerator. If handled very carefully to avoid bruising, it may be stored

for a month or two on a shelf in a cool cellar. Some homemakers can eggplant, but in processing it loses its color and becomes mushy. It is too watery to be frozen raw with good results. The best method of storage seems to be the freezing of partially cooked eggplant combination dishes. Do not thaw them before reheating.

Peeling is unnecessary in preparing tender, young eggplant, as is the salting and draining process so often recommended. Just remove the stem and top before cooking. Eggplant can be halved, sliced, cubed, or diced; baked, steamed, fried, stuffed, broiled, sautéed, breaded or sauced; served alone or in casserole combinations; eaten hot, at room temperature, or even cold. It combines especially well with cheeses, tomatoes, onions, garlic, herbs and meats. One pound (two or three medium-sized eggplants) will serve four.

Though some people consider the eggplant a meat substitute, this is due to its substantial nature and its frequent preparation as a main dish, rather than to its protein content. Eggplant is high in carbohydrates, but low in calories.

EGGPLANT AND TOMATOES

1 medium eggplant
2 large or 3 small tomatoes
1 small onion, chopped
2 tablespoons oil
¼ teaspoon salt
  dash of black pepper
1 teaspoon oregano
  several leaves fresh basil, minced
1 tablespoon chopped parsley

1. Wash eggplant and cut into cubes. Core and chop tomatoes.
2. Brown onion in oil, then add eggplant, tomatoes, and seasonings. Cover and simmer for about 30 minutes, until vegetables are tender. Serve over steamed brown rice.

Makes 4 servings

BAKED EGGPLANT WITH PARSLEY

Preheat oven to 350°F.

1 firm, medium eggplant, with stem removed
¼ cup olive oil
½ to 1 pound lean ground lamb
1 medium onion, chopped
1 teaspoon green garlic, chopped fine
3 ripe tomatoes, quartered
½ a red sweet pepper, chopped
2 tablespoons parsley, chopped fine
½ teaspoon salt
   fresh-ground black pepper
   a whisper of powdered oregano
½ cup vegetable liquid (stock from celery, green beans,
   mushrooms, etc.)
1 tablespoon grated Romano or Parmesan cheese

1. Slice your eggplant across, thinly, (more than 3 slices to an inch); sauté the slices in oil in heavy skillet over medium heat. Use enough oil so slices are brown on both sides.
2. Line the bottom and sides of a shallow earthenware or glass baking dish, such as a deep pie pan, with the cooked slices as they are removed from the skillet. One-third to one-half can be reserved in a plate, leaving the skillet empty.
3. In the same skillet, gently sauté the ground meat with the onion and garlic, stirring now and then. Add the skinned tomatoes, the sweet pepper and parsley, and mix gently. Season with salt, pepper and oregano. If you have fresh celery leaves, add them instead of the oregano or use less.
4. When the ground meat shows no red, drain off the excess fat and transfer the contents of the skillet to the baking dish, on top of the eggplant slices, level the top and lay the remaining eggplant slices over this.
5. Pour in the vegetable stock and top with cheese. Bake at 350°F. until bubbly and cheese is melted—15 to 20 minutes.

Makes 4 to 6 servings

"MOCK CAVIAR" EGGPLANT APPETIZER

Preheat oven to 400°F.

1 eggplant
½ small onion, chopped
2 tablespoons vegetable or olive oil
1 teaspoon vinegar
   salt and pepper to taste

1. Bake eggplant on oven rack at 400°F. for 1 hour. Peel thin outer skin.
2. Mash seeds and flesh, then add chopped onion, oil, vinegar, and seasonings.
3. Chill and serve on a bed of crisp lettuce and tomato.

Makes 3 servings

MOUSSAKA

Preheat oven to 400°F.

3 large, firm eggplants
3 tablespoons finely chopped onion
2 tablespoons butter
1 pound lean lamb or beef, ground
3 large, ripe peeled tomatoes
¼ cup dry red wine
   salt and black pepper to taste
1 teaspoon minced parsley
½ teaspoon minced garlic
2 tablespoons olive oil
1 tablespoon potato flour
½ cup stock
4 tablespoons grated cheese
½ cup buttered whole wheat bread crumbs

1. Peel eggplants and cut in ½-inch slices.
2. Sauté onion in 1 tablespoon of butter for 3 minutes, add ground meat and cook about 15 minutes, stirring occasionally. Add cut-up tomatoes and wine. Season lightly with salt and pepper, and simmer until meat is tender (about 20 minutes). Add parsley and garlic; remove from heat.
3. Sauté eggplant slices in oil till each slice is golden brown on both sides. While eggplant browns, melt remaining butter in a small saucepan, add the flour, stir and cook without browning for 3 minutes. Gradually add stock while stirring, bring to a boil and add cheese. Stir while the sauce simmers for 6 minutes.
4. Cover the bottom of a greased baking dish with a layer of eggplant, then a layer of meat, and so on, with an eggplant layer on top. Pour on cheese sauce, sprinkle on a little additional grated cheese and the crumbs. Brown in a hot oven. Serve hot.

Makes 8 servings

HERBED EGGPLANT

½ cup olive oil
1 clove garlic, minced
½ teaspoon basil
⅛ teaspoon thyme
1 tablespoon chopped fresh parsley
    salt and pepper to taste
1 medium eggplant
    wheat germ, optional

1. Combine oil and seasonings and let stand for 15 minutes.
2. Cut eggplant in thin, lengthwise slices and arrange on broiler pan.
3. Baste eggplant with seasoned oil and broil until tender, about 5 minutes. If desired, sprinkle with wheat germ.

Makes 6 to 8 servings

SIMPLE EGGPLANT

Preheat oven to 400°F.

1 medium eggplant, cut in ½-inch slices
   oil
   salt
   pepper
1 small onion, grated
   chopped chervil or parsley
   grated cheese, about ⅔ cup

1. Arrange eggplant slices on a baking sheet. Brush slices with oil; sprinkle with salt, pepper, and grated onion.
2. Bake at 400°F. about 5 minutes. Turn and brush other side with oil; bake 5 minutes more, or until tender.
3. Sprinkle with chopped chervil or parsley and your favorite grated cheese, and run under broiler to melt cheese.

Makes 4 to 6 servings

Note: A quick, easy and most delicious way to prepare eggplant.

RATATOUILLE

Preheat oven to 350°F.

6 tablespoons olive oil
2 large onions, sliced
4 cloves of garlic, minced
3 zucchini, sliced
1 red bell pepper, seeded and sliced
1 medium eggplant, diced
3 medium tomatoes, quartered
   salt and freshly ground pepper, to taste
2 teaspoons fresh basil, chopped
⅓ cup minced parsley

1. In a Dutch oven, heat the oil and sauté onions and garlic, until onions are limp. Add zucchini and pepper and sauté a few minutes longer.
2. Remove from heat and add eggplant and tomatoes, salt and pepper, and basil.
3. Bake at 350°F. for 45 minutes or until vegetables are tender.
4. Sprinkle with parsley and serve immediately.

Makes 6 servings

Note: Ratatouille is also delicious cold. Try it with dark bread, fresh butter and cheese for a picnic treat.

STUFFED EGGPLANT

Preheat oven to 375°F.

1 cup grated mozzarella cheese
½ cup grated Parmesan cheese
⅓ cup ricotta cheese
2 eggs
¼ cup chopped parsley
   salt and pepper to taste
2 tablespoons whole wheat flour
⅓ cup milk
1 tablespoon salad oil
2 eggplants
   whole wheat flour
¼ cup olive oil
2 tablespoons butter
   tomato sauce

1. In mixing bowl combine mozzarella, Parmesan, ricotta, 1 egg, 1 tablespoon parsley, salt and pepper to taste. Blend to a smooth paste. Chill mixture thoroughly.
2. In another bowl, mix flour, add remaining egg, milk, and oil. Beat until smooth. Peel eggplants. Cut into thin, lengthwise slices. Dip in flour and

shake off excess. Heat olive oil and butter together. Dip eggplant slices in prepared batter until they are coated. Sauté in hot oil until browned on both sides. Drain. Place 2 tablespoons of chilled cheese mixture on each slice. Roll loosely. Arrange rolls seam side down on baking pan. Cover with tomato sauce.

3. Bake in moderately hot (375°F.) oven for 15 minutes. Sprinkle with the remaining chopped parsley and serve immediately.

Makes 6 servings

Greens

Among the most maligned and mistreated members of the vegetable kingdom, leafy greens are at their best when served in a fresh, crisp salad or lightly steamed to bring out their very brightest color. Greens are easy to grow, high in nutritional value, and extremely versatile. Many of the recipes in this section can be interchanged with those for chard and spinach. As a rule, 1 to 1½ pounds of greens will serve four.

BEET GREENS

Beet greens are very much like spinach, and can be treated much the same way. When young and tender, they can be used in salads; large, older leaves are at their best when lightly steamed. Beet greens are rich in vitamin A, calcium, and iron, and also offer substantial amounts of vitamins B and C.

COLLARDS

Collards, slowly simmered with salt pork, have long been a favorite in

the South. This hardy member of the cabbage family somewhat resembles kale, and like kale, it is staunchly resistant to cold. In fact, a few light frosts improve its flavor. When the temperature drops below 20°F., collards will benefit from a good layer of mulch.

When harvesting collards, you can either cut whole young plants, or just pick the tender leaves at the top. Collards mature from the bottom up, so when harvesting whole plants, cut them as soon as the lower leaves are ready. Clusters of leaves may be picked a few at a time, as needed, but pick the leaves before they mature or they will be tough.

To prepare collards for cooking, wash them thoroughly and remove the tough stems. They can be served cooked or as salad greens. Collards are among the most nutritious of greens, containing large amounts of calcium, iron and vitamin A, and sizable quantities of potassium, vitamin C and B vitamins as well.

DANDELIONS

Dandelions are probably never cultivated in gardens, but many of us grow abundant crops in our lawns without even trying. Dandelions are a real springtime delicacy, at their best early in the season when the leaves are small. As the leaves grow larger they take on an unpleasant bitterness.

Dandelions are easily harvested by digging up the entire plant with a small trowel or knife. The roots are cut off, and the leaves washed thoroughly. They are delicious dressed with sour cream and chives or a cooked dressing. Like other kinds of greens, dandelion contains iron, calcium and vitamin A.

ENDIVE AND ESCAROLE

Endive and escarole are often regarded as kinds of lettuce, but they differ from lettuce in several important ways. For one thing their leaves possess an unusual, slightly bitter flavor quite unlike the taste of lettuce. Endive is often blanched to reduce the bitterness, but blanching also reduces food value and is not a good practice. Actually, the bitter quality of the leaves can become a savory asset when cooked with other greens, or added to bland soups. Endive and escarole also pep up the salad bowl.

Endive generally matures in late fall. The plants can be pulled up with a good-sized ball of earth around their roots, and carefully set in a dark corner of a cool, unheated cellar for storage. Although they can withstand light frost, the plants should be pulled before a hard freeze.

Endive contains lots of vitamin A, and fair amounts of calcium, phosphorus, iron, potassium, and vitamin B.

KALE

Kale is one of the most resilient members of the cabbage family, being resistant to both heat and cold. It is most popular as a winter vegetable, and is harvested far into autumn or even winter. In the South, a winter crop is planted about two months before the first frost.

Kale is harvested either by cutting the whole plant, or by picking the larger leaves while they're still young. Old kale becomes stringy and tough, so it must be harvested as soon as it's fully grown.

Kale can be served like any other green, although its coarse texture makes it rather unpopular in salads. To prepare it for cooking, wash it well and remove the leaves from the tough stems. Kale is quite rich in vitamin A, calcium and iron, and also contains vitamins B and C, and assorted minerals.

MUSTARD GREENS

Mustard greens can be used either raw or cooked. The tangy leaves are harvested as they mature; keeping up with the harvest will allow the plants to continue producing.

SORREL

Sorrel is often thought of as a weed, but some varieties are cultivated for their piquant leaves. French gardeners would consider their gardens incomplete without sorrel. Sorrel is generally used in soups or salads.

121

TURNIP GREENS

Turnip greens are actually richer in vitamins A, B₁ and B₂ than turnip roots. They are used much the same way as mustard greens or collards. Young, tender leaves are the best, and may be cut in judicious quantities from the plants as they grow.

WATERCRESS

Watercress belongs to the same family as turnips, cabbage and mustard. This pungent-flavored little plant grows best in cool, gently flowing water. Watercress contains appreciable amounts of vitamin C, iron and iodine. An established bed of watercress will provide cuttings each spring and fall.

CHEF SALAD DELUXE

1 cup grated carrots
1 cup grated fresh beets
½ pound fresh endive, kale, spinach, or favorite greens
1 cup grated green and/or red cabbage
1 cup grated turnips
1 cup raw, fresh green beans or cauliflower
1 cup sprouts
1 cup nuts and/or seeds
1 cup cheese and/or cottage cheese

1. Arrange vegetables around the cheese or toss all together.
2. Top with *gomazio* (see page 290) and your favorite dressing.

Makes 8 to 10 servings

Note: Any leftover cooked grains may also be added to this salad. One mother we know serves all the vegetables for this salad separately, and family members all select their own combinations of colors and toss the salad in their own bowls.

HOT ESCAROLE AND POTATOES VINAIGRETTE

4 tablespoons oil
2 medium-sized potatoes, scrubbed but unpeeled
1 clove garlic, finely chopped
2 small onions, sliced and separated into rings
1 large head escarole
¼ teaspoon basil
   salt and pepper to taste
2 to 3 tablespoons cider vinegar

1. Heat oil in large skillet over medium heat.
2. Slice potatoes ¼-inch thick and sauté with garlic until potatoes are almost tender, and golden on both sides.
3. Add onions, stir, reduce heat, cover pan and cook slowly 5 minutes or until potatoes are tender.
4. Separate escarole into leaves, discard any damaged leaves and root end; break leaves into 1- to 2-inch pieces. Place in skillet with potatoes and onions, basil, salt and pepper to taste. Cook for a few minutes, covered, only until escarole is wilted.
5. Remove from heat and toss with the vinegar. Serve immediately.

Makes 6 servings

SNAPPY TOSSED SALAD

1 cup beet greens, chopped
1 cup mustard greens, chopped
½ cup onion, minced
½ cup mayonnaise
2 hard-boiled eggs, sliced

1. Stir together the greens and onion.
2. Toss with mayonnaise and garnish with eggs.

Makes 2 servings

SPRING GREENS

6 cups greens, washed clean and broken up roughly
1 onion, or 4 stalks Egyptian or Welsh perennial onions
2 tablespoons oil or chicken fat
2 tablespoons vinegar
1 tablespoon molasses (or brown sugar)

1. Measure the greens after washing. Use several waters, lifting greens from the water each time so that sand or dirt will sink to the bottom of the pan.
2. Steam greens or cook briefly in just the water that clings to the leaves.
3. Drain thoroughly and save the liquid to use in soups. Chop greens somewhat or cut through with a knife.
4. Slice onion and sauté in oil or fat until golden. In a small bowl, mix vinegar and molasses, then add to the onion and heat thoroughly. Add greens, mix well and heat again.

Makes 3 to 4 servings

Note: This recipe can be used for beet or turnip greens, spinach, chard or any of your favorites. But by all means try it with a mixture of early spring greens such as dandelion and wild winter cress, and the leaves of perennial herbs such as sour sorrel, good-King-Henry, and Russian broad-leaf comfrey. These fresh spring greens are ready long before spinach or beet greens can be picked, and this tasty dish costs almost nothing.

● *Old cookbooks sometimes recommend that when endive is cooked in salted water, it should be kept constantly under the water to prevent it from turning black.*

ENDIVE WITH SWEET-SOUR DRESSING

1 head endive (about 1 pound)
3 slices nitrite-free bacon
2 eggs
⅓ to ½ cup honey
½ cup vinegar or lemon juice
½ cup cold water

 ¼ teaspoon dry mustard (or 1 teaspoon prepared
  mustard)
 ½ teaspoon salt
 ⅛ teaspoon black pepper

1. Wash endive and tear into pieces about 1½ inches long. Wrap in paper towels to dry thoroughly.
2. Chop bacon and fry in skillet until crisp and brown.
3. Beat eggs; add honey, vinegar, water, mustard, salt and pepper.
4. Pour egg mixture into hot bacon fat and stir until mixture thickens.
5. Pour dressing over the endive. Stir thoroughly and serve immediately.

Makes 4 to 6 servings

Note: This dressing may also be used for dandelion greens.

GREENS AND VEGETABLES SAUTÉ

 1 onion, peeled and chopped
 3 tablespoons oil
 1 small zucchini, thinly sliced
 ½ pound mushrooms
 1 pound greens, coarsely torn
 ¾ teaspoon salt
 ⅛ teaspoon pepper
 1 teaspoon sweet basil
 1 teaspoon chopped chives
 2 teaspoons lemon juice

1. In a large skillet, sauté onion in oil until tender, about 10 minutes. Add zucchini and mushrooms, and sauté until tender, another 7 to 10 minutes.
2. Add greens gradually, and continue cooking just until they are wilted. Add seasonings and lemon juice, stir well, and serve immediately.

Makes 6 servings

GARDEN-FRESH WATERCRESS SOUP

 1 large bunch watercress
 2 green onions with tops
 2 or 3 new potatoes, depending on size (1½ cups diced)
 1 cup chicken stock or light cream
 ⅛ teaspoon salt
  dash pepper
 ⅛ teaspoon celery salt
 ½ teaspoon chopped fresh basil
 4 teaspoons chopped fresh parsley

1. Clean vegetables and chop coarsely. Drop vegetables into 1 quart of boiling water and cook until potatoes are tender.
2. Allow to cool slightly, then blend for a few seconds in the blender. Return to the pan and add stock (or cream) and seasonings. Heat gently.
3. Top each serving with a teaspoon of chopped parsley.

Makes 4 generous servings

ENDIVE TEMPURA

  peanut or vegetable oil
 1 egg
 1 cup flour
 1 cup water
  salt to taste
  Belgian endive

1. Heat oil in deep-fryer to 400°F.
2. Mix together egg, flour, water, and salt. Batter will be lumpy.
3. Wash and pat dry leaves of endive. Dip into the batter, a few at a time, and fry until batter is golden brown.

Note: All sorts of vegetables can be "tempura-ed"—cauliflower, zucchini, squash, asparagus, some beans, and also sugar peas.

ITALIAN CHICKEN-ESCAROLE SOUP

¼ small chicken (breast quarter or leg quarter)
2½ quarts water
1 medium onion, chopped
1 stalk celery, chopped
  salt and pepper to taste
1 medium head fresh escarole—cleaned, washed and
  cut into 1-inch pieces
1 egg, beaten
2 tablespoons grated Parmesan or Romano cheese

1. In a large saucepan combine chicken, water, onion, celery and seasonings. Cook until chicken is tender. Remove chicken and take meat from bones, tearing into small pieces. Return chicken pieces to broth.
2. Cook escarole in small amount of water until just tender. Drain and add to chicken broth.
3. When ready to serve, mix beaten egg and cheese. Stir briskly into the boiling soup.

Makes 6 to 8 servings

KALE WITH YOGURT

1 pound kale
½ cup chicken stock
¼ teaspoon salt
  dash of nutmeg
½ cup yogurt
¼ teaspoon prepared mustard

1. Wash the kale thoroughly and strip leaves from the heavy stems. Cook leaves in chicken stock about 10 minutes or until tender. Add salt and nutmeg.
2. Top with yogurt, to which you've added the mustard.

Makes 4 servings

GARDEN QUICHE

Preheat oven to 375°F.

2 tablespoons minced onion or leeks
½ cup grated carrots
2 tablespoons butter
1½ cups chopped, blanched greens
3 eggs
1 cup milk or cream
¼ cup grated sharp cheddar or Swiss cheese
1 baked pie shell
    chopped parsley for garnish

1. Sauté onion and carrots in butter until tender.
2. Steam greens and drain well.
3. Beat eggs with milk; add cheese.
4. Mix all ingredients together; pour into pie shell and bake at 375°F. for 30 minutes, or until set.
5. Sprinkle with parsley and serve.

Makes 4 to 6 servings

Note: This *quiche* works well with the Whole Wheat-Rice Pie Shell in the Accompaniments chapter, page 292.

COLCANNON (OR CURLY KALE)

1 pound kale, very finely chopped
1 pound potatoes
    salt and pepper to taste
    pinch of mace
2 carrots (optional)
2 small leeks or green onion tops
1 cup milk or cream
½ cup butter

1. Cook finely chopped kale separately in salted water until tender.
2. Peel potatoes, cook and mash well. Two carrots can be cooked with the potatoes, if desired. Add seasonings.
3. Chop up the leeks or onion tops and simmer them in milk or cream to just cover, until soft. Add to mashed potatoes.
4. Drain the kale and blend into mashed potatoes. Blend in till "the greens and scallions mingle like a picture in a dream."
5. Serve in a warmed casserole. Make a well in the middle for the butter.

Makes 6 servings

Note: This traditional Irish dish is a welcome treat on a chilly evening. Leftovers are served as potato cakes, sautéed in butter, and are as delicious as newly made colcannon.

WILTED DANDELION GREENS

6 quarts tender young dandelion leaves
6 slices nitrite-free bacon, fried and crumbled (optional)
3 tablespoons bacon fat or oil
4 tablespoons cider vinegar
3 tablespoons minced shallots
1 to 2 teaspoons honey
¼ teaspoon salt
  dash of pepper
3 hard-boiled eggs, chopped

1. Wash greens and place in a large kettle. Add water to just cover; bring to a boil. Remove from heat and let stand for a few minutes. Drain well.
2. Meanwhile, fry bacon or heat oil in a large skillet. Stir in vinegar and shallots, and heat briefly. Add honey, salt and pepper and cook on low heat for a few minutes.
3. Gradually stir drained greens into dressing, cover, and simmer a few minutes more. Serve garnished with hard-boiled eggs.

Makes 6 servings

KALE AND BROWN RICE

Preheat oven to 350°F.

2 cups cooked brown rice
1 cup grated cheddar cheese
4 eggs, beaten
2 tablespoons chopped parsley
½ teaspoon salt
⅛ teaspoon black pepper
1 pound kale
1 tablespoon oil
2 tablespoons wheat germ
2 tablespoons soft, whole grain bread crumbs

1. Combine the cooked rice, cheese and beaten eggs. Add parsley, salt and pepper.
2. Wash kale, strip off leaves and steam until almost tender.
3. In an oiled casserole, lay alternate layers of rice and kale, ending with rice.
4. Combine oil, wheat germ, and crumbs, and top casserole with the mixture.
5. Bake at 350°F. for 30 minutes.

Makes 6 servings

SORREL SOUP

1 pound beef short ribs
8 cups water
1 carrot, chopped
1 large potato, diced
1 large onion, chopped
½ teaspoon chopped basil
    salt and pepper to taste
3 cups washed sorrel
2 hard-boiled eggs, finely chopped
2 tablespoons parsley
    sour cream

1. Combine beef and water and cook 1½ hours.
2. Add carrot, diced potato, onion, and basil and cook for 20 minutes more. Add salt and pepper to taste.
3. Separately cook 3 cups of washed sorrel in a minimum of water for about 5 minutes. Puree in a blender, then add to the soup.
4. Add eggs and parsley and heat briefly. Serve with sour cream.

Makes 8 servings

Note: This exceptionally delicious soup can be made with spinach or beet greens instead of sorrel.

● *When watercress is young, it is light green in color. When a bit older, it takes on more of a bronze tone. At this point it is more pungent.*

MUSHROOM AND WATERCRESS SALAD

VINAIGRETTE DRESSING:
   4 parts olive oil or vegetable oil
   1 part wine vinegar
      salt and fresh ground pepper to taste

1 pound very fresh mushrooms
2 bunches watercress, cut with kitchen shears
2 tablespoons chopped parsley
2 tablespoons finely cut chives

1. Beat dressing ingredients with a whisk, or shake in covered jar. Taste for seasoning. Correct, if necessary.
2. Slice the mushrooms very thin and combine with watercress. Toss with vinaigrette dressing, and sprinkle with chopped parsley and chives. Serve immediately.

Makes 6 servings

Note: This salad may be served at once, or made ahead and refrigerated for a few hours to allow the flavors to develop. Fresh, young spinach may be substituted for the watercress if you prefer.

131

BRAISED BELGIAN ENDIVE AU GRATIN

Preheat oven to 350°F.

8 stalks endive (4 if very large)
½ cup chicken stock
   salt to taste
2 tablespoons melted butter
½ cup whole wheat bread crumbs
1 tablespoon wheat germ or bran
½ cup grated, sharp cheddar cheese

1. Wash endive under running water. Leave stalks whole if they are small; if large, cut in half lengthwise. Place in skillet, add stock and salt (if needed). Cook slowly until almost tender, about 15 minutes.
2. Arrange in a greased, shallow baking dish.
3. Combine butter, whole wheat bread crumbs, wheat germ or bran, and cheese. Sprinkle mixture over endive and bake at 350°F. until the cheese melts and crumbs are brown, about 15 minutes.

Makes 4 servings

LUNCH SPECIAL

1 medium potato
½ cup steamed beet greens
   wheat germ (optional)
2 eggs, fried
¼ cup grated sharp cheese
2 tablespoons chopped parsley

1. Cook and mash the potato and mix together with the steamed, drained beet greens.
2. Form into 2 patties, dip in wheat germ if desired and sauté in a small amount of oil until lightly browned.
3. Top each with a fried egg and grated cheese. Garnish with parsley.

Makes 2 servings

SCOTCH BROTH

4 cups stock
¾ cup barley
½ cup dried or frozen green peas
1 small turnip
2 medium-large carrots
1 leek or onion
2 cups kale, chopped in bite-sized pieces
3 sprigs parsley
   salt and pepper to taste

1. Put stock in pan and bring to a boil. Wash barley and peas and add to stock.
2. Dice turnip. Cut up one carrot and grate the other. Add vegetables to stock.
3. Let soup simmer for 45 minutes to an hour. Season with salt and pepper to taste.

Makes 8 servings

WATERCRESS CREAM SOUP

1 large bunch watercress
2 tablespoons flour
6 cups milk
3 tablespoons minced onion
1 teaspoon chopped fresh basil
2 teaspoons salt

1. Wash watercress and pat dry. Saving 6 sprigs for garnish, finely chop the remaining cress and set aside.
2. Make a paste of the flour and ¼ cup of the milk in a large saucepan. Slowly stir in remaining milk, minced onion, chopped basil and salt. Cook, stirring constantly, until mixture comes to a boil. It should thicken slightly.
3. Stir in chopped watercress and simmer 3 minutes, not longer. Serve immediately. Garnish each serving with a sprig of watercress.

Makes 6 servings

Kohlrabi

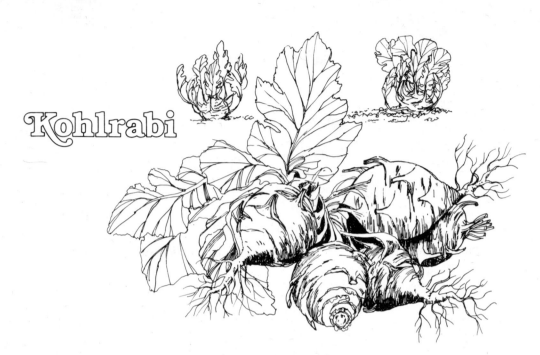

Though common in Chinese cuisine and popular in Europe, kohlrabi is little known in the United States. Gardeners often mistreat this misunderstood vegetable by letting it grow to baseball size. At this size kohlrabi is apt to be tough, woody, and bitter. On the other hand, if harvested when about two inches in diameter, it has a remarkably mild, sweet, turnip-like flavor and crisp, tender flesh.

Kohlrabi has been called the "mongrel of the vegetable kingdom" because it is rather like a "turnip growing on a cabbage root." It is actually a biennial herb, related to cabbage and cauliflower. Kohlrabi is grown for its bulbous stem, from which leaves arise. Don't let the bulb get larger than two inches in diameter. Though kohlrabi is usually harvested by pulling up the entire plant, if they're planted too close to one another it's better to cut the stem below the bulb, thereby not disturbing the roots of neighboring plants.

If the bulbs are not needed immediately, store them in the refrigerator for a few days. Kohlrabi can also be stored for two or three months in a cool, frost-free spot—a root cellar, cool basement, or outdoor storage pit. Remove all but about a half inch of the tops, and pack in layers of moist sand or peat moss in bins or boxes. They should keep fresh and crisp well into the winter.

Raw kohlrabi, washed, peeled and sliced goes well on a relish tray with

a dip. It can also be cooked, in its skin, then peeled and mashed with butter and salt like turnips. In Chinese cooking, kohlrabi is peeled, sliced, or diced, and used like bamboo shoots in soups and stir-fry dishes, or steamed with meat, poultry, fish, or other vegetables. Kohlrabi is rich in calcium and has a good amount of vitamin C.

KOHLRABI DIP

2 large kohlrabi, peeled and finely grated (about 2 cups)
2 teaspoons lemon juice
2 tablespoons mayonnaise
¼ teaspoon honey
   salt and pepper to taste
½ teaspoon celery salt
1 teaspoon prepared mustard

Mix all ingredients well. Chill before serving as a vegetable dip or with crackers.

Makes about 2 cups

Note: Try this dip with the crackers suggested in the Accompaniments chapter, pages 290-291.

KOHLRABI SALAD

2 cups sliced kohlrabi
¼ cup sour cream or yogurt
¼ cup mayonnaise
1 teaspoon mustard
½ teaspoon dill seed, crushed
1 tablespoon lemon juice
   salt, to taste

1. Peel and slice the kohlrabi, being careful not to use the tough center fibers.
2. Combine sour cream, mayonnaise, mustard, dill seed and lemon juice in a bowl and add kohlrabi, and salt to taste. Cover and chill until serving.

Makes 4 servings

CONFETTI SALAD

4 kohlrabi, diced
1 parsnip, diced
3 carrots, diced
8 radishes, diced
1 cup beet greens, chopped
1 tablespoon yogurt
2 tablespoons honey
1 tablespoon vinegar

1. Combine and mix vegetables in a bowl.
2. Stir together the yogurt, honey and vinegar and add to vegetables.
3. Chill several hours before serving.

Makes 3 to 4 servings

● *One gardener whose family has always grown kohlrabi told us she can't remember her grandmother ever doing anything with this unusual vegetable. They'd pull it up, wash and peel it, and eat it like an apple!*

HERBED KOHLRABI

1 to 1½ pounds kohlrabi, peeled and cut into ½-inch
  cubes (about 3½ cups)
2 tablespoons chopped parsley
1 teaspoon chopped basil
1 tablespoon butter or oil
½ teaspoon salt
  dash of black pepper

1. Steam or boil kohlrabi until just barely tender, about 8 minutes.
2. Add parsley and basil and toss in hot butter or oil until well-blended. Add salt and pepper to taste.

Makes 4 servings

KOHLRABI SAUTÉ

1 onion, chopped
1 tablespoon butter
1 tablespoon oil
1½ pounds kohlrabi, peeled and thinly sliced
¼ cup chicken stock
  salt and pepper to taste

1. Sauté onion in butter and oil for 2 or 3 minutes.
2. Add sliced kohlrabi and continue to sauté 15 minutes longer, stirring occasionally.
3. Add chicken stock; cover and simmer for about 10 minutes or until kohlrabi is tender. Add salt and pepper to taste.

Makes 4 servings

Lettuce

By far the best loved of salad greens, lettuce joins beans and tomatoes as a standard fixture in backyard vegetable gardens. Lettuce is really a lot more versatile than many cooks give it credit for. In addition to its usual contributions to salads and sandwiches, lettuce can be wilted or creamed, cooked with peas, stuffed like cabbage, served with stewed tomatoes, or braised like celery. Cultivated lettuce may be conveniently divided into four types:

LOOSE LEAF

This variety does not form heads, and is probably the easiest of all to grow. The leaves can be picked off one at a time as they are ready, usually from the outside first, without disturbing the growing plant. Or, if the leaves are cut off at ground level, and the roots are left undisturbed, the plant will send up new leaves for a second crop. Young leaves are the sweetest and most tender—if allowed to grow too large, they turn somewhat bitter. Loose leaf lettuce is best when used raw, in salads and sandwiches.

BUTTERHEADS

As their name implies, these types form soft, buttery heads, yellowish in color almost to the center, with darker green outer leaves. The inner leaves feel smooth and almost oily to the touch. Butterheads are rather delicate, and must be handled carefully, but they are a great asset to salads. Among the more popular varieties are 'Boston' and 'Mignonette'.

CABBAGEHEADS OR CRISPHEADS

These form firm, crisp heads like those of the familiar iceberg lettuce. They contain lots of water, and are lower in nutritional value than the leafier varieties. They are also the most difficult to grow, requiring just the right conditions to form large, firm heads.

COS OR ROMAINE

This member of the lettuce family forms tall, elongated heads with stiff, upright leaves shaped somewhat like the bowl of a spoon. The delightfully crunchy leaves start out a deep, rich green color at the outer edge and pale to white at the inner ribs.

Knowledgeable gardeners say that lettuce should always be picked early in the day to preserve the crispness brought on by cool nighttime temperatures. Wash lettuce thoroughly but quickly as soon as it's harvested, then dry it immediately with paper towels to prevent vitamin loss. If you can't use it the same day, you can refrigerate it in an airtight crisper or plastic bag for up to five days before it starts to deteriorate.

When using lettuce that has been stored for several days, don't soak it before serving, even though it is a bit wilted. Soaking will crispen the lettuce, but it destroys a good deal of the vitamin content in the process. All varieties of lettuce contain assorted minerals, vitamin A and vitamin C in varying amounts.

LAYERED VEGETABLE SALAD

1 head lettuce, chopped fine
6 stalks celery, chopped fine
1 large onion, chopped fine
3 green peppers, seeded and chopped fine
1 pound green peas, cooked until tender
2 cups mayonnaise
⅓ cup Parmesan cheese, grated
3 hard-boiled eggs, chopped fine
3 tomatoes, chopped fine
1 pound crisp fried nitrite-free bacon, crumbled

1. In a covered 9 x 13 pan layer the lettuce, celery, onion, peppers, and peas in that order. Spread the mayonnaise over the top and refrigerate—tightly covered—for 4 hours.
2. On top of the mayonnaise, sprinkle the cheese, then the eggs and tomatoes. Crumble the bacon over the top. Refrigerate overnight. Serve.

Makes 16 servings

Note: All that "chopped fine" business makes this begin to sound mushy—but it is a delightful combination of flavors, and is easily served and eaten buffet style—a truly successful "make-ahead" salad. This recipe is easily cut in half to serve fewer people.

LETTUCE IN SOY SAUCE (WITH MUSHROOMS)

1 tablespoon peanut oil
1 cup sliced mushrooms
1 small onion, sliced
3 tablespoons tamari soy sauce
½ teaspoon honey
1 head lettuce (about 1 pound) coarsely torn into
　2-inch pieces
1 tablespoon sesame seeds, optional

1. In a large skillet heat oil, then add mushrooms and onion and sauté for about 5 minutes.
2. Add soy sauce and honey. Turn off heat and gradually add lettuce. Stir and toss until lettuce is slightly wilted and thoroughly covered with sauce.
3. Add sesame seeds and serve immediately.

Makes 4 servings

● *Tearing lettuce in pieces rather than cutting it with a knife will help to keep the cut edges from turning dark.*

GREEN SUMMER SALAD

lettuce, 2 or 3 of your favorite varieties, torn in bite-size pieces
2 stalks celery, with leaves, chopped
1 cucumber, cubed
3 scallions, thinly sliced, or 1 tablespoon chopped chives
several sprigs of watercress, or chervil to taste

DRESSING:
3 tablespoons olive oil
⅓ teaspoon salt
1 teaspoon green or cured garlic, minced
1 tablespoon wine vinegar
freshly ground black pepper
1 tablespoon blue cheese, crumbled

1. Combine salad ingredients in a large salad bowl.
2. Shake all dressing ingredients together in a glass jar, pour over salad and toss lightly.

Makes 4 to 5 servings

Note: If you prefer, substitute ½ teaspoon of paprika or a chopped hard-boiled egg for the blue cheese.

WILTED LETTUCE

6 strips bacon, cut in ½-inch pieces
2 tablespoons unbleached flour
1 egg
1½ tablespoons honey
4 tablespoons vinegar
    pinch of salt
1 cup water
1 pound lettuce, coarsely torn

1. In a large skillet, cook bacon until crisp. Remove from pan and pour off fat.
2. Mix together flour and egg. Add honey, vinegar, salt and water, and beat together well.
3. Pour into skillet and cook, stirring, until thickened. Turn off heat and gradually stir in lettuce. Continue stirring until lettuce is wilted and coated with dressing.

Makes 4 to 5 servings

● *Juice extracted from lettuce was long used in England as a sleep-inducing potion. The juice was dried and made into white cakes that were given to patients both before and after operations.*

HOT LETTUCE-SAUERKRAUT SALAD

1 head lettuce (about 1 pound)
1 cup sauerkraut, firmly packed
1 tablespoon oil
1 apple, chopped but not peeled
½ cup chopped dates (or raisins)
½ cup chopped walnuts

1. Wash lettuce, tear into 2-inch pieces and dry on paper towels.
2. Drain sauerkraut.
3. Heat oil in skillet, add apple and sauerkraut and sauté for about 5 minutes to blend flavors.
4. Over very low heat, add lettuce, dates (or raisins) and nuts. Toss until lettuce is slightly wilted. Serve at once, piping hot.

Makes 4 servings

Mushrooms

Mushrooms are easier to grow than most people think. When their darkness, humidity, and temperature needs are satisfied, mushrooms require little care and are great fun to cultivate These fungi delight the palate and add a touch of elegance to any meal.

Most seed dealers sell mushroom spawn which usually comes in a brick containing sterilized growing medium, permeated with germinated spores. Mushrooms grow best in regions where the temperature drops below 60°F. and stays down for at least three months, and where the atmosphere is not too arid. Having no chlorophyll, these plants do not need sunlight. However, they demand rich compost on which their spores can sprout and grow.

Three weeks after the spawn is planted in the medium, it will be ready for casing (covering with a layer of soil). Clusters of tiny white dots will appear in about three more weeks, if the proper temperature and moisture conditions are met. After another 10 days, the largest will be ready for picking. The harvest must not be rushed; only those whose caps have broken away from the stem should be picked. These ripe mushrooms will taste much better than the "green" immature ones which commercial growers must ship to avoid bruising.

143

Careful picking is necessary whether you are growing the tiny button mushrooms or the giant-size varieties. Don't pull them up, or you could injure others that are just breaking through the soil. Instead, press the soil down around the bottom of the stem with one hand and twist off the stem at ground level with your other hand. Or, use a sharp knife to cut the stem at its base. Selective harvesting is suggested; by picking every day, the beds will produce for as long as six months.

After the entire bed is harvested, the mushroom compost can be used as soil conditioner. In fact, the gardener can plan his or her schedule around the cultivation of mushrooms. By starting the mushrooms in the fall, and harvesting them throughout the winter, used mushroom compost will be available in the spring to fertilize your garden.

Mushrooms are at their best when firm and white, but dark spots do not necessarily signify decay. Darkening may mean that the mushrooms have been bruised by careless harvesting or handling.

Mushrooms can be refrigerated in a plastic bag for a couple of days. They can be kept for a week when laid on a shallow tray and covered with a damp cloth under refrigeration. Mushrooms are rich in B vitamins and contain fair amounts of calcium and assorted minerals. They are quite low in calories by themselves but will absorb butter, oil and sauces when cooked.

To prepare mushrooms for cooking, wash them gently or wipe them with a damp cloth, but don't soak them. Stem ends should be trimmed off just when you're ready to use the mushrooms, to keep the cut parts from turning dark. Plan about a pound of mushrooms for four to six servings.

MUSHROOMS CONTINENTAL

1 tablespoon oil
1 tablespoon butter
1 tablespoon dry, white wine (optional)
1 to 2 tablespoons shallots, finely chopped
½ pound fresh mushrooms, sliced
1 tablespoon tamari soy sauce
1 tablespoon dry, white wine (optional)
¼ teaspoon dried thyme
¼ teaspoon dried marjoram

1. Heat oil, butter and first tablespoon of wine together in frying pan. Add the shallots and cook gently about 3 minutes, until shallots are tender.
2. Add the mushrooms and cook for 1 to 2 minutes, then add soy sauce, second tablespoon of wine (if desired) and herbs. Stir well.
3. Simmer for 5 to 10 minutes, until mushrooms are tender and most of the liquid is absorbed.

Makes 3 to 4 servings

Note: This makes an elegant accompaniment to fish.

MUSHROOM QUICHE

Preheat oven to 400°F.

1 8-inch pie crust, unbaked

FILLING:
    1 tablespoon onion, chopped
    2 tablespoons oil or butter
    1 cup mushrooms, sliced
    3 eggs
    ½ pound cottage cheese
    ½ teaspoon salt
    ½ teaspoon kelp
      pinch of pepper or paprika
    2 tablespoons chopped fresh parsley

1. Sauté the onion lightly in a little oil or butter till soft. Add mushrooms and cook just until they begin to soften.
2. Beat the eggs and mix well with the cottage cheese. Add the mushrooms and the seasonings and parsley.
3. Pour into prepared pie crust and bake for 15 minutes at 400°F. Lower the heat to 350°F. and bake for 40 or 50 minutes more or until the filling is firm.

Makes 8 servings

CREAM OF MUSHROOM SOUP

½ pound fresh mushrooms, finely chopped
2 small slices onion, chopped
1 quart milk
1 cup light cream, evaporated milk or one of the nut creams
1 teaspoon salt
2 tablespoons butter

1. Place the mushrooms and onion slices in top of a double boiler, add the milk and cook over boiling water, stirring occasionally, until mushrooms are tender (about 45 minutes).
2. Now add the cream or evaporated milk, the salt, and stir in the butter. Serve piping hot.

Makes 5 servings

STEAMED WHOLE MUSHROOMS

½ pound small, whole mushrooms
2 tablespoons butter
    dash celery powder
    seasoned salt to taste
1 tablespoon chopped fresh chives

1. Wipe the mushrooms clean but do not peel.
2. In the top of a double boiler, melt butter over hot water. Sprinkle mushrooms with seasonings, and cook in butter 20 minutes, or until as tender as you prefer.

Makes 3 to 4 servings

Note: Serve steamed mushrooms as a side dish with meat or fowl, or as a luncheon dish on whole wheat toast.

GLORIOUS MUSHROOMS

1 pound mushrooms
2 tablespoons vegetable oil or butter
1 onion, chopped
   dash oregano
   sprig of fresh parsley or 3 tablespoons dried parsley
3 tablespoons sweet apple cider

1. Peel or wipe mushrooms, then slice, including the stems.
2. Put oil or butter in pan; brown onion until just golden. Add mushrooms, herbs and sweet cider.
3. Cover and cook gently for about 20 minutes, until mushrooms are tender.

Makes 6 servings

Note: An unusual but quite tasty way to serve mushrooms.

● *Don't peel your mushrooms. Much of their distinctive flavor lies in the skin, and will be lost by peeling.*

KASHA AND MUSHROOMS

1 egg, beaten
1 cup buckwheat groats
2 tablespoons oil
1 cup mushrooms, sliced
2 cups fat-free chicken broth or meat stock
½ teaspoon salt

1. Beat the egg well and add groats. Mix together very well to coat all the grains.
2. Brown mixture gently in oil in a heavy skillet. Add the sliced mushrooms.
3. Bring chicken broth to a boil and add to the mixture together with the salt. Mix well and cook very slowly, covered, until all liquid is absorbed and kasha is nice and fluffy. Add a little more broth if necessary.

Makes 6 servings

MUSHROOMS STIR-FRIED WITH CELERY

1 bunch washed celery
½ pound fresh mushrooms
2 tablespoons oil
2 tablespoons tamari soy sauce
1 teaspoon salt
1 teaspoon honey

1. Cut the celery diagonally in one-inch pieces. Cut clean mushrooms lengthwise in ¼-inch slices.
2. Heat the oil in a skillet, add mushrooms, and stir-fry over high heat for 1 minute.
3. Add the seasonings and celery, stir-fry all together for 3 minutes. Serve at once.

Makes 4 to 5 servings

Note: If you prefer a more delicate flavor, decrease the amounts of seasonings.

Okra

Primarily a hot-weather vegetable, okra thrives in the warmth of the deep southern states, where two crops can be grown in a single year. It may come as a surprise, then, that this tall annual, which belongs to the same family as cotton, can also be successfully cultivated in northern gardens.

Okra's most distinctive feature is its thick, gluey sap, which oozes out of the sliced pods as they are cooked. This sap is used to thicken various kinds of soups and stews, and makes okra an essential ingredient in any true southern gumbo. The young pods also possess a pleasant flavor, and are often served as a vegetable, with vinaigrette or hollandaise sauce.

For best quality, okra should be harvested a few days after the flowers fall, while the pods are quite young. The pods will be from one to four inches long, depending on the variety. They should still be soft, and the seeds should be only half grown. If left to mature, the pods become so tough and fibrous that they are indigestible. Picking the pods as soon as they are ready (every day if necessary) allows the plants to continue producing.

Okra should be used as soon as possible after picking, as the pods toughen quickly. If you find it necessary to store the pods for longer than 24 hours, spread them out in a cool, well-ventilated place, and keep them a bit moist. The ventilation is extremely important, because okra tends to heat up when stored in closed crates or boxes.

Okra can be preserved by freezing, canning or drying. Of the three methods, drying is least desirable because it cuts the vegetable's vitamin A content in half. When fresh, okra provides calcium, phosphorus, and iron, in addition to vitamins A and C.

To prepare okra for cooking, remove the stem ends and wash the pods. If the pods are used whole, the slippery juice will stay inside, and the pods will take on a crisp, crunchy texture if not overcooked. Depending upon how it's used, 1 pound of okra will serve four to six people.

CHICKEN GUMBO

1 small stewing chicken
1 ham bone
2 quarts water
1 onion, chopped
4 to 5 green shallots
2 cloves garlic, finely chopped
1 cup okra, chopped
½ cup celery leaves, chopped
4 bay leaves
    sprig of thyme
2 cups peeled, chopped tomatoes
2 tablespoons chopped parsley
    salt and pepper to taste
    shrimp or crabmeat, optional

1. Place the chicken, ham bone and water in a heavy pot and simmer for an hour or two. Remove any meat from the bones, and return it to the pot.
2. Strain the liquid back into the pot and add the onion, shallots, garlic, okra, celery leaves, bay leaves and thyme. Simmer for 45 minutes, then add tomatoes, parsley and seasonings.
3. Simmer a few minutes more, then serve. For extra flavor, shrimp or crabmeat may be added to the soup.

Makes 8 servings

OKRA SOUP

½ pound lean beef, cut into small pieces
1 onion, chopped
1 carrot, chopped
2 tablespoons oil
1 quart water
2 cups fresh okra, finely chopped
1 teaspoon chopped chives
½ teaspoon chopped basil
   salt and pepper to taste

1. Brown the meat, onion and carrot in oil. Add water and let simmer about 1 hour.
2. Add the okra and seasonings and cook about 25 minutes longer.

Makes 4 to 6 servings

OKRA DIP

1 pound very young, fresh okra with stems
¼ teaspoon salt

DIP:
   ¼ cup homemade mayonnaise
   ¼ cup yogurt or sour cream
   ½ teaspoon prepared mustard
   1 tablespoon chopped onion

1. Steam or cook okra in salted water until just tender. Chill.
2. Combine remaining ingredients and use as dip for okra (eating with fingers).

Makes 4 to 6 servings

Note: When okra pods are cooked whole in this manner they stay crisp instead of becoming slippery.

151

PIEDMONT PICKLED OKRA

2 pounds young okra pods (not more than 3 inches long), cut with stems
3 to 4 small, whole cayenne peppers (1 per jar of pickles)
3 to 4 teaspoons dill seed (1 teaspoon per jar)
2 cloves garlic (½ clove per jar)
2 cups vinegar
¾ cup water
¼ teaspoon turmeric
¼ cup salt

1. Leave about ¼ inch of stem on the okra pods, and wash them well. Pack the okra, peppers, dill seed and garlic into boiled pint jars.
2. Mix the vinegar, water, turmeric and salt in a pan; bring to a boil, reduce heat, and simmer briefly. Pour hot brine solution into jars to within ½ inch of the top.
3. Place jars in a pan of boiling water for 15 minutes, making sure the water will not boil over into them. Remove jars and seal. Allow at least 3 weeks before using the okra, and chill before serving.

Makes 3 to 4 pints

OKRA SALAD

2 cups okra, cut into 1-inch slices
1 large tomato, cut into wedges
½ green pepper, coarsely chopped
½ sweet red pepper, coarsely chopped
½ cup chopped celery
2 tablespoons chopped parsley
1 tablespoon chopped onion
½ teaspoon salt

DRESSING:
  1 tablespoon lemon juice
  ½ cup oil
  1 teaspoon prepared mustard

1. Cook or steam okra until just tender, about 8 minutes. Cool.
2. Add remaining salad ingredients and chill.
3. Prepare dressing:
   Mix lemon juice, oil, and mustard. Pour dressing over vegetables and toss until well-combined. Serve on salad greens.

Makes 4 to 6 servings

OKRA PILAF

  4 slices nitrite-free bacon, diced
  ½ pound okra, cut into ½-inch slices
  1 medium onion, chopped
  ½ green pepper, chopped
  2 cups tomatoes, peeled and quartered
  1 cup brown rice
    salt and freshly ground pepper, to taste
  2½ cups chicken broth

1. Fry bacon in large frying pan over medium heat until slightly browned, about 3 minutes.
2. Add okra, onion, and pepper, sauté about 5 minutes.
3. Add tomatoes, rice, salt, pepper, and broth, and mix well with a fork, so that everything is coated with bacon fat.
4. Bring to a boil, then cover and reduce heat. Simmer for 25 minutes, or until rice has absorbed the liquid.

Makes 6 servings

Note: This dish is a good complement to seafood.

STEWED OKRA

1½ pounds fresh okra
2 tablespoons butter
1½ cups finely chopped onions
8 medium-sized firm ripe tomatoes, finely chopped
2 teaspoons finely chopped garlic
2 teaspoons salt
½ teaspoon freshly ground black pepper
1½ teaspoons chili powder

1. Wash the okra under cold running water and, with a small, sharp knife, scrape the skin lightly to remove any surface fuzz. Cut ⅛ inch off the stem at the narrow end of each pod.
2. In a heavy 10- to 12-inch skillet, melt the butter over moderate heat. When the foam begins to subside, drop in the onions and, stirring frequently, cook for 5 minutes, until they are soft and transparent but not brown. Stir in the tomatoes and garlic, and cook, covered, for 5 minutes.
3. Add the okra, salt, pepper, and chili powder, and turn the pods about with a spoon to coat them on all sides. Reduce the heat to low, cover tightly, and simmer for 15 to 20 minutes, or until the okra is tender. Serve at once.

Makes 6 to 8 servings

OKRA CREOLE

1 onion, chopped
1 green pepper, chopped
½ sweet red pepper, chopped
½ cup chopped mushrooms
1 clove garlic, finely chopped
2 tablespoons oil
2 tomatoes, skinned and chopped
    salt and pepper to taste
1 pound okra, cut into 1-inch pieces
2 tablespoons chopped parsley

1. Sauté onion, green pepper, red pepper, mushrooms, and garlic in oil for about 5 minutes.
2. Add tomatoes, seasonings, and okra and simmer slowly for 15 to 20 minutes.
3. Serve immediately, garnished with chopped parsley.

Makes 4 to 5 servings

FRIED OKRA

2 eggs, slightly beaten
½ teaspoon salt
⅛ teaspoon black pepper
¾ cup cornmeal
2 tablespoons wheat germ
1 pound okra, sliced in ¼-inch rounds
2 tablespoons oil
  tomato sauce

1. Combine eggs, salt, and pepper in a bowl.
2. In another bowl, combine cornmeal and wheat germ.
3. Dip okra in egg mixture, then in cornmeal mixture. Fry in hot oil until tender and golden brown, 12 to 15 minutes.
4. Serve with your favorite tomato sauce.

Makes 4 to 6 servings

Note: An unusually crispy and delicious way to serve okra.

Onions

Gardeners have grown onions since ancient times. Egypt, in the days of the pharaohs, was famous for its mild onions. Today's gardener and cook is faced with a wide variety of onions, from the large, mild Bermuda onion to the pungent little scallion; from the subtle, thick-stemmed leek to the piquant, sophisticated shallot and the versatile garlic.

Onions are planted in early spring, traditionally after the last snowfall (the "onion snow"). Planting the sets a little closer together than is generally recommended will allow you to thin for green onions early in the season. Onions grow slowly, and don't mature until late summer or fall. As the plants mature, their tops shrivel and fall to the ground. A day or two after the tops have fallen, the onions are pulled and left lying on the ground for a few days to cure in the sunlight and air. It's best to let onions mature fully before you pull them, but do harvest them before a heavy frost.

After your onions have cured, bring them indoors and spread them out in an airy, dry place until cold weather arrives. Then you can hang them in bunches or put them in crates or net bags in a cool, dry attic, garage or cellar. As long as they are dry, onions won't be hurt by slight freezing, however, they should not be handled while frozen.

It's a good idea to keep a few onions in the refrigerator for immediate

use. Refrigerating onions before peeling and slicing or chopping them reduces tears.

Mature onions are not terribly rich in nutrients, but they do contain iron and vitamins A and C. In addition to being employed for their flavoring ability, onions are traditionally served whole, in a cream sauce or glaze.

SCALLIONS

Scallions are actually young onions which are pulled before the bulbs have formed, as soon as they are edible. Green onions are allowed to partially develop before being harvested. When scallions are grown, several pullings are usually made, removing the largest plants each time and allowing the rest to continue growing.

Scallions may be eaten raw, in salads or with dips, or cooked.

To prepare scallions for cooking or serving, wash them well, trim off the roots and remove the outer skin, leaving the lower stem clean and white. Many times the tops are used along with the white portions, to add color and additional flavor to the dish.

GARLIC

Garlic is grown in much the same manner as onions. It is planted in early spring and harvested in summer, when the tops turn dry and fall over. Like onions, garlic needs to be cured. The bulbs are spread out to dry, and are then cleaned by trimming the roots close to the bulb and removing the loose, outer skin.

Garlic may be stored like onions, tied in bunches or braided into the kind of strings sometimes seen in grocery stores. Keep it in a cool, dry place until needed. To use garlic, remove from the bulb as many cloves as you need, peel off the outer shells, and mince, crush or slice as desired.

LEEKS

The *leek* is an onion-like plant which is used much like the mature onion, but which is milder in flavor. Like parsnips and salsify, leeks are a cold-

weather crop. They can be harvested in the fall when they mature, or left in the ground and dug as needed throughout the winter. Although it will mean sacrificing some of the long, white stem, you'll have an easier time digging up leeks in the winter if you don't plant them too deep.

When leeks are prepared for cooking, they need to be washed very carefully to get the dirt out from between all the layers. It is often helpful to slit the stems lengthwise (but not all the way through) to rinse out the soil.

SPRING SOUP

5 bunches leeks
2 tablespoons oil
4 average-sized potatoes, thinly sliced
2 green stalks of celery and the leaves, sliced
2 quarts vegetable or chicken stock
1 pint milk or cream
2 tablespoons sour cream
1 tablespoon fresh or dried parsley
  pepper to taste
2 tablespoons sherry, optional

1. Cut up only the white part of the leeks and sauté slowly in oil along with potatoes and celery. Be careful not to brown. Add vegetable or chicken stock and simmer for 30 minutes.
2. Press this through your food mill or strain and put through blender. Keep the liquid—you need it! Combine liquid and puree, then add milk and sour cream.
3. Add parsley, and pepper to taste. For an interesting flavor, add a vigorous dash of nutmeg.
4. Add 2 tablespoons sherry if desired and reheat carefully—but do not boil.

Makes 6 to 8 servings

Note: A sprinkling of chopped olives adds color and taste to each bowl of leek soup—which perks up the winter-weary palate. The same soup may be served cold during the heat of summer, but don't forget the chopped olives, hot or cold.

MACARONI-VEGETABLE DINNER

Preheat oven to 375°F.

1½ cups whole wheat macaroni, cooked and drained
3 eggs, lightly beaten
1 cup milk
½ cup whole wheat bread crumbs
½ cup wheat germ
3 tomatoes, cored and chopped
½ cup shredded carrots
1 small green pepper, chopped
3 scallions, thinly sliced (with tops)
2 cups grated cheddar or other strong-flavored cheese
1 teaspoon salt
¼ teaspoon pepper

Combine all ingredients and mix thoroughly. Bake in a large, greased casserole at 375°F. for 30 minutes, or until eggs are set and vegetables are tender.

Makes 4 to 6 servings

• *Stewed and roasted onions were long a favorite supper dish in Scotland, and were believed to have medicinal properties.*

BAKED ONIONS

6 large onions, unpeeled

1. Steam onions until tender, 20 to 30 minutes, depending on their size.
2. Cut the bottoms off of the onions and slip off the skins. Place them around a roast of beef, about 20 minutes before serving the meat, and baste with the beef juice. Arrange whole, baked onions around the roast on serving platter.

Makes 6 servings

Note: The steamed onions may be served as soon as they are tender, to accompany meat or game, instead of being baked with the roast.

AKAAKAI (POLYNESIAN GREEN ONION SOUP)

3 tablespoons sesame seeds
1½ pounds beef short ribs
9 cups water
6 tablespoons tamari soy sauce
1 teaspoon salt
6 bunches green onions with tops, cleaned and cut into
    2-inch pieces
    freshly ground pepper, to taste

1. Heat the sesame seeds in a small pan until golden.
2. Wipe the short ribs with a damp cloth.
3. Into a Dutch oven, put water, short ribs, soy sauce, salt, and the sesame seeds. Simmer, uncovered, for 2 hours, or until the meat is tender.
4. Remove ribs, cut meat from bone, trim away fat and discard with bones.
5. Skim soup for fat, and replace meat. Add onions and cook, covered, for 30 minutes over medium heat.
6. Sprinkle each serving with freshly ground pepper.

Makes 4 servings as a meal
     8 servings as a soup course

SANTA CRUZ TOFU SPREAD

½ pound tofu (bean curd)
3 green onions, minced
1 stalk celery, minced
½ teaspoon salt
½ teaspoon celery salt
1 teaspoon sesame oil
½ cup sprouts, chopped
1 teaspoon dillweed
1 teaspoon cayenne pepper flakes
2 tablespoons plain yogurt
   chopped dillweed or parsley, for garnish

1. Mash *tofu* well and mix with remaining ingredients. Add more yogurt, if needed, for a more moist spread.
2. Serve on bread or crackers, garnished with dillweed or chopped parsley.

Makes 1 cup

ONIONS AU GRATIN

8 medium onions, sliced
¼ cup oil
½ cup grated Romano cheese
¼ cup grated cheddar cheese
paprika

1. Sauté onion slices in oil 10 to 12 minutes. Remove to baking dish.
2. Sprinkle cheese over top, along with paprika. Broil 5 inches from heat until cheese melts.

Makes 6 servings

GLAZED ONIONS

12 small onions
4 tablespoons butter or oil
2 tablespoons honey
½ teaspoon salt, optional

1. Steam the onions until barely tender, about 15 minutes. Cut off bottoms, slip off skins, and set aside.
2. In a saucepan, melt the butter, add honey, and heat for a minute. Add salt if desired.
3. Add onions and simmer for about 10 minutes, being careful not to scorch. Stir often to coat onions with glaze.

Makes 6 servings

Note: This dish is very good served with lamb.

ONION SOUP EXCELLENCE

4 large yellow onions, chopped
4 tablespoons butter or oil
2 quarts beef stock
4 white onions, finely grated
2 large red onions, sliced and separated into rings
   salt to taste
1 teaspoon pepper

1. Lightly sauté chopped yellow onions in butter or oil. Do not brown.
2. Pour in beef stock and simmer for about 10 minutes.
3. Add grated onion, onion rings, and seasonings, and simmer 20 to 30 minutes more. Serve with a piece of hot toast and some grated Parmesan cheese in each bowl.

Makes 6 to 8 servings

FRENCH LEEKS

12 leeks
¼ cup olive oil
6 tomatoes, peeled and quartered
   small can pitted black olives
2 tablespoons lemon juice
2 teaspoons grated lemon rind
   salt and freshly ground pepper to taste
¼ cup chopped parsley

1. Clean the leeks and cut them into 2-inch lengths. Heat the oil in a medium-sized saucepan, add the leeks, and steam for 10 minutes over low heat.
2. Add the tomatoes, olives, lemon juice and rind, and salt and pepper. Cover and cook another 10 minutes. Cool, sprinkle with parsley, and serve.

Makes 6 to 8 servings

FISH STUFFED WITH VEGETABLES

Preheat oven to 375°F.

1 4- to 5-pound fish (red snapper, striped bass, or
   salmon), cleaned and ready for stuffing
   salt as needed
3 tablespoons butter or oil
1 clove garlic, minced
⅓ cup chopped onion
¼ cup chopped green pepper
2 tablespoons chopped sweet red pepper
1½ cups shredded carrot
¼ cup chopped celery
2 tablespoons chopped fresh chives
2 tablespoons chopped fresh parsley
⅛ teaspoon rosemary
¼ teaspoon thyme
½ teaspoon dill
¼ teaspoon salt
¼ teaspoon paprika
⅛ teaspoon black pepper
2 tablespoons butter, melted

1. Wash fish, pat dry with paper towels, and rub with salt, inside and out.
   Place in an oiled, shallow roasting pan.
2. Melt 3 tablespoons butter or heat oil in a skillet. Sauté garlic and vegetables
   until tender. Remove pan from heat and add seasonings. Mix together well.
3. Spoon stuffing into fish and close cavity with wooden toothpicks or string.
   Brush fish with remaining 2 tablespoons of melted butter.
4. Bake at 375°F. until fork-tender, 45 to 50 minutes. Baste often. Serve
   with parsley butter or lemon butter if desired.

Makes 6 to 8 servings

● *Be careful not to overcook onions; if cooked too long, the sulfur in onions
breaks down, and they give off a bad smell.*

LEEKS FOR A COLD WINTER NIGHT

8 or 10 good-sized leeks
4 cups chicken or beef broth (with small slivers of meat if desired)
salt to taste
crumbled cheese, optional

1. Cut off all but 1 or 2 inches of the green plume-like tops. Wash leeks very carefully.
2. Put leeks in a saucepan, add broth, bring to a boil, then cook, covered, over moderate heat until leeks are tender but not broken down. Add salt to taste.
3. Serve in soup bowls; bits of crumbled cheese may be put into the bowls before the leeks and stock are poured in.

Makes 3 to 4 servings

Variation: For a different taste, the leeks may be cooked in water until tender, then drained. Add milk and butter to leeks and heat on low for a few minutes. Cheese may be added to soup bowls if desired.

● *In the ancient poetry of Northern Europe, heroic young men, rather than being called the flowers of their tribe, were called the leeks.*

CLASSIC ONION PIE

Preheat oven to 375°F.

8 slices nitrite-free bacon
½ cup chopped onion or shallots
3 eggs, beaten
1 cup milk
¾ teaspoon salt
½ teaspoon Worcestershire sauce
1 cup shredded Parmesan cheese
1 9-inch pastry shell or 6 small tart shells, baked

1. Fry bacon until crisp. Drain and crumble coarsely.
2. In bacon fat (or oil, if you prefer), sauté onion until nearly tender.
3. Beat eggs together with milk, salt and Worcestershire sauce. Stir in shredded cheese, bacon and onions. Pour into pastry shell.
4. Bake at 375°F. for 30 minutes, or until golden brown.

Makes 6 servings

● *How can you keep from crying when you work with strong onions? Next time, try peeling them under cold running water, or holding a piece of bread in your mouth while you chop them.*

POACHED EGG SOUP

¼ cup butter
3 stalks celery, diced
3 leeks, diced
2 turnips, diced
4 cups broth
   salt
1 teaspoon honey
2 cups peas
6 eggs
   parsley for garnish

1. Melt the butter in a Dutch oven and sauté the celery, leeks and turnips for 10 minutes, stirring occasionally. Keep the pot covered when not stirring.
2. Add the broth, salt, and honey, and cook until turnips are tender.
3. Add peas.
4. Break eggs into a saucer and add, one at a time, to the soup when it is just below the boiling point.
5. Cover and simmer until all eggs are set.
6. Garnish with parsley and serve with or over grilled cheese sandwiches.

Makes 6 servings

PEPPER-ONION RELISH

6 sweet red or yellow peppers, finely chopped
6 green peppers, finely chopped
6 large onions, finely chopped
½ cup honey
1 quart vinegar
4 teaspoons kosher salt

1. Combine all ingredients and bring to a boil.
2. Cook until slightly thickened, about 45 minutes, stirring from time to time.
3. Pack boiling-hot relish into clean, hot jars, filling them to the top. Seal tightly and store in refrigerator.

   OR, if extended storage is desired, process relish in a boiling water bath. Pack boiling-hot relish into clean, hot jars, leaving ½ inch of space at the top. Adjust jar lids. Process in boiling water for 5 minutes (starting to count time when water in canner returns to a boil). Remove jars, complete seals if necessary. Set jars several inches apart on a wire rack to cool.

Makes 2 one-pound jars

Parsnips

In a season where fresh vegetables are few and far between, parsnips add a fresh, earthy quality to meals whether served raw or cooked. In the eastern and northern states, parsnips can be left in the garden to be dug whenever convenient all winter long. In more temperate climates, it's best to plant them in the fall so their growth occurs during the cooler winter months.

Wait at least until after the first heavy frost to harvest parsnips. Freezing changes the carbohydrates in the roots to sugar, giving them a sweeter and more delicate flavor. The roots can be safely left in the ground until the spring, but must be dug before new shoots appear, for once new growth starts, the roots become limp, stringy, and tough.

Parsnips can be refrigerated for a week or two and can be frozen, canned, or root-cellared for longer storage. But leaving them in the garden takes the least effort and produces the most satisfactory results. If parsnips are to be dug while the ground is frozen, mulch the rows to make the harvest easier. If stored in a root cellar they should be spread out in the very coldest part of the room and covered with moss or moist earth.

About a pound and a half of parsnips will serve four people. The small- to medium-sized roots taste best. Scrub them well, and then slice and serve raw for an interesting addition to a salad. Parsnips can also be steamed, boiled

and mashed, or sautéed. Peel them, if desired, after cooking. They marry well with many spices, apples, and their carrot cousins. Parsnips are a good source of minerals.

MOCK CRABMEAT SALAD

2 cups shredded, raw parsnips
1 cup finely chopped celery
1 tablespoon chopped pimento
½ cup quartered ripe olives
½ cup mayonnaise
1 tablespoon lemon juice
2 teaspoons thinly sliced green onion
¾ teaspoon salt or kelp powder
shredded salad greens

1. Combine parsnips, celery, pimento and olives.
2. In a separate bowl, blend mayonnaise, lemon juice, onion, and salt. Add to parsnip mixture and toss lightly.
3. Serve over shredded greens.

Makes 4 to 5 servings

● *Parsnips are not considered worth eating by those in the know until after the first heavy frost, which mellows and sweetens their flavor. Parsnips were once so popular in England that when sweet potatoes were first introduced they were accepted largely because they tasted sweet, like parsnips.*

CANDIED PARSNIPS

1 pound small, young parsnips
2 tablespoons butter
1 tablespoon honey
⅛ teaspoon nutmeg

1. Wash and cook parsnips in boiling, salted water about 30 minutes, or until tender when pricked with a fork.
2. Drain and remove skins. Slice lengthwise.
3. In a frying pan, melt butter and add honey and nutmeg. Add parsnips and sauté until glazed, heated through, and delicately browned.

Makes 4 to 6 servings

PARSNIP VICHYSSOISE

2 large leeks
3 stalks celery, sliced
3 tablespoons butter
6 medium parsnips, diced
1 cup peas
1 cup wax beans
4 cups chicken broth
1 pint half-and-half or whole milk
   salt and pepper to taste
   parsley for garnish

1. Sauté leeks and celery in butter in a heavy pot.
2. Add parsnips, peas, wax beans and broth, and cook in the top of a double boiler until the parsnips are very soft.
3. Put through a food mill or blender to make a smooth soup.
4. Pour back into the pot and add the half-and-half. Heat until hot but do not boil. Add salt and pepper to taste.
5. Garnish with parsley and serve.

Makes 6 to 8 servings

PINTO-VEGETABLE SOUP

1 cup pinto beans
3 cups water
2 cups tomato juice
1 parsnip, chopped
1 onion, chopped
1 carrot, chopped
¼ teaspoon sage
   salt and pepper to taste

1. Soak beans for several hours.
2. Cook beans for 1 hour. Add remaining ingredients and cook 30 minutes more. Serve piping hot.

Makes 4 servings

OVEN-FRIED PARSNIPS

Preheat oven to 350°F.

8 large parsnips
4 cups water or vegetable stock
2 tablespoons oil or melted chicken fat
   chopped parsley

1. Wash parsnips, but do not scrape or peel; the roots have better flavor if the skins are kept on.
2. Parboil parsnips in water or stock for about 10 minutes. They should be firm, not tender.
3. Drain thoroughly. Peel off the skin and slice roots lengthwise in 3 or 4 portions. (Some parsnips have an inner core that is difficult to remove if the slices are cut crosswise.)
4. Brush slices with oil and lay strips in shallow baking pan. Bake 30 minutes at 350°F. or until parsnips are golden-brown. The inside should be tender and the outside crisp. Garnish with chopped parsley.

Makes 4 to 6 servings

● *Parsnips discolor easily so they should be cooked unpeeled or in water with a little lemon juice added.*

PARSNIP FIESTA SALAD

2 cups parsnips, cooked and diced
2 cups sugar peas, cooked
2 onions, thinly sliced and separated into rings
1½ cups carrots, finely chopped
½ cup onion tops, finely chopped
2 cups young beet greens
1 clove garlic, minced
12 radishes, thinly sliced (red and white), loose leaf
   lettuce

Combine all ingredients in a large salad bowl. Toss with your favorite dressing and serve.

Makes 4 to 6 servings

CURRIED PARSNIP PANCAKES

8 medium-sized parsnips (1 pound), scraped and sliced
2 eggs, lightly beaten
1 tablespoon vegetable oil
2 tablespoons whole wheat flour
1½ teaspoons curry powder
1 teaspoon salt
    vegetable oil for frying

1. Cook the parsnips in lightly salted boiling water until they are very tender. Drain thoroughly, return them to the pan, and shake them over low heat for a minute or so, until they are dry.
2. With a table fork or a potato masher, mash the parsnips as thoroughly as possible. Add the eggs, vegetable oil, whole wheat flour, curry powder, and salt, and beat vigorously together with a large spoon until all the ingredients are well combined.
3. Place enough oil into a large, heavy saucepan to cover the bottom. Heat the oil, then drop the parsnip mixture into the hot oil by heaping table-spoons. Fry the pancakes until they are brown on one side, then turn and flatten to fry on the other side.

Makes about 12 pancakes

PARSNIP-CABBAGE SALAD

1 cup shredded parsnips
1 cup shredded cabbage
1 cup diced celery
1 to 2 tablespoons dill seed
2 tablespoons vinegar
2 tablespoons honey

1. Stir together the vegetables and dill seed.
2. In a small saucepan, heat the vinegar and honey.
3. Pour dressing over vegetables and toss lightly.

Makes 4 servings

Peas

Traditionally the first seeds to go in the ground, peas should be planted as soon as the soil can be worked. And the instant that the pods are bright green and bulging with peas is the instant they should be picked. Ideally, you should split the pod open with your thumb and roll the perfect small sweet peas into your mouth right then and there. To store fresh peas even for 24 hours is to sacrifice sugar, vitamins, and texture—to store them for several days is to condemn your garden peas to the sorry state of those sold commercially.

Don't wait for your peas to mature before harvesting. At maturity a chemical change takes place which causes the sugar content to decrease rapidly, as the pea dries to seed and becomes starchy and hard. Harvest your peas while they are still young and tender. The pods should be bright green, velvety to the touch, and well-filled. When overripe, peas take on a spotty, yellowish color and a swollen appearance.

Be careful picking your peas. Hold the vine with one hand, and pull off the pods with the other. Tearing or jerking the pods from the vine may injure the plants and cause them to stop producing. For best results, peas should be shelled and eaten within an hour of picking. Like corn, peas deteriorate rapidly after being picked; their sugar content starts to turn to starch within two hours.

If you have to store peas before you can use them, don't shell them. Place them, uncovered, in the coldest part of the refrigerator until just before you're ready to use them. Rinse them, if necesary, before shelling, but not after. They're best cooked with the least possible amount of water—the French method is to use the moisture on wet lettuce leaves. They line a saucepan with the damp greens and a few pea pods, pour in the peas, cover with more lettuce, and steam over high heat for a few minutes. Butter, salt, and pepper the peas before eating.

For long-term storage peas can be canned, but freezing them is preferred because the frozen product tastes closer to the fresh. If part of your crop has gotten beyond you, you can dry it to use as you'd used dried beans, or to use for next year's seed. Allow the peas to stay on the bush until the peas are dried and the pods are wrinkled. Then, pull the vines and lay them on a rack in the sun for a few days. Strip off the pods, and allow the peas to dry for a few more days on a rack in partial shade. Shell the peas, and store in envelopes in a cool, dry place if you want them for next year's seed.

If you plan to use them as dried peas, you'll want to disinfect the crop by heating it in an oven for 30 minutes to an hour at a constant temperature of 135°F. Spread the peas in shallow pans for this treatment, and don't let the temperature vary significantly. Then store them in airtight containers in a dry place.

Two pounds of peas in the shell will produce about two cups of peas, enough to serve three or four people. Peas are rich in vitamin A and the B vitamins.

SUGAR PEAS

Sugar peas, snow peas, or edible-podded peas are appearing more frequently in home gardens. This is due, perhaps, to the growing popularity of Chinese cooking, of which they are a featured part, and also to the ease with which they are prepared. They are picked before the peas form, and the entire pod is eaten—no shelling is necessary. The pods lack the fibrous inner lining of regular peas, and therefore this vegetable can be treated like green beans, simply steamed or stir-fried before serving.

A luxuriant producer, sugar pea plants can yield almost double the quantity of the same number of sweet pea plants. Once harvest starts, the

plants should be checked regularly. Don't let the pods fill out with peas; they're rarely as sweet as shelling peas. To preserve the pods' natural sweetness, prepare them as soon as possible after picking. If you have a bumper crop (almost a sure thing with this heavy yielder) they can be frozen, though the frozen sugar pea will never equal the delicacy and crispness of its fresh counterpart.

To prepare for cooking, all that need be done is to rinse and remove any withered blossoms. Cut the larger pods in half, and steam as you would regular peas, or stir-fry in a *wok* with a bit of sesame or peanut oil. When properly cooked, they're still crunchy and have a brilliant emerald green color. Nutritional content is similar to that of regular peas, but sugar peas have only half the calories.

DRESSED-UP PEAS

Preheat oven to 350°F.

1 small onion, chopped
2 cups cherry tomatoes (whole)
1 tablespoon butter, melted
½ cup grated cheese
3 cups peas
1 mild or hot chili pepper, chopped
½ teaspoon salt
⅛ teaspoon pepper
½ cup grated cheese
1 chili pepper, cut in lengthwise strips

1. Mix the onion, tomatoes, butter, cheese, peas, and chopped chili pepper together. Add salt and pepper.
2. Pour into a baking dish and cover with the additional cheese and lengthwise strips of chili pepper.
3. Bake at 350°F. for 20 minutes.

Makes 6 servings

Note: This dish offers a particularly delicious combination of flavors.

INDIAN PEAS

Preheat oven to 350°F.

2 tablespoons chopped onion
2 cups shelled peas
⅔ cup cornmeal
1 cup milk
1 egg, beaten
½ teaspoon salt
4 teaspoons chopped parsley

1. Sauté onion in a small amount of oil until clear.
2. Place peas and onion in a greased, 1½ quart casserole.
3. Stir the cornmeal into the milk and blend well.
4. Stir in the egg and salt, and pour over the peas and onions.
5. Sprinkle with chopped parsley and bake at 350°F. for 20 to 30 minutes, stirring a few times.

Makes 4 servings

PUNGENT PEAS 'N ONIONS

1 cup tiny, white onions
1 tablespoon butter
4 cups shelled, fresh peas
½ teaspoon ground dillweed
1 tablespoon butter
   salt to taste

1. Sauté onions in butter until tender but not brown.
2. Meanwhile, cook peas until just tender.
3. Combine peas and sautéed onions. Add dillweed, butter, and salt. Heat over very low heat until piping hot. Serve immediately.

Makes 6 to 8 servings

FINGER SALAD

Assorted vegetables, enough to serve your family:
 carrots
 beets
 snap beans
 asparagus spears
 cherry tomatoes
 peppers
 kohlrabi
 sugar peas
 Jerusalem artichokes
 green onions

DRESSING:
 1 cup olive or sesame oil
 ¼ cup lemon juice
 ½ teaspoon salt
 ⅛ teaspoon black pepper

parsley to garnish

1. Lightly steam carrots, beets, beans, and asparagus separately, then chill.
2. Slice all vegetables in uniformly thin slices, except pea pods, cherry tomatoes and green onion.
3. Mix dressing and marinate kohlrabi, pea pods, peppers, asparagus, artichokes, onion and snap beans in it overnight.
4. Arrange all the vegetables on individual plates or large serving platters in pretty designs or rows.
5. Garnish with chopped parsley and serve with a vegetable or cheese dip.

● *For an interesting variation on green pea soup, slice a cucumber or two, drain as much of the water from the slices as you can (by patting them with a cloth), dip them in flour, sauté in butter till lightly browned, and add them to the soup right when you are ready to serve it.*

GREEN PEA SOUP

6 cups green peas, shelled
1 onion, sliced
1 large potato, cubed
1 large carrot, diced
    few sprigs fresh mint
4 cups water or chicken broth
    salt and pepper to taste

Cook vegetables and mint in water or broth until all are tender. Remove mint and put soup through a food mill. Add seasonings, reheat if necessary, and serve.

Makes 6 to 8 servings

Note: If you prefer a thicker soup, add a mixture of butter and flour until the desired consistency is reached. For a cream soup, substitute milk for half the broth, adding it after the soup has been put through the mill.

● *If peas are allowed to stand in their cooking water after they are cooked, they quickly lose their color.*

PARSNIPS AND PEAS

1 onion, peeled and chopped
2 teaspoons sesame oil
1 pound parsnips, scrubbed and sliced
1 pound fresh black-eyed peas (2 cups, shelled)

Sauté onion in oil until clear, about 5 minutes. Add parsnips and peas, and simmer over low heat about 30 minutes, until tender.

Makes 4 to 6 servings

GREEN MASHED PEAS

6 cups green peas, shelled
1 onion, sliced
½ cup fresh parsley, coarsely chopped
½ cup water
2 tablespoons butter
   salt and pepper to taste

1. Cook peas, onion and parsley in water over moderate heat until tender, about 5 minutes.
2. Drain off the water, reserving it to use in soups. Put the peas through a food mill.
3. Add the butter and seasonings, and whip the mixture with a fork until peas are light and fluffy—like mashed potatoes. Reheat if necessary.

Makes 6 to 8 servings

Note: This is a good way to use the large, tough peas from your garden that got overlooked in earlier pickings. However, if the peas are dried up and the pods are wrinkled, save them for seed to plant next year.

●   *Pea pods have all the flavor of the peas and can be used to make a tasty pea soup. Wash the empty pods, discarding any hard ones, and cook them for an hour in water to cover, in a tightly covered pan. Drain them well, press out the juice, and use this juice as the base for making a clear pea soup.*

Peppers

The peppers grown for use as vegetables all belong to the *Capsicum* family, and are in no way related to the Asiatic vines whose berries are used for white and black pepper seasonings. Garden peppers fall into two groups; sweet, or mild varieties, and hot chili types. Peppers originated in the tropics, and moved gradually northward until, today, they have become a popular summer garden crop in many parts of the United States. Although peppers are killed by frost, the growing season is long enough to permit their cultivation in most parts of the United States.

Peppers are an outstanding source of vitamin C. Sweet peppers are usually picked when they have almost reached their full size but are still solid and bright green in color. However, if green peppers are allowed to mature fully and turn red before picking, their vitamin C content will be much higher.

Chili peppers come in many varieties, ranging from milder varieties like fresnos to stinging hot types such as jalapeños, and cayenne, from which cayenne pepper is ground. Hot peppers may be picked either when green or when fully ripe and red. They are somewhat sweeter and milder when green, and are generally preferred at this stage for stuffing and baking.

When picking peppers, it's better to cut them from the plant with a half inch of stem attached, rather than to just pull them off. Pulling is likely to

damage the plant. They can be kept in an airtight container in the refrigerator for about 5 days before their quality seriously declines. Peppers will keep longer if the core and seeds are removed first.

To prepare peppers for cooking, wash them well and remove the cores, seeds and membranes, leaving only the green or red shells. The seeds of green peppers are extremely bitter, and the seeds of chili peppers are stingingly hot, so they are always discarded.

Sweet peppers may be preserved by freezing, in fact, they are one of the few vegetables that can be frozen without blanching first. Prepare them as you would for cooking, removing cores and seeds, then chop or cut in strips to freeze. Of course, frozen peppers lose their crunchiness, but they are fine for use in casseroles, soups, or sauces which require long cooking.

Sweet peppers may also be canned; they are generally pickled or included in relishes and chutneys. Hot peppers are sometimes pickled but are usually preserved by canning or drying.

Two large or 4 small sweet peppers will serve four people as a side dish.

CHILI RELLENO BAKE

Preheat oven to 350°F.

6 sweet green chili peppers
½ to ¾ pound cheddar or Monterey Jack cheese, sliced
1 medium onion, finely sliced or diced
4 eggs, separated
1 tablespoon water
2 tablespoons flour
½ teaspoon salt

1. Remove stems from peppers; slit lengthwise and remove seeds. Stuff peppers with generous slices of cheese and sliced (or diced) onion.
2. Combine egg yolks, water, flour, and salt. Beat well. Beat the egg whites until stiff and fold gently into the egg yolk mixture.
3. In a buttered, shallow casserole, put a small layer of the egg mixture, then arrange the stuffed chilis in a single layer, and top with the remaining egg mixture.

4. Bake at 350°F. until egg sets and is golden brown, about 25 minutes.

Makes 4 to 6 servings

Note: Many people prefer to peel chili peppers, as the skins tend to be tough. To peel peppers, arrange them close together on a broiler pan. Place the pan one inch from the broiler, and turn the peppers often until the skins are blistered and lightly browned all over. Drop peppers into a plastic bag and close bag to retain the moisture. When peppers are cool enough to handle, peel off the loosened skin with a knife. Then proceed with Step 1.

GARDEN-STYLE STUFFED PEPPERS

4 to 6 green or red peppers, uncooked
2 cups cooked brown rice
1 large carrot, shredded
¼ cup raw green peas
1 stalk celery, chopped
½ cup raw cauliflower, chopped
2 scallions, thinly sliced
2 hard-boiled eggs, chopped

DRESSING:
2 tablespoons oil
2 tablespoons vinegar
1 tablespoon lemon juice
1 teaspoon salt
1 teaspoon dry mustard

1. Slice tops off peppers and remove seeds and membranes. Dice tops and combine with rice, remaining vegetables, and chopped eggs.
2. Combine dressing ingredients and pour over rice mixture. Chill at least 1 hour to blend flavors. Taste and correct seasoning.
3. Pack stuffing into peppers and serve immediately or chill until needed. The cold rice mixture can be stored in the refrigerator for a day if necessary.

Makes 4 to 6 servings

SEED-STUFFED PEPPERS

Preheat oven to 375°F.

6 green peppers
½ pound pumpkin seeds
½ pound sunflower seeds
1 onion, finely chopped
1 carrot, coarsely grated
1 stalk celery, finely chopped
1 tablespoon chopped fresh parsley
   dash sage
   dash thyme
   dash rosemary
   dash curry powder
   salt and pepper to taste
2 tomatoes, cut in wedges

1. Steam peppers until tender; cut in half lengthwise and remove cores, seeds and membranes.
2. Grind the pumpkin and sunflower seeds together. Mix together with all remaining ingredients except tomato wedges. If mixture seems dry, add a tablespoon or so of oil to moisten it.
3. Stuff seed mixture into steamed peppers, and surround with tomato wedges.
4. Bake, uncovered, at 375°F. until heated through, about 25 minutes.

Makes 6 to 8 servings

CHEESE-STUFFED PEPPERS

Preheat oven to 350°F.

4 medium peppers, seeded and cored
½ pound sharp cheddar cheese, grated (there should
   be at least 2 cups of grated cheese)

1 medium onion, finely chopped
1 stalk celery, finely chopped
4 eggs, beaten
⅓ cup milk
   parsley, paprika, and salt or kelp to taste

1. Steam peppers until tender, then cut in half lengthwise.
2. Mix together cheese, onion and celery. Stuff this mixture into the prepared peppers, and lay them in a fairly shallow, oiled casserole, or individual custard cups.
3. Beat eggs and milk together. Pour over the peppers.
4. Sprinkle all with parsley, paprika, and salt or kelp.
5. Bake at 350°F. until the eggs are set, about 20 minutes.

Makes 4 servings

SALAD-STUFFED PEPPERS

5 large green peppers
4 cups cottage cheese
½ cup mayonnaise
3 scallions, finely chopped
2 teaspoons fresh parsley, finely chopped
1 teaspoon dry mustard
   salt, paprika, caraway seeds to taste

1. Split peppers lengthwise; remove stems, seeds and membranes. Set aside.
2. Blend remaining ingredients together thoroughly.
3. Fill pepper halves with cottage cheese mixture and chill for a few hours to blend flavors.

Makes 5 servings

Note: This mixture may also be used as a dip for chunks of pepper and other vegetables. When using it as a dip, make it with whipped cottage cheese.

PEPPERS WITH SPICY MEXICAN SAUCE

Preheat oven to 375°F.

5 large green peppers
1 cup cooked brown rice
1 pound lean ground beef
1 onion, finely chopped
1 to 2 cloves garlic, pressed
1 teaspoon fresh summer savory or sweet basil leaves
    dash each, marjoram and thyme
    salt and pepper to taste
2 teaspoons soy grits
2 teaspoons wheat germ

SAUCE:
    1 large onion, finely chopped
    1 clove garlic, minced
    2 jalapeño (mildly hot) peppers, seeded and finely chopped
    3 tablespoons oil
    4 tomatoes, peeled and chopped
    ½ teaspoon honey
    ¼ teaspoon chili powder
    1 teaspoon oregano
    ½ teaspoon salt
    freshly ground pepper to taste
    ¼ cup grated cheddar cheese

1. Wash peppers, split in half lengthwise and remove cores, seeds and membranes. Steam until barely tender, 5 to 8 minutes. Drain peppers and set aside until cool enough to handle.
2. Mix rice, beef, onion, garlic, seasonings, grits, and wheat germ together and pack into the pepper halves. Bake at 375°F. for 20 minutes.
3. Meanwhile, make sauce:
   Sauté onion, garlic and peppers in oil until tender.
4. Add tomatoes, honey, chili powder, oregano, salt, and pepper. Cook

down to thicken slightly, and pour over the nearly baked peppers.

5. Sprinkle grated cheese over the sauce and run under broiler until cheese is melted.

Makes 6 to 8 servings

● *The Aztecs ascribed medicinal properties to chili peppers, and it seems they knew what they were talking about. One large, green chili pepper has as much vitamin C as an orange; ripe, red chili peppers contain large quantities of vitamin A.*

CHILAQUILES

6 corn tortillas
1 large bell pepper, with seeds and membranes removed
1 fresh, hot chili pepper, with seeds and membranes removed
1 onion
2 cloves garlic, peeled
   oil
2 tomatoes, cored and chopped
3 beaten eggs
½ teaspoon salt
1 cup tomato or enchilada sauce
½ cup grated cheese

1. Cut the tortillas into fat strips (1½ inches by 2 inches). Chop peppers and onion; mince garlic.
2. Sauté tortilla strips in oil until they are crisp. Add peppers, onion, and garlic and sauté until barely tender.
3. Add chopped tomatoes, beaten eggs and salt; cook, stirring occasionally, until the egg coats everything and sets.
4. Heat the sauce, pour it over the egg mixture and top with grated cheese. Serve immediately.

Makes 4 servings

Note: This dish is a kind of Mexican hash—all kinds of leftover vegetables can be added to the basic recipe.

'BURGERS HAWAIIAN IN PEPPER RINGS

2 large green or red peppers
1 pound lean ground beef or beef heart
4 teaspoons wheat germ
1 egg, beaten
1 to 2 teaspoons tamari soy sauce
1 teaspoon molasses
¼ teaspoon ground ginger
   black pepper to taste

TOPPING:
   pineapple rings
   molasses

1. Slice off tops of peppers, remove seeds and membranes, and cut into rings about ½ inch thick.
2. Combine remaining ingredients (except topping) and form into 'burgers on top of pepper rings.
3. Broil 'burgers under high heat for about 4 minutes. Turn and broil the other side 3 minutes. Top each 'burger with a pineapple ring brushed with molasses, and broil another minute. Serve immediately.

Makes 4 to 6 servings

● *Be careful not to overcook peppers, or they will turn bitter.*

SAUTÉED PEPPERS AND TOMATOES

1 medium onion, chopped
3 to 4 tablespoons oil
4 large bell peppers, cored and cut in chunks
1 teaspoon salt
3 large tomatoes, cored and cut in chunks
1 teaspoon dried basil

1. Sauté onion in oil for 5 minutes.
2. Add peppers and salt, and sauté about 8 minutes more.
3. Add tomatoes and basil, cover and simmer until peppers are tender, about 3 to 5 minutes.

Makes 4 servings

Note: This dish is especially good when served with grilled meats and barbecue dishes.

Potatoes

Growing potatoes at home offers a double dividend—both the tiny, tender-skinned new potatoes harvested before the plant matures and the tougher-skinned staple that keeps an entire winter when properly stored.

New potatoes can be dug anytime after the plant flowers, but they should be dug carefully, by hand, so as not to disturb the formation of other tubers. Marble-sized, immature potatoes, rich in vitamin C, are at their best simply washed, boiled until tender, and served hot, in their skins, with melted butter and perhaps some chopped parsley. They are also used in salads and can be canned.

Potatoes intended for root cellar storage must be left to mature fully. The tubers will grow underground until the vines wither, and they can be left in the ground up to six weeks after that if the weather is not too warm or too wet. Try to time your potato harvest for a day when the soil is dry. Dig up the potatoes with a pitchfork, taking care not to damage their skins, and allow them to dry for an hour or two on top of the ground. Examine your crop and set aside for immediate use any potatoes that are bruised or cracked. Perfect potatoes should be stored in a humid, cool, but frost-free place. If they are stored where light can get at them, they will turn green and develop a toxic substance called solanine. All such green portions should be cut off

and discarded, though the rest of the potato can be eaten. Properly stored, potatoes will keep for months. For best keeping and cooking quality, store potatoes where the temperature is about 45° to 50°F. They can also be frozen partially cooked, but should not be thawed before they are reheated.

Before cooking, scrub potatoes well and remove any bad spots, sprouts, or eyes. It's rarely necessary to peel potatoes for they can be baked, mashed, scalloped, fried, and prepared in many other ways with their skins intact. Many nutrients lie just below the potato's surface and are lost when the vegetable is pared. If you do decide to peel your potatoes, wait until just before they are cooked or they will turn dark. Allowing at least 1 four-inch potato per serving, count on four servings from a pound of potatoes.

Although they are mostly starch, potatoes contain a fair to large amount of vitamin C and supply minerals as well.

POTATOES IN PEPPER BOATS

Preheat oven to 325°F.

2 medium-sized green peppers
2 cups mashed potatoes
½ cup non-instant dry milk powder
1 egg, beaten
½ cup grated cheddar cheese
¼ cup chopped parsley
½ teaspoon celery salt
½ teaspoon paprika
1 tablespoon wheat germ

1. Cut slice from stem end of peppers. Cut in half; remove seeds and tough white membrane. Cook in boiling water for 5 minutes. Drain.
2. Combine remaining ingredients, mix well, and mound onto the pepper halves.
3. Bake in buttered, shallow casserole about 20 minutes at 325°F.

Makes 4 servings

SAUERKRAUT COTTAGE PIE

Preheat oven to 350°F.

1 cup cooked hamburger, drained of fat
1 cup drained sauerkraut
1 egg, slightly beaten
⅔ cup beef or chicken stock
   salt to taste
½ teaspoon caraway seeds
¼ teaspoon thyme
¼ teaspoon black pepper
½ cup finely chopped onion
⅓ cup finely chopped sweet red peppers
1 clove garlic, minced
1 tablespoon oil
2 cups mashed potatoes, salted to taste
1 tablespoon butter
   paprika

1. Combine meat, sauerkraut, beaten egg, stock and seasonings. Add salt.
2. Sauté onion, sweet peppers, and garlic in oil for 5 minutes. Do not brown. Add to meat mixture; mix.
3. Turn into lightly oiled baking dish.
4. Top with mashed potatoes. Dot with butter and sprinkle with paprika. Bake at 350°F. or until potato is golden, about 30 minutes.

Makes 4 servings

CHEESE-TOPPED POTATOES

6 medium potatoes, scrubbed and cut in halves or quarters
2 tablespoons butter
½ to 1 cup milk
   salt and pepper to taste
⅔ cup grated Parmesan or sharp cheddar cheese

1. Cook potatoes until tender, not mushy, 15 to 20 minutes. Drain well.
2. Mash potatoes with butter and enough milk to make a fluffy consistency. Add salt and pepper to taste.
3. Spread mashed potatoes in a shallow casserole or on a baking sheet, top with grated cheese, and broil about 5 minutes, until cheese melts and browns slightly.

Makes 4 to 5 servings

● *The starch content of potatoes increases with age. Starchy potatoes are best suited for baking and french frying.*

POTATO-CARROT PANCAKES

2 cups peeled, cubed uncooked potatoes
1 cup sliced carrots
2 eggs, slightly beaten
¼ cup whole wheat flour
½ teaspoon double-acting baking powder
½ teaspoon salt
½ teaspoon onion salt
  dash pepper
  butter
  sour cream

1. In 2-quart saucepan over medium heat, in 1 inch of boiling water, heat potatoes to boiling; reduce heat to low; cover and cook 5 minutes. Add carrots and continue cooking 15 minutes more; drain.
2. With potato masher, mash potatoes and carrots until potatoes are smooth (carrots will still be lumpy). Add remaining ingredients except butter and sour cream, and mix well. Let stand 5 minutes.
3. In a 10-inch skillet over medium heat, melt about 1 teaspoon butter (or more as needed); add potato mixture by rounded tablespoonfuls. Using back of tablespoon, press each mound into a 2½-inch pancake. Fry pancake until golden on underside, about 2 minutes; turn and brown other side. Remove pancakes to platter; keep warm.
4. Repeat with remaining potato mixture. Serve with sour cream.

Makes 4 servings

BLUE CHEESE POTATOES

Preheat oven to 400°F.

4 medium baking potatoes
   oil
½ cup sour cream
1 teaspoon chopped fresh chives
¼ cup blue cheese, crumbled
   milk as needed
4 tablespoons butter
¾ teaspoon salt
   dash of black pepper
   parsley for garnish

1. Brush potatoes with oil. Bake in hot oven (400°F.) 1 hour.
2. Remove potatoes from oven; cut a lengthwise slice from the top of each potato.
3. Scoop out inside and mash; add sour cream, chives, cheese, milk, butter, salt, and pepper. Beat until fluffy.
4. Spoon mixture back into jackets. Place on baking sheet and return to hot oven for 15 minutes. Serve garnished with parsley.

Makes 4 servings

● *Potatoes stored where the temperature is below 45°F. for more than a week may develop a sweet taste, because some of their starch turns to sugar. To improve their flavor, store them at 70°F. for a week or two before you use them.*

PAN-BROILED POTATOES

4 large baking potatoes
4 tablespoons oil
3 tablespoons onion, minced or grated
   salt and pepper to taste
1 tablespoon chopped parsley or chives

1. Scrub the potatoes but don't peel them. Shred or grate them rather coarsely.
2. Heat the oil in a large skillet, and spread the potatoes and onion over the bottom of the pan. Cover and cook over medium heat until browned on the bottom.
3. Turn the potatoes and continue cooking until the other side is brown. Season with salt and pepper to taste, garnish with chopped parsley or chives, and serve immediately.

Makes 5 to 6 servings

● *When sprouts appeared on stored potatoes in the nineteenth-century household, the potatoes were dropped into boiling water for a few minutes, the sprouts were rubbed off, and the potatoes were dried and put back into bags.*

POTATO-SCALLION SOUP

2 potatoes
2 scallions or small onions
2 to 3 tablespoons butter
2 medium-sized carrots
4 cups water
½ cup kale, beet or turnip greens, or other fresh greens in season
¼ cup thin egg noodles
½ teaspoon salt
⅛ teaspoon pepper
½ teaspoon basil
1 teaspoon chopped parsley

1. Cut potatoes into small cubes, and thinly slice scallions or onions. Sauté both in butter until golden brown.
2. Grate carrots. Bring water to a boil, add all ingredients and simmer until potatoes are tender.

Makes 4 servings

CREAMED POTATO CASSEROLE

Preheat oven to 350°F.

6 large potatoes, peeled
2 cups large-curd cottage cheese
1 cup yogurt
1 to 2 cloves garlic, put through a press
1 teaspoon salt
2 to 3 scallions, finely chopped
1 cup grated cheddar cheese
   caraway seeds

1. The potatoes should be boiled until they are just barely tender, not yet soft. Cut them up into rather small cubes and combine them with the cottage cheese, yogurt, garlic, salt, and scallions.
2. Turn the mixture into a buttered casserole and sprinkle the grated cheddar cheese over the top. Sprinkle with caraway seeds and bake at 350°F. for about 30 minutes. Serve hot.

Makes 6 to 7 servings

● *Potatoes can be ruined by being cooked in too much water—the water should just cover them in the pan. Pour off the water as soon as the potatoes are done—if you let them stand in the water, they'll quickly become waxy and watery.*

POTATO-BEAN LOAF

Preheat oven to 350°F.

1 cup dry navy beans
3 cups stock
8 medium potatoes
2 to 3 tablespoons butter
1 cup milk
½ cup onion, diced
½ cup green pepper, chopped
½ cup celery, diced
¼ cup celery leaves, chopped

1 clove garlic, minced
¾ cup cheese, grated
salt to taste

1. Soak beans overnight. Drain and cook in stock for 2 hours. Drain excess stock and save to use in soups.
2. Cook potatoes until tender; mash with butter and milk. Meanwhile, sauté vegetables lightly in small amount of oil or melted butter.
3. Fold beans and vegetables into mashed potatoes. Stir in ½ cup of cheese, and salt to taste, and put into an oiled casserole.
4. Sprinkle with remaining ¼ cup cheese and bake at 350°F. for 25 minutes.

Makes 8 to 10 servings

● *A dark ring under a potato's skin means that the potato was left in the ground too long, and was hit by frost.*

SCALLOPED POTATOES

Preheat oven to 350°F.

5 medium potatoes
1½ teaspoons salt
¼ teaspoon pepper
¼ cup whole wheat flour
2 to 3 tablespoons butter
1 small onion, thinly sliced, optional
2 cups milk, or more as needed

1. Oil a 1½- or 2-quart casserole. Scrub potatoes and slice thinly (don't peel them).
2. Put a layer of potatoes in the bottom of the casserole, sprinkle with salt, pepper and flour; dot with butter. Top with onion slices if desired.
3. Repeat process until all the potatoes are used. Pour milk over top.
4. Bake for 60 to 70 minutes at 350°F., until potatoes are tender and dish is bubbly.

Makes 6 servings

Sweet Potatoes & Yams

Not really a potato at all, the sweet potato actually belongs to the morning glory family. When grown in the tropics it produces a long trailing vine and lavender morning glory-like blossoms. Grown in cooler climates, it seldom blossoms, but will produce tubers if given five months of hot days and warm nights, as well as plenty of room to vine. Yams are distinguished from sweet potatoes by their orangey, moist flesh.

Early sweets may be dug when they are large enough to cook, a quality which can be determined only by digging them up and taking a look. If intended for winter storage they can stay in the ground until the first frost hits the leaves. Then the vines should be cut immediately, and the tubers dug as soon as possible, preferably on the same day. Dig slowly and with care, for any bruise on the skin will form rot in storage. The tubers may be allowed to dry in the sun, but should not be left out overnight.

Once properly cured, sweet potatoes can be stored under the right conditions for up to four months. To toughen their skins, they should be held at a temperature of about 85°F. in a place where the humidity is about 90 percent for 10 to 14 days. These conditions can be approximated by placing the sweets in wooden crates stacked with wooden strips between (to ensure air circulation) next to a furnace or warm chimney. The crates should be

covered with plastic sheeting to maintain high humidity. At the end of this initial curing process, the sweets can be moved to a dry, well-ventilated place where the temperature hovers at about 55°F. Temperatures below 50°F. encourage decay.

Once sweet potatoes are finally stored, they should not be moved unnecessarily. During storage, some of the starch in sweet potatoes turns to sugar, improving their flavor with little nutritional loss. Sweet potatoes can also be canned or frozen for long-term storage. For short-term storage, keep them in a closed box or bag at room temperature. Do not refrigerate.

Before cooking, sweet potatoes should be thoroughly scrubbed, but peeling is unnecessary. They can be baked or boiled like white potatoes and take very kindly to herbs, spices, and fruit flavorings. Allow one medium-sized sweet potato or about ⅓ to ½ pound per serving.

Sweet potatoes are exceptionally rich in vitamin A and also provide some vitamin C.

SWEET POTATO PUDDING

Preheat oven to 325°F.

3 eggs
¾ cup molasses and/or honey
½ cup milk
½ cup butter, melted
½ teaspoon nutmeg
½ teaspoon salt
3½ cups diced, raw sweet potato
½ cup chopped raisins or nuts, optional

1. In blender, place eggs, molasses, milk, butter, nutmeg, salt and 1 cup of diced sweet potato. Cover and blend until smooth.
2. Remove cover while blender is running and slowly add the remaining sweet potato. Add raisins or nuts if desired, blending at low speed until well mixed.
3. Pour into a buttered baking dish and bake at 325°F. for 1¼ hours.

Makes 6 servings

HAM AND YAM SURPRISE

Preheat oven to 350°F.

4 sweet potatoes or yams (about ¾ pound)
1 slice ham, ¾-inch thick (about 1 pound)
¼ pound dried apricots
2 tablespoons minced onions
1 tablespoon butter
1 tablespoon whole wheat or unbleached flour
¼ teaspoon salt
1½ teaspoons prepared mustard
½ teaspoon Worcestershire sauce
1½ teaspoons vinegar
¼ teaspoon ground cloves
1 tablespoon honey
  fresh parsley for garnish

1. Parboil sweet potatoes 20 minutes in water to cover. Peel and slice into greased casserole.
2. Cut ham into 4 sections and place on potatoes.
3. Cook apricots for 5 minutes in water to cover. Drain partially, reserving ½ cup of liquid, and mash.
4. Sauté onions in butter until tender; add flour, salt, mustard, Worcestershire sauce, vinegar, cloves, and honey. Add apricots and ½ cup apricot juice. Simmer for 5 minutes until well-blended. Pour over ham.
5. Bake at 350°F. for 40 minutes. Garnish with parsley.

Makes 4 servings

CRANBERRY CANDIED SWEET POTATOES

Preheat oven to 350°F.

4 medium-sized potatoes, cooked, peeled, and halved
½ cup whole cranberry sauce
3 tablespoons lemon juice

⅓ cup honey
1 tablespoon melted butter

1. Place potatoes in an oiled, shallow baking dish. Combine cranberry sauce and lemon juice, mixing well. Spread cranberry mixture over potatoes.
2. Combine honey and butter; pour over sweet potatoes. Bake at 350°F. for 25 minutes, basting occasionally.

Makes 4 generous servings

Note: Even people who don't usually go for candied sweet potatoes like this dish.

SWEET POTATO AND PECAN PIE

Preheat oven to 375°F.

¼ cup butter, softened
⅓ cup honey
   dash salt
2 cups mashed sweet potatoes
3 eggs, well beaten
½ cup milk
1 teaspoon vanilla
½ teaspoon cinnamon
½ teaspoon ginger
½ teaspoon nutmeg
1 cup pecan halves
1 unbaked 8-inch whole wheat pastry shell

1. Cream butter, honey and salt together.
2. Combine sweet potatoes, eggs, milk, vanilla, spices and pecan halves. Mix well. Add butter-honey mixture and mix until well blended.
3. Pour into pastry shell. Bake at 375°F. for 50 to 55 minutes or until knife inserted in center comes out clean.

Makes one 8-inch pie

HONEY-GLAZED SWEET POTATOES

4 sweet potatoes, cooked until tender
3 tablespoons butter
   juice and grated rind of one orange
2 tablespoons honey
1 tablespoon chopped parsley
1 tablespoon chopped chives

1. Slice cooked sweet potatoes into thin chips.
2. Melt butter in a skillet and add orange and honey. Add sweet potato chips and toss in the sauce until coated and heated through.
3. Sprinkle with parsley and chives, and serve.

Makes 4 servings

SWEET POTATO SOUFFLÉ

Preheat oven to 350°F.

2 cups cooked, mashed sweet potatoes (about 3 whole potatoes)
2 egg yolks
½ cup pecans, optional
1 cup milk, scalded
2 to 4 tablespoons honey, to taste
½ teaspoon salt
3 tablespoons butter
½ cup raisins
½ teaspoon nutmeg
2 egg whites, stiffly beaten

1. Mix together all ingredients, folding in beaten egg whites last.
2. Pour into an oiled 1½- or 2-quart casserole and bake at 350°F. for 1 hour or until set as a custard.

Makes 4 servings

SPANISH BOILED DINNER

Preheat oven to 350°F.

2 cloves garlic, minced
4 tablespoons butter
1 large onion, chopped
2 tomatoes, chopped
1 green pepper, seeded and chopped
1½ pounds beef stew meat
   salt, and freshly ground pepper, to taste
1½ teaspoons honey
6 ears corn kernels (cut off the cob)
3 potatoes, diced
3 sweet potatoes, peeled and diced
2 cups beef broth, or 2 cans beef consommé
1 small pumpkin

1. Sauté garlic in butter until golden, add onions and cook in a Dutch oven until they become limp.
2. Add tomatoes, pepper, beef cubes, salt and pepper, and honey. Cook and stir until meat is browned.
3. Add corn, potatoes, and beef broth and simmer for 40 minutes, covered. Water may be added if mixture appears dry.
4. Meanwhile, remove the top, seeds and membranes from the pumpkin. Place it in a shallow baking dish, well salted and peppered, and with all cut surfaces buttered. Bake in 350°F. oven for 45 minutes.
5. When pumpkin and boiled dinner are done, fill the pumpkin with the meat mixture. Serve hot.

Makes 8 servings

SWEET POTATO BREAD

Preheat oven to 375°F.

2 tablespoons dry yeast
½ cup warm water
½ teaspoon salt
2 tablespoons honey
2 tablespoons vegetable oil
1 cup cooked sweet potatoes, mashed
½ cup cornmeal
1 cup whole wheat flour
4 tablespoons butter
½ cup whole wheat flour

1. Sprinkle yeast over water and allow to stand until yeast is dissolved.
2. Add salt, honey and oil. Stir to mix. Add sweet potatoes, cornmeal and a cup of whole wheat flour. Mix well and allow to stand 10 minutes in a warm place covered with a towel.
3. Break up the butter in small pieces and drop over dough. Fold dough over and knead the butter into the dough, adding ½ cup whole wheat flour. Knead about 5 minutes, adding more flour if necessary.
4. Place in buttered 8 x 8 square pan, cover with a warm towel, and allow to rise until double. Bake at 375°F. 40 to 45 minutes. The top will be golden brown but not hard. Cool on rack, and cut into squares.

Radishes

The name "radish" comes from the Latin *radix,* meaning a *root.* One of the earliest recorded cultivated vegetables, radishes were grown in ancient Egypt, Greece, and Rome, and have been used for centuries in China and Japan. Now eaten primarily as an appetizer or as part of a salad, radishes may also be cooked and have the added attraction of being just about the fastest growing vegetable—going from seed to table in just four weeks.

There are three common types of garden radishes. Early or spring radishes are harvested before the heat of summer sets in; the more heat resistant summer or midseason varieties are grown during summer months; winter radishes are grown in the cool fall weather and may be left in the ground until frost comes.

Radishes can range in color from pure white to gold and the familiar red, as well as pink, violet, and black; in size they range from cherry-sized bulblets, to large globes, to long carrot-like roots, to 50-pound mammoths. French varieties are small, colorful types that are well-suited for eating raw. Chinese or Japanese varieties form larger roots of mild flavor which can be eaten either raw or cooked. There are at least two varieties called Spanish, one of which forms a long root, and the other a beet-sized globe, both with black skins and white flesh. The Oriental and Spanish varieties are usually winter types and are often suitable for long-term storage.

Early and summer radishes should be pulled as soon as they attain full growth, while they are still smooth and firm. They should not feel spongy when pressed. Leaving them in the ground even a few days longer than necessary may cause them to turn bitter. Winter radishes can be left in the ground until after frost, then dug and stored in a root pit or damp cellar where they'll keep through the winter. Radishes will keep in the refrigerator for a few weeks if their tops have been removed.

To prepare radishes for serving, cut off the greens and wash the roots thoroughly. Though they do supply a small amount of vitamin C and some minerals, radishes are more useful as appetite stimulants than as nutriment.

CREAMED RADISHES ON TOAST

18 radishes (about 3 cups sliced)
½ teaspoon salt
2 tablespoons butter
2 tablespoons whole wheat or unbleached flour
2 cups milk
½ teaspoon salt
  dash of black pepper
1 teaspoon chopped chives
6 slices whole grain bread
  chopped parsley for garnish

1. Wash radishes. Remove tops and roots. Slice or quarter. Cover with boiling salted water and cook for 5 minutes. Drain thoroughly.
2. Melt butter in skillet; add flour and stir until flour begins to brown. Pour in milk and stir until thick and bubbly.
3. Add the seasonings and radishes, and simmer until heated through. Meanwhile, toast bread.
4. Serve creamed radishes over toast, and garnish with parsley.

Makes 6 servings

BATTER-FRIED RADISHES

½ pound long, white radishes, or round, red radishes,
   grated
1 egg, beaten
¼ cup milk
½ cup whole wheat flour
1 teaspoon salt
½ to ¾ cup grated sharp cheddar cheese
   oil for sautéing

1. Beat all ingredients except radishes and oil together to make a batter. Stir in grated radishes.
2. Drop by spoonfuls into a small amount of hot oil, and sauté until golden on both sides. Drain excess oil and serve hot.

Makes 4 servings

● *For a light, slightly peppery sandwich filling, use radish thinnings, first cutting off the hairy taproots. Slices of crisp raw radishes can also make a colorful, snappy addition to sandwiches.*

BAKED RADISHES

Preheat oven to 350°F.

½ pound radishes, long white, or round (cut long ones
   into 1 inch pieces; leave round ones whole or cut in
   half)
1 tablespoon honey
1 tablespoon butter
⅛ teaspoon cinnamon

1. Steam radishes for 5 minutes; drain and arrange in a shallow baking dish.
2. Combine honey, butter and cinnamon in a small saucepan to make glaze. Pour over radishes and bake uncovered at 350°F. until tender, about 30 to 35 minutes.

Makes 4 servings

RADISH SALAD

2 cups thinly sliced radishes
2 cups sliced cucumbers
1½ cups sliced scallions
1 teaspoon honey
2 teaspoons salt
¾ cup sour cream
2 hard-boiled eggs
1 tablespoon minced parsley or scallions

1. Combine radishes, cucumbers and scallions and chill well.
2. In a separate bowl, combine honey and salt with sour cream.
3. Top chilled vegetables with the sour cream dressing. Sprinkle with chopped whites of hard-boiled eggs, and minced parsley or scallions.

Makes 4 servings

Rhubarb

Rhubarb, like asparagus, is an economical plant that produces year after year with a minimum of care. Once its roots are established they send up sturdy stalks topped with large, red-veined leaves each spring. Only the stalks of rhubarb are edible—the leaves must be discarded because they contain oxalic acid and its salts, which can be fatally poisonous.

Stalks can be picked as they are needed once the plants have had a full year in the garden. To harvest, grasp the stalk near its base and twist away from the plant's crown. It should separate easily. Do not cut the stalks from the plant, and harvest only those stalks which are at least one inch thick and ten inches long. Leave any that are too thin or too short to feed the roots for next year's growth. Cut off the leaves and throw them on the compost pile on your way into the kitchen.

Though some hardy souls do eat rhubarb raw, munching on the tart stalks as though they were celery, most people prefer it cooked, with some sweetening added. To cook rhubarb, cut the stalks into one-inch or one-and-one-half-inch pieces and stew them in just a tiny bit of water until tender. Only a little water is needed, because rhubarb releases a great deal of moisture as it cooks. Rhubarb can also be baked or steamed. Also known as pie-plant, rhubarb does make delicious pies, whether used alone or combined with

207

other fruits or a custard. But it can also be used like other fruits, to make re-freshing tonic-like beverages, tangy relishes to accompany game or grain dishes, and pleasing cobblers or crunches to be served with ice cream. It can be frozen, raw, in chunks to be used for winter pies, or canned as a juice or sauce. One pound of rhubarb makes about a pint of sauce—three or four servings. Rhubarb supplies vitamins A and C and calcium and iron.

RHUBARB BREAD

Preheat oven to 325°F.

1½ cups brown sugar, or ¾ cup honey
½ cup oil
1 egg
1 tablespoon baking soda
1 cup buttermilk
2½ cups whole wheat flour
1 tablespoon salt
1½ cups rhubarb, diced
1½ teaspoons vanilla
½ cup finely chopped nutmeats, optional

TOPPING:
   ½ cup brown sugar
   1 teaspoon cinnamon
   1½ tablespoons butter

1. Mix brown sugar or honey and oil; add egg and beat well.
2. Dissolve soda in buttermilk. Set aside.
3. Sift flour and salt together. Add to sugar-oil mixture alternately with butter-milk. Stir in rhubarb, vanilla and nutmeats. Pour into 2 greased bread pans.
4. Combine topping ingredients and sprinkle over batter. Bake in 325°F. oven for 1 hour. Remove from pans and cool on wire rack.

Makes 2 loaves

RHUBARB RAISIN PIE

Preheat oven to 375°F.

4 cups diced rhubarb
¼ cup flour
1¼ cup brown sugar
¾ cup raisins
1 cup nuts
2 tablespoons grated lemon rind
2 tablespoons butter
1 unbaked 9-inch, 2-crust pastry shell

1. Mix the rhubarb, flour, sugar, raisins, nuts and rind together well and pour into pastry shell.
2. Dot with butter; cover with crust.
3. Bake at 375°F. for 40 minutes.

Makes 6 to 8 servings

RHUBARB CUSTARD PIE

Preheat oven to 400°F.

3 cups rhubarb, cut in 1-inch pieces
1½ cups raw sugar or ¾ cup honey
¼ cup flour
2 eggs
1 unbaked 8-inch pastry shell

1. In a large bowl combine rhubarb, sugar (or honey), flour, and eggs; mix lightly.
2. Pour into your favorite 8-inch pastry shell and bake at 400°F. for 55 minutes.

Makes one 8-inch pie

STEAMED RHUBARB PUDDING

1 cup rhubarb, cut in small chunks
½ cup honey
2 eggs
1 cup whole wheat bread, about 3 slices, crumbled
½ cup milk
1 cup raisins or chopped figs
½ teaspoon cinnamon
   dash of cloves or nutmeg
1 teaspoon grated orange rind
1 tablespoon butter

1. Use some of the butter to grease the top section of a glass or enamel double boiler.
2. Mix rhubarb and honey, add beaten eggs and bread crumbs. Add milk, fruit, flavoring of your choice and orange rind, then butter.
3. Pour into greased top section over boiling water, and steam for 45 minutes. Serve hot with honey slightly thinned with orange juice or slivers of orange peel.

Makes 4 servings

Salsify or Oyster Plant

The most commonly grown variety of salsify is quite like the parsnip—a slender white taproot sown in spring and harvested after the cold weather develops. Unlike parsnips, however, salsify tastes very much like oysters. Its flavor is improved after a frost, and harvest should be delayed until then. The crop can be dug and buried in layers of sand or peat moss in the root cellar, but for storage with the least effort, just leave it in the garden. The roots can be dug in early spring, or whenever desired all winter long. If the crop is left in the garden, cover the row with a thick layer of mulch to prevent alternate freezing and thawing, and to make the salsify easier to dig up.

Salsify roots discolor and shrivel upon exposure to air, and should be cooked unpeeled, or immediately after peeling, in water to which some lemon juice has been added. Salsify can be cooked in much the same way as parsnips. Plan 2 roots for each average size serving.

Although it does not provide many vitamins, salsify does contain a substantial amount of minerals, including calcium, phosphorus and iron.

MOCK OYSTER STEW

⅓ cup oil
6 salsify, cut in ½-inch pieces (about 6 cups)
1 large onion, chopped
½ cup celery, chopped
¼ cup whole wheat flour
6 cups milk
2 tablespoons kelp powder
1 teaspoon celery greens, chopped
   salt to taste

1. Place oil in a large kettle. Add salsify and brown.
2. Stir in onion and celery and simmer for 10 minutes.
3. Stir in flour.
4. Gradually add milk, stirring well. Simmer for 15 minutes.
5. Add kelp, celery greens and salt to taste.

Makes 6 servings

OVEN-FRIED SALSIFY

Preheat oven to 350°F.

10 or 12 salsify roots
4 cups water or stock
2 tablespoons oil
   chopped parsley

1. Wash salsify but do not peel. Parboil in water or stock for about 10 minutes. They should still be firm.
2. Drain thoroughly. Peel and cut in half lengthwise.
3. Brush slices with oil and arrange in a shallow baking dish. Bake 30 minutes at 350°F. or until salsify is golden brown. The outside should be crisp and the inside tender. Garnish with chopped parsley.

Makes 4 to 6 servings

SALSIFY WITH HERB HOLLANDAISE

2 pounds salsify

SAUCE:
    ¼ cup butter
    2 egg yolks
    ¼ teaspoon salt
    1 teaspoon tarragon
    1 tablespoon lemon juice

1. Wash and peel or scrape salsify. Cut into 1-inch pieces and steam or cook in boiling water to cover until tender (about 8 to 10 minutes). Drain.
2. Meanwhile, make sauce:
   Melt the butter in a small pan. Place egg yolks, salt and tarragon in blender, turn on to high speed. Slowly pour in the hot butter. Add lemon juice, then turn off blender.
3. Pour sauce over salsify and serve at once.

Makes 4 servings

SALSIFY FRITTERS

4 salsify roots, cut in 1-inch slices
1 tablespoon butter
½ teaspoon salt
⅛ teaspoon pepper
   dash of nutmeg
½ cup whole wheat or rye flour
3 tablespoons oil

1. Steam or cook salsify until tender, about 30 to 35 minutes. Mash. Add butter, salt, pepper and nutmeg.
2. Shape into small flat cakes, roll in flour and brown on both sides in hot oil.

Makes 4 servings

SALSIFY WITH PARSLEY AND GARLIC

1 pound salsify, scraped and cut into ½-inch cubes
   (about 2½ cups)
1 tablespoon butter
1 clove garlic, minced
2 tablespoons chopped parsley
½ teaspoon salt
⅛ teaspoon pepper

1. Steam salsify until tender, about 10 minutes.
2. Melt butter in a large skillet, add garlic and parsley, and toss 1 or 2 minutes.
3. Add salsify, salt, and pepper, and simmer 1 or 2 minutes longer, until heated through.

Makes 4 servings

Note: This dish is a delicious accompaniment to lamb.

SALSIFY PUDDING

Preheat oven to 325°F.

2 cups grated salsify
2 tablespoons chopped onion
2 tablespoons chopped sweet red peppers
2 tablespoons chopped parsley
2 eggs, lightly beaten
2 cups scalded milk
1½ tablespoons melted butter
½ teaspoon salt
⅛ teaspoon pepper

Combine all ingredients and put in a buttered baking dish. Set in a pan of hot water and bake at 325°F. until firm (about 40 minutes).

Makes 4 to 6 servings

Soybeans

Soybeans are among the most versatile crops the home gardener can grow. They are an excellent source of protein and can be combined with grains and/or milk products and/or seeds for a meal that rivals meat in protein value. A single planting can produce both green "shell beans" for immediate use and dried beans for storage. They can be ground into flour, or made into soy milk or soybean curd, called *tofu,* which is often used in Oriental dishes. Since the dried beans can also be sprouted, one packet of seed can actually produce three different vegetables.

For use as green shell beans the pods should be harvested when well-rounded and almost mature, but before they start to turn yellow. The harvest period lasts only about a week, and a few days more than that will result in beans better left on the vine to dry. Before you try to shell soybeans, wash and blanch them for five minutes to make it easier to remove the beans from the pods. Drain, cool, and squeeze out the beans. They can be frozen or canned without further blanching. To serve, boil in salted water for 15 minutes, and eat with butter or cream sauce. They'll have a firm texture and a nutty flavor. Two cups of cooked beans should provide four to six servings.

For dry soybeans, pick the pods just as they are dry, while the stems are still green; otherwise the shells may shatter and drop their beans. Shell the

215

beans, and spread in single layers on cookie sheets. To kill weevil eggs, heat the crop in an oven for from 30 minutes to an hour at 135°F. Store in airtight containers in a dry place. The soybean is most often used in its dried form. Because of their high protein content, soybeans need longer soaking and cooking than other dried beans. The traditional method of soybean cookery requires soaking the soybeans for at least eight hours, then cooking them for two to three hours more. A much easier way is to cook soybeans in a pressure cooker. This way, they require no soaking and are done in only 20 to 25 minutes. Another method is to soak the beans for an hour or two at room temperature, then put them in the freezer overnight. Next day, they can be cooked for two to three hours. Because they have a rather bland flavor, soybeans are best served in distinctively seasoned dishes.

Soybeans in any form are valued chiefly for their protein content. They are 34 percent protein; other legumes contain about 20 to 24 percent. Soybeans are also rich in iron, calcium and phosphorus, and contain substantial amounts of vitamins A, B, D and E.

SOY LOAF

Preheat oven to 350°F.

1 onion, grated
2 cloves garlic, crushed
2 stalks celery, finely chopped
2 cups cooked, pureed soybeans
½ cup wheat germ
¼ cup non-instant milk powder
3 eggs
3 tablespoons oil
1 teaspoon salt
½ cup cashew bits
1 teaspoon fresh thyme
1 teaspoon fresh dillweed
1 teaspoon fresh sage
½ cup grated cheese
½ cup sautéed mushrooms

1. Sauté onion, garlic and celery until tender.
2. Mix together with remaining ingredients, except mushrooms and cheese.
3. Press half the mixture into an oiled loaf pan. Sprinkle with cheese and mushrooms; cover with rest of soy mixture.
4. Bake at 350°F. for 40 minutes. Serve with the following brown gravy.

Makes 4 servings

BROWN GRAVY

2 tablespoons whole wheat flour
2 tablespoons oil
1 tablespoon tamari soy sauce
1 cup cold water or beef stock

1. In a heavy skillet, brown flour in oil, stirring constantly. Stir in soy sauce.
2. Add water or stock and cook over medium heat, stirring, until thickened.

Makes 1 cup

BEAN DIP

2 cups soybeans or other beans, cooked
3 cloves garlic
1 teaspoon cumin
1 tablespoon olive oil
1 teaspoon salt

1. Put all ingredients in blender. Blend, adding just enough water or bean juice (water the beans were cooked in) to give a smooth-spreading consistency to the dip.
2. Serve as a dip with raw vegetables and the homemade crackers found on pages 290-291.

Makes 4 to 6 servings

STIR-FRIED SOYBEANS

3 cups fresh soybeans
1 onion
2 carrots
4 mild to hot chili peppers
2 tomatoes
1 cup fresh pineapple chunks
2 cloves garlic
2 tablespoons oil

SWEET AND SOUR SAUCE:
   ½ cup cider vinegar
   ½ cup brown sugar or ¼ cup honey
   ½ cup stock
   1 tablespoon cornstarch
   2 tablespoons cold water
   2 tablespoons soy sauce
   2 tablespoons white wine
   ¼ teaspoon freshly grated ginger (powdered ginger
     will do)

1. Soak the soybeans overnight. Drain off the soaking water and cook in fresh water until tender, 2 to 3 hours. Drain and reserve any liquid for the sauce.
2. Cut the onion, carrots, peppers, tomatoes and pineapple into uniform chunks, and keep them separate. Mince garlic. Set aside.
3. Meanwhile, make sauce:
   Combine the vinegar, sugar, and stock in a saucepan and bring to a boil. Mix the cornstarch and cold water well, and then add to the vinegar mixture. Stir over low heat until sauce thickens. Add the rest of the ingredients and stir in. Set aside.
4. In a large frying pan or *wok* heat the oil. Add the onion, carrots and garlic, stirring in the oil until they are just beginning to get tender and are still crisp.

5. Add the peppers and tomatoes and pineapple; stir in well. Then add the soybeans and sweet and sour sauce. Stir to coat everything, and cook 2 to 3 minutes longer.

Makes 6 servings

SOYBEAN SALAD

3 cups cooked soybeans
½ cup chopped celery
1 white or red onion, sliced
4 hard-boiled eggs, diced
3 to 4 mild chili peppers, chopped (or hotter if you like)
¼ cup chopped parsley
⅓ cup chopped sweet pickles
⅔ cup pitted olives (green or ripe)
10 cherry tomatoes, cut in half

DRESSING:
½ cup buttermilk
1 cup yogurt
¼ cup crumbled blue cheese
1 teaspoon dillweed
1 teaspoon dry mustard
salt or seasoned salt and pepper to taste

1. Combine all vegetables and the hard-boiled eggs.
2. Prepare dressing:
Mix all ingredients together. Pour dressing over salad and chill for a few hours.
3. Serve on leaves of Romaine lettuce and garnish with alfalfa sprouts.

Makes 6 to 8 servings

TUTTI-FRUTTI BEANS

1 cup soybeans
2 cups stock
¼ cup whey
¼ cup whole wheat flour
1 apple, chopped
1 carrot, chopped
1 cup onion, chopped
½ cup raisins
1 teaspoon basil
   salt to taste

1. Soak soybeans in water in refrigerator overnight.
2. Drain beans and cook in fresh water for 2 hours.
3. Drain and discard excess liquid.
4. Heat stock. Make a paste of the whey and flour and stir into stock. Stir until thickened.
5. Add beans and other ingredients. Simmer 15 minutes. Serve over noodles or rice.

Makes 4 to 6 servings

SOYBEAN PATTIES

Preheat oven to 350°F.

1 cup dry soybeans (2 cups cooked)
1 cup wheat grits
¼ cup sesame seeds
2 carrots, grated
1 onion, grated
1 egg
2 tablespoons brewers yeast
1 teaspoon thyme
1 tablespoon parsley
1 cup tomato juice

1. Soak soybeans in water overnight in refrigerator.
2. Cook beans for 2 hours, drain, and mash.
3. Cook grits in 3 cups of water for 20 minutes.
4. Combine cooked soybeans, grits, and sesame seeds. Add grated vegetables. Stir in egg, yeast and herbs.
5. Form into patties and arrange in shallow baking dish. Pour tomato juice over all.
6. Bake at 350°F. for 20 to 30 minutes.

Makes 6 to 8 servings

● *Soybeans tend to boil over more readily than other kinds of beans, so you'll need to keep an eye on them when you cook them.*

Spinach

The mildest and most popular of the potherbs, spinach demands cool weather, an acid soil, and careful irrigation. If these conditions are not met, your spinach may unexpectedly bolt, or the leaves may yellow, wilt or become tough. For these reasons many gardeners prefer the heat resistant, less temperamental New Zealand variety, which, while not a true spinach, will provide spinach-like greens all through the summer and fall. It can be substituted in recipes calling for spinach with comparable results.

Spinach is ready to be harvested when six or more of its leaves are seven inches long, though the tender outer leaves may be picked for salads before that time. The entire plant can be pulled at once, ending that plant's production, or individual outer leaves can be picked, allowing the inner rosette of smaller leaves to mature for later harvest.

Before cooking or storing, spinach should be inspected and carefully washed. All damaged or yellow leaves should be removed, or they may make the rest of the leaves spoil as well. Trim off the roots, and wash the spinach in a sinkful of warm water, being careful to get all the grit out of the crumpled leaves. Spinach that is especially sandy should be washed in two or more waters. Lift the leaves out of the final water, allowing the grit to settle in the sink. Rinse in cold running water and drain well. Whirl the leaves in a salad

basket to remove excess moisture. Spinach can be stored in a plastic bag in the refrigerator crisper drawer for from three to five days. For long-term storage, spinach is best frozen, but can also be canned.

Before cooking spinach, rinse the leaves again and chop large or coarse leaves. The spinach can be steamed in a covered skillet with only the water that clings to the leaves, or a small amount of additional water. It can be served with butter and lemon juice or a few drops of vinegar. Count on about three servings from a pound of spinach.

The fresh taste and pleasing texture of spinach is also a wonderful addition to salads. If served raw, spinach provides a large amount of vitamin A, a good amount of vitamin C, and sizable quantities of calcium, iron, potassium, and other minerals.

SPINACH RING

Preheat oven to 300°F.

½ teaspoon lemon juice
1 pound spinach leaves, cooked and finely chopped (about 2 cups)
2 tablespoons butter, melted
2 eggs, slightly beaten
1 cup milk
1 tablespoon grated onion
 dash of nutmeg
 salt and pepper to taste

1. Add lemon juice to spinach.
2. Mix butter, eggs, milk, onion, nutmeg, and salt and pepper.
3. Add spinach to custard mixture and mix well.
4. Bake in a buttered 1-quart ring mold at 300°F. about 25 minutes, or until firm.
5. Unmold onto serving dish and fill center with creamed vegetables or chicken.

Makes 4 servings

BROTHCHAN FOLCHEP SOUP

6 leeks, cut in 1-inch pieces
2 tablespoons butter
1 quart milk
2 tablespoons oatmeal, cooked
½ teaspoon salt
4 cups spinach or nettles, chopped

1. Sauté leeks in the butter in a heavy, 2-quart pot.
2. Add the milk and simmer until leeks are tender. Stir frequently and do not boil.
3. Add oatmeal, salt, and chopped greens. Cook until greens are tender.

Makes 6 servings

Note: This is an Irish peasant soup—very mild and good.

● *Spinach can be steamed in just the water that clings to its leaves after washing, though if the greens are bitter, it may be preferable to boil them in water.*

SPINACH-RICOTTA DUMPLINGS

1 pound fresh spinach leaves, finely chopped
1½ cups ricotta cheese
¾ cup dry whole wheat bread crumbs
¼ cup wheat germ
2 eggs, beaten
1 clove garlic, minced
¼ cup chopped onion
¼ cup grated Parmesan cheese
½ teaspoon salt
1 teaspoon basil
   dash of nutmeg
   whole wheat or rye flour
2 quarts boiling water
1 teaspoon salt
   tomato or mushroom sauce

1. Combine first 11 ingredients.
2. Form into 1-inch balls and roll lightly in flour. Chill.
3. Bring water to a boil in a deep saucepan. Add salt and turn down heat. Drop spinach balls into simmering water and cook until they rise to the top (about 4 to 5 minutes).
   Remove with slotted spoon and serve with tomato or mushroom sauce.

Makes 6 to 8 servings

Note: A delicious new way to serve spinach!

SPINACH-SESAME SOUFFLÉ

Preheat oven to 350°F.

1 pound fresh spinach leaves, steamed, drained and pressed
1 tablespoon butter
2 ounces grated Parmesan cheese
3 egg yolks
½ teaspoon salt
⅛ teaspoon black pepper
8 egg whites, stiffly beaten
2 tablespoons sesame seeds

1. Put spinach through a food mill or puree in blender. You should have about 2 cups. Simmer spinach puree in butter to dry out or remove any excess liquid.
2. Remove from heat and add grated cheese. Then add egg yolks, salt and pepper.
3. Add stiffly beaten egg whites; fold in quickly but do not beat.
4. Fill a buttered soufflé dish to within about ½ inch of the top. Bake at 350°F. for 20 minutes. Top with sesame seeds and bake 10 minutes more.

Makes 4 to 6 servings

SPINACH CROQUETTES

2 pounds fresh spinach
1 small onion, chopped
1 teaspoon salt
⅛ teaspoon pepper
1 teaspoon chopped fresh chives
¼ cup whole wheat bread crumbs
¼ cup wheat germ
1 egg

1. Sort through spinach leaves and pick out any coarse stems or mushy leaves. Wash quickly in cold water to remove any dirt or sand.
2. Place spinach in a saucepan with just the water that clings to the leaves; cover and cook 5 minutes or until tender.
3. In a large bowl, combine cooked spinach, onion, seasonings, crumbs, wheat germ and egg. Mix well and shape into 3-inch patties.
4. Sauté briefly on each side in oil until light brown.

Makes 4 to 6 servings

DARK GREEN AND ORANGE SALAD

1 bunch leaf lettuce, shredded (use a dark green variety)
  about 2 cups
2 cups torn spinach leaves
1 bunch watercress, shredded (about 2 cups)
1 large carrot, sliced into curls
½ cup sprouts (any kind you may have)
4 chopped green onions
12 pitted ripe olives
12 raw almonds or cashews

Combine greens, carrot curls, sprouts and onions. Stuff olives with the nuts. Add to salad. Just before serving, toss with your favorite dressing.

Makes 6 servings

SPINACH SALAD WITH COOKED DRESSING

½ pound spinach, washed and drained

DRESSING:
    4 strips nitrite-free bacon, cut in ½-inch pieces
    2 teaspoons honey
    ¼ teaspoon salt
    1½ tablespoons vinegar
    ⅛ teaspoon dry mustard
      dash paprika
    ¼ cup thinly sliced green onions

1. In a large salad bowl, tear or cut spinach coarsely.
2. Prepare dressing:
   Cook bacon in a skillet until crisp, remove, drain, and reserve. Add remaining ingredients to pan, bring to a boil, and remove from heat right away.
3. Pour hot dressing over spinach and toss lightly. Sprinkle with bacon bits. Serve at once.

Makes 4 servings

Sprouts

Sprouts are a gardener's dream. They can be grown and harvested all year 'round, without benefit of light or soil, and they mature in three to five days. They don't need any compost or mulch, they require no special equipment, and you need give them only a few minutes of attention while they grow.

One word of caution before you set out to grow your own sprouts: make sure that the seeds or beans you use are intended for eating and cooking. The kind meant for planting are sometimes treated with insecticides and fungicides. Use dried beans and seeds that you've grown in your garden, or purchase them at a grocery or health food store. Soybeans, lentils, wheat berries, alfalfa seeds, mung beans, and most other kinds of dried beans can be sprouted. Here's how it's done:

Soak one-quarter cup of beans in warm water for eight hours, or overnight. Then rinse them under warm tap water and pour them into a quart jar. Cover the top of the jar with cheesecloth, and turn the jar upside down so that any remaining moisture can escape.

Keep the jar in a warm, dark place, such as next to the hot water pipe under the sink. Rinse and drain the sprouts two or three times each day, until they are an inch or two long. Rinsing the sprouts is important to prevent mold from growing. When the sprouts reach their desired length, give them a

final rinse and refrigerate them in a covered jar for not longer than a day or two before you use them.

Sprouts need no preparation for cooking or serving. They can be added to fresh salads or tucked into sandwiches. Stir them into soups or add them to Oriental dishes just before serving. The versatility of this vegetable is limited only by your imagination.

Sprouts are low in calories, and loaded with vitamins A and C, in addition to assorted minerals.

LEBANESE-STYLE TABBOULI

1 cup bulgur
½ cup olive oil
¼ cup lemon juice
2 scallions, finely chopped, including green tops
2 tablespoons minced parsley
4 tomatoes, very finely chopped
1 small bunch celery, very finely chopped
2 cucumbers, finely chopped
1 cup sprouted wheat berries
   salt and freshly ground pepper to taste

1. Place the bulgur in the bottom of a large ceramic bowl or crock. Add olive oil and lemon juice.
2. Layer the vegetables in this order: scallions, parsley, tomatoes, celery, cucumbers, and sprouted wheat berries. Sprinkle with salt and pepper.
3. Cover crock closely and store in refrigerator until ready to serve, at least 24 hours, or up to 2 weeks.
4. To serve, toss salad until well mixed. Check for seasonings and add more if desired.
5. Serve on a bed of lettuce, or wrapped in individual lettuce leaves.

Makes 6 servings

Note: This traditional Lebanese salad is easy to make, and popular with adults and children alike.

CURRIED TURKEY AND SPROUTS

2 cups turkey stock
⅓ to ½ cup whole wheat flour
1 cup bean sprouts
½ cup carrots, chopped
½ cup onion, chopped
½ cup green pepper, chopped
½ cup celery, chopped
2 cups turkey, cooked and diced
1 teaspoon curry powder
2 cups cooked brown rice

1. Bring stock to boil. Stir in flour until thickened.
2. Add vegetables and simmer for 20 minutes, until vegetables are tender.
3. Add turkey and curry powder, and cook a few minutes more. Serve on a bed of brown rice.

Makes 4 servings

WHEAT BERRY BREADSTICKS

Preheat oven to 425°F.

1 tablespoon dry yeast
1½ cups lukewarm water
1 tablespoon honey
4 cups whole wheat flour
1 teaspoon salt
1 cup sprouted wheat berries
1 egg, beaten with—
½ teaspoon water, for glaze
  coarse salt, grated cheese, poppy seeds, or sesame seeds for topping

1. Dissolve yeast in lukewarm water, adding honey. Leave to "work" for about 5 minutes.

2. Combine whole wheat flour and salt. Stir in yeast mixture and wheat berries, reserving ½ cup flour for kneading.
3. Turn dough onto a lightly floured board and knead until smooth and satiny. Divide dough into approximately 48 pieces and roll each into a rope about ½ inch in diameter and about 9 inches long. Place on a buttered baking sheet.
4. Brush with egg and water glaze, and sprinkle with desired topping. Let rise for 20 minutes.
5. Bake at 425°F. for 12 to 15 minutes, until golden brown.

Makes 48 sticks

Note: For crunchy breadsticks, cool them after baking and place in a slow oven (250°F.), turning occasionally, for 45 to 60 minutes, until evenly browned. Cool on racks. Served from a tall glass, these breadsticks are an elegant complement to your favorite Italian dishes.

STIR-FRIED BEAN SPROUTS

> 1 tablespoon peanut oil
> 1 carrot, cut into shoe-string strips (about 1 inch long)
> 1 stalk celery, cut into shoe-string strips (about 1 inch long)
> ½ green pepper, cut into shoe-string strips (about 1 inch long)
> 1 small onion, coarsely chopped
> 2 cups bean sprouts
> 1 to 2 tablespoons tamari soy sauce

1. Heat oil in a large skillet or *wok*. Add carrot, celery, pepper and onion and stir-fry for about 5 minutes.
2. Add bean sprouts and stir-fry for 1 minute longer.
3. Add soy sauce, mix well, and serve immediately.

Makes 4 servings

Note: A light and colorful side dish.

WHEAT BERRY-SUNFLOWER SEED LOAF

6 teaspoons dry yeast
1 cup lukewarm water
1 tablespoon honey
4 tablespoons oil
1 egg
4 tablespoons honey
2 teaspoons salt
2 cups lukewarm water
9 cups whole wheat flour
½ cup soy flour
2 tablespoons brewer's yeast
½ cup skim milk powder
4 tablespoons wheat germ
⅓ cup sunflower seeds
⅔ cup sprouted wheat berries
2 tablespoons butter
1 egg
¼ teaspoon water
¼ cup sesame or sunflower seeds

1. Sprinkle dry yeast over surface of 1 cup lukewarm water. Add 1 tablespoon honey and leave to "work."
2. Place oil, egg, honey, salt and 2 cups lukewarm water in large electric mixer bowl. Add yeast mixture and beat on low speed. Add half (4½ cups) of the whole wheat flour and beat on medium speed for about 10 minutes.
3. Add soy flour, brewer's yeast, skim milk powder, wheat germ, and 4 more cups whole wheat flour, reserving ½ cup for kneading.
4. Knead for 8 to 10 minutes, until dough is springy and elastic.
5. Place dough in an oiled bowl, turning it over to oil the surface. Cover with a damp cloth and let rise in a warm, draft-free place for 1 hour.
6. Punch down dough. Divide into three equal parts. Spread sunflower seeds on floured board and shape one part of dough into a loaf, working in sunflower seeds until they are well distributed. Repeat procedure with wheat

berries and remaining two parts of bread. Place loaves in 3 well-buttered 9 x 5 x 3 pans.

7. Combine egg and water, and brush tops of loaves. Sprinkle with sesame or additional sunflower seeds. Let rise in warm place for 45 minutes to 1 hour.

8. Do not preheat oven. Bake loaves in 400°F. oven for 15 minutes, then turn oven to 375°F. and continue baking for 35 minutes or until loaves are golden brown and sound hollow when tapped on top.

Makes 3 loaves

GROUND BEEF CHOP SUEY

1 tablespoon oil
2 cups thinly sliced celery
½ cup sliced onion
1 pound lean ground beef
2 tablespoons arrowroot flour or cornstarch
2 tablespoons water (or more, as needed)
¼ cup tamari soy sauce
½ teaspoon salt
3 cups chopped cabbage
1 cup sprouts
4 cups cooked brown rice

1. Heat oil in a large skillet; add celery, onion, and meat, and cook about 5 minutes, until meat begins to brown.

2. Blend arrowroot flour with water, then stir in soy sauce and salt. Add this mixture to the meat mixture.

3. Cook, stirring constantly, until sauce thickens. Stir in cabbage and sprouts, and cook about 5 minutes more. Serve over cooked brown rice.

Makes 8 servings

Note: This tasty dish is quick to make, and quick to disappear, especially when served to children.

MOLDED SPROUT SALAD

3 tablespoons unflavored gelatin
2 cups cold water
2 cups unsweetened pineapple juice
1 whole lemon, quartered
6 carrots, diced
1 small red beet
½ cup alfalfa or other sprouts
2 tablespoons honey
    additional sprouts

1. Stir gelatin into cold water in a stainless steel pan. Put on stove immediately over lowest heat and let dissolve, stirring occasionally.
2. Put pineapple juice and lemon into blender. Start to blend, then add diced carrots and red beet. Blend until very fine, or just until pieces are chopped small, according to your preference. Add ½ cup sprouts and blend fine to disguise or leave whole for a different effect.
3. By this time, the gelatin should be melted and look clear. Add honey and stir until dissolved, then pour blended vegetables into gelatin and mix well. Pour into a circular mold and chill.
4. When ready to serve, unmold gelatin onto a bed of green sprouts for an attractive color contrast.

Makes 6 servings

SPROUT OMELET

8 eggs
4 tablespoons water
    salt to taste
    freshly ground pepper to taste
3 tablespoons butter
1½ cups lentil, alfalfa or mung bean sprouts
    chopped parsley for garnish

1. Break eggs into a bowl, beat lightly. Add water and beat briefly. Add salt and pepper.
2. Heat butter in a heavy skillet, to medium-high heat. Pour in egg mixture, just enough to cover bottom of the pan. Continue cooking, without stirring, till bottom is golden.
3. Sprinkle with sprouts and parsley.
4. Using spatula, flip over so omelet is a half-moon shape. Carefully turn out onto warm platter; serve immediately.

Makes 6 servings

● *Sprouts are unequaled as a garnish or topping. Add a handful to a bowl of soup— they add a touch of freshness. Steamed vegetables can be topped with your favorite sprouts, either whole or chopped, raw or lightly sautéed. Any kind of sprouts can be served with your breakfast eggs as the filling for an omelet.*

SPROUT SOUP

1 potato, cut into chunks
1 carrot, cut into chunks
1 small onion, diced
1 stalk celery, chopped
1 cup sprouting water, or vegetable or chicken stock
¼ teaspoon salt
　 dash of pepper
2 cups coarsely chopped sprouts
2 tablespoons tamari soy sauce
2 tablespoons chopped parsley

1. Cook potato, carrot, onion and celery in stock for about 10 minutes. Add salt and pepper.
2. Blend in blender until thick and smooth.
3. Return to saucepan; add sprouts and soy sauce and simmer for 3 minutes.
4. Garnish with parsley and serve immediately.

Makes 3 to 4 servings

VEGETABLE GEL

2 envelopes unflavored gelatin
½ cup cold water
2 cups boiling water or bouillon
1 tablespoon tamari soy sauce
   juice of one lemon
2 tablespoons honey
2 cups cold water
½ teaspoon salt
4½ cups sliced or grated vegetables such as:
   carrots
   parsley
   radishes
   sprouts
   whole peas
   celery
   cabbage
½ cup chopped nuts
½ cup raisins
⅔ cup sliced pitted olives

1. Sprinkle gelatin in ½ cup cold water and stir until it dissolves.
2. Stir in 2 cups boiling water or bouillon.
3. Add soy sauce, lemon juice, honey, and 2 cups cold water. Allow gel to cool but not set.
4. Add the remaining ingredients and pour into a ring mold. Chill.
5. Serve on a bed of lettuce with mayonnaise or yogurt or your favorite dressing in the center.

Makes 6 to 8 servings

Summer Squash

In all their diversity, and with their well-known prolific and dependable habits, summer squash should be included in every garden. Varieties include: zucchini and cocozelle, which are cylindrical and dark green; crookneck and straightneck, which are yellow and shaped as their names describe; and patty pan, which is flat, has scalloped edges, and is white to pale green in color. All the summer squashes are easy to grow, though their rambling and luxuriant foliage tends to take over any portion of a garden plot to which they are allotted. Keeping up with your summer squash harvest will ensure a continuous crop of small, tender, non-seedy fruits until the first frost. They should be picked when very young, while the rind is still soft enough to be easily broken when pressed with a thumbnail. Ideally, zucchini, cocozelle, and the yellow squashes should be used before they are eight inches long, and the patty pans when they are between one and four inches in diameter. If you allow your squash to grow to maturity, the vine's production will slow down or stop altogether.

Although they are best when served soon after picking, summer squash will keep as long as one week in the refrigerator when stored in airtight containers. They can be frozen in cooked casserole dishes, as purees, or as gratings which have been wrung out in a muslin towel to remove excess moisture.

237

Many gardeners substitute zucchini for cucumbers in pickle recipes or bake it, shredded, into a fruitcake-like bread which they freeze. Some report success in storing the mature, hard-rinded fruits in single layers on newspapers in a steady temperature of about 50°F.

If harvested when young, squash can be served without paring or removing the seeds. Raw, they add a fine, soft crunch to salads or a plate of *crudités*. To prepare summer squash for cooking, wash, trim off the ends, and cut or slice as directed in the recipe. If a few squashes have escaped notice and have grown large enough to develop tough skins and seedy centers, they should be peeled and the seed cavities scraped out before they are used. Larger squashes are often suitable for stuffing and baking, in which case they need not be peeled. Figure on two tender, young squash for each serving.

Summer squash, like cucumbers, are mostly water, but they do contain a good amount of vitamin A, particularly the yellow varieties.

SUMMER SQUASH SAUTÉ

1 clove garlic, minced
3 tablespoons butter or olive oil
1 medium onion, sliced
6 fresh mushrooms, sliced
½ teaspoon dried rosemary
¼ teaspoon ground cardamom
4 to 5 cups yellow squash or zucchini, thinly sliced on
   a slant
2 tablespoons sour cream or yogurt
⅛ teaspoon black pepper
   salt to taste

1. In a large skillet, gently simmer garlic in butter until yellow. Add onion and mushrooms; cook on low heat for 5 minutes.
2. Add rosemary, cardamom and squash to skillet; stir and cook another 5 minutes, then cover and cook gently for 8 minutes.
3. Add sour cream or yogurt, pepper and salt to taste. Cover, turn off heat, and let stand 4 minutes. Serve immediately.

Makes 6 servings

SQUASH AND MUSHROOMS

1 tablespoon oil
6 small summer squash (about 2 pounds), unpeeled and
    cut into small cubes
1 large onion, chopped
1 cup tomato sauce
½ cup dry, white wine
½ pound mushrooms, sliced
½ teaspoon oregano
    salt and pepper to taste

1. Heat oil in a large skillet. Add squash and onion and sauté for 2 minutes, stirring to coat pieces with oil.
2. Add remaining ingredients and simmer 5 to 7 minutes longer, until vegetables are tender. Serve immediately.

Makes 6 servings

ZUCCHINI CASSEROLE

Preheat oven to 350°F.

1 cup cooked brown rice
1 cup cheddar cheese, grated
2 pounds zucchini, thinly sliced
⅓ cup parsley, chopped
½ cup green onion, sliced
¼ cup olive oil
2 to 3 eggs, beaten
    salt, garlic salt or garlic powder, to taste
½ teaspoon oregano, to taste

Mix all ingredients together in a greased casserole and bake at 350°F. for 1 hour, or until eggs are set and zucchini is tender.

Makes 3 servings

ZUCCHINI ROUNDS

⅓ cup biscuit mix
¼ cup Parmesan cheese, grated
⅛ teaspoon pepper
2 eggs, slightly beaten
2 cups shredded zucchini, unpeeled
2 tablespoons butter

1. In mixing bowl, stir together biscuit mix, cheese and pepper.
2. Stir in beaten eggs just until mixture is moistened. Fold in zucchini.
3. In skillet, melt 2 tablespoons butter over medium heat. Using 1 heaping serving-size tablespoon for each round, drop by spoonfuls into skillet and cook four at a time. Cook 2 to 3 minutes on each side or until brown.
4. Keep finished rounds warm while others are cooking.

Makes 12 rounds (6 servings)

Note: Combine with a meat dish for a complete meal. Serve fresh fruit for dessert.

● *A simple way to serve zucchini is to slice it in half lengthwise, brush it with oil, and broil. It will cook through, yet stay firm. If you sprinkle the top with Parmesan cheese for the last few minutes of cooking, your squash will have a tasty crunchy crust.*

ZUCCHINI AND TOMATOES

1 medium-sized zucchini, thinly sliced and quartered
2 tablespoons olive oil
1 fresh tomato, cored, sliced, and quartered
   salt and pepper to taste
1 teaspoon oregano

1. Sauté zucchini in olive oil for about 5 minutes, until tender.
2. Add tomato and seasonings, and cook for 5 minutes more. If desired, place mixture in shallow baking dish, top with mozzarella cheese, and run under broiler until cheese melts.

Makes 4 to 6 servings

EGGS IN A NEST

3 1-inch slices of vegetable spaghetti squash, seeds removed
2 cups tomato juice
3 eggs
1 teaspoon each of basil, thyme and parsley

1. In a heavy skillet, arrange the rings of spaghetti squash.
2. Pour in juice and simmer for 20 minutes.
3. Break one egg into each circle and sprinkle with herbs.
4. Cover and cook until eggs are set.

Makes 3 servings

YELLOW SQUASH IN SOUR CREAM SAUCE

2 medium yellow summer squash (about 2 pounds)
1 small onion, chopped (about ¼ cup)
2 tablespoons oil
1 cup sour cream
¾ teaspoon salt
¼ teaspoon paprika
1 tablespoon parsley, chopped

1. Cook the squash until tender in a small amount of boiling water. Drain well and slice.
2. Sauté onions in oil until clear. Add squash and toss until slices are coated with oil.
3. In a separate pan, combine sour cream, salt, and paprika and heat gently. Do not boil.
4. Add the vegetables to the sour cream and heat gently until piping hot, again not allowing sauce to boil. Serve sprinkled with parsley.

Makes 4 servings

STUFFED ZUCCHINI

Preheat oven to 350°F.

2 small zucchini
    boiling, salted water
2 eggs, lightly beaten
⅓ cup whole grain bread crumbs
⅓ cup Parmesan cheese
¼ cup oil
1 small onion, minced
    few sprigs of parsley, minced (about 1 tablespoon)
    salt, garlic salt, pepper, thyme

1. Parboil whole zucchini in boiling, salted water 15 minutes, until barely tender. Drain, trim ends, and cut in half lengthwise. Scoop out inside.
2. Arrange shells in greased baking dish. Mash the pulp. Add eggs, crumbs, cheese, oil, onion, parsley and seasonings to taste.
3. Mix together well. Sprinkle shells with salt and pepper and fill with the pulp mixture.
4. Bake uncovered at 350°F. for 25 to 30 minutes.

Makes 4 servings

BULGUR SQUASH CASSEROLE

Preheat oven to 350°F.

4 cups boiling water
2 cups bulgur
1 teaspoon salt
1 teaspoon paprika
2 cups yogurt
¼ cup sesame oil
½ teaspoon salt
1 egg, beaten

¼ cup chopped chives or green onions
5 cups summer squash, cubed
⅓ cup grated cheese
⅓ cup toasted sesame seeds
   whole wheat bread crumbs
   butter

1. Pour boiling water over bulgur and let stand until water is absorbed. Stir salt and paprika through bulgur.
2. Stir yogurt, sesame oil, salt, beaten egg and chives or green onions together.
3. In baking pan, 7 x 11, spread bulgur. Arrange cubed squash over bulgur. Sprinkle grated cheese over squash. Pour yogurt sauce over mixture. Now top with bread crumbs and toasted sesame seeds and dot with butter.
4. Bake at 350°F. until squash is tender.

Makes 10 to 12 servings

CRUNCHY ZUCCHINI SLICES

1 medium-sized zucchini
1 egg, slightly beaten
¼ cup milk
1 teaspoon oregano
   salt and pepper to taste
½ cup wheat germ
2 tablespoons olive oil
   mozzarella or other good melting cheese, grated

1. Thinly slice zucchini.
2. Combine egg, milk and seasonings. Dip zucchini into egg mixture, then into wheat germ.
3. Sauté in oil until tender, about 5 to 10 minutes.
4. Top with cheese and run under broiler briefly, to melt cheese.

Makes 4 to 6 servings

SUMMER SQUASH WITH TOMATOES AND CORN

Preheat oven to 350°F.

3 tablespoons oil or butter
1 small onion, chopped
1 clove garlic, minced
1 large or 2 small summer squash, unpeeled and thinly
   sliced
2 tomatoes, cored and cut in chunks
   kernels cut from 2 ears of corn
1 teaspoon fresh mint, chopped
¼ teaspoon ground coriander
1 teaspoon salt
1 cup milk or light cream
1 teaspoon chili powder
3 ounces cream cheese, diced (or grated cheddar)

1. In a skillet or heavy casserole, heat oil and sauté onion and garlic briefly.
2. Add squash, tomatoes and corn, and toss to coat pieces. Stir in the mint, coriander and salt, cover pan and simmer about 15 to 20 minutes, stirring occasionally, until vegetables are tender. Transfer to a casserole dish.
3. Add the milk and bake at 350°F. in a covered casserole for another 15 to 20 minutes.
4. Mix in the chili powder and top with cream cheese. Return to oven to allow cheese to partially melt.

Makes 4 servings

ZUCCHINI BREAD

Preheat oven to 325°F.

3 eggs
1 cup honey
2 teaspoons vanilla

1 cup oil
1 teaspoon salt
¼ teaspoon baking powder
1 teaspoon baking soda
3½ teaspoons cinnamon
2 cups whole wheat flour
¼ cup wheat germ
¼ cup bran
2 cups grated zucchini, unpeeled
¾ cup chopped nuts
½ cup raisins, optional

1. Beat eggs and honey together. Stir in vanilla and oil.
2. Combine dry ingredients and add to first mixture, beating well.
3. Stir in zucchini, nuts and raisins. Pour into 2 greased loaf pans and bake at 325°F. for 60 to 70 minutes.
4. Cool in pans before serving.

Makes 2 loaves

Note: This bread freezes well.

VEGETABLES ITALIANO

3 cups zucchini slices
1 cup onion, sliced
3 tablespoons butter
1 cup chopped tomatoes
    salt and pepper to taste
1 teaspoon oregano
    Parmesan cheese

1. Sauté zucchini and onion in butter for 10 minutes. Add tomatoes and seasonings, and continue cooking over low heat 5 minutes more.
2. Sprinkle with cheese and serve.

Makes 4 to 6 servings

ZUCCHINI-TOMATO SALAD

3 medium zucchini (about 1 pound)
2 or 3 tomatoes
1 cup chick-peas

DRESSING:
3 tablespoons vinegar
½ cup olive oil
1 teaspoon salt
1 teaspoon honey
½ teaspoon pepper
¼ teaspoon dry mustard
⅓ cup chopped parsley
1 teaspoon basil

1. Cut zucchini into 2-inch strips.
2. Slice tomatoes.
3. Place tomatoes, zucchini and chick-peas in bowl. Combine remaining ingredients and pour over vegetables. Chill about 2 hours, covered. Stir occasionally. Remove vegetables from dressing to serve.

Makes 6 servings

STIR-FRIED SUMMER SQUASH

5-6 small summer squash (zucchini, scallop, cocozelle, or whatever)
1 onion
1 clove garlic
1 bell pepper, sliced
3 large tomatoes
1 teaspoon fresh thyme
2 tablespoons oil
3 eggs, slightly beaten
¾ cup grated sharp cheese
1 teaspoon tamari soy sauce

1. Slice all the vegetables thin and mince the thyme.
2. Stir-fry the vegetables and thyme in oil in a hot frying pan.
3. When just tender, add eggs, cheese and soy sauce; cook this quickly into the vegetables.

Makes 4 to 5 servings

SAVORY SPAGHETTI SQUASH "GAI CHOW"

1 large spaghetti squash
1 tablespoon butter
2 green peppers, seeded
4 medium carrots
   vegetable oil
1 cup sliced mushrooms
1 cup diced, drained pineapple (optional)
¼ to ½ cup soy sauce
1 3-pound chicken, cooked, boned, and diced (about 3
   cups of meat)
   salt and pepper to taste

1. Cook squash 30 minutes in rapidly boiling water, cool, cut in half, remove seeds, and scrape out pulp using edge of spoon. Melt butter over medium heat. Sauté squash 3 minutes, stirring to avoid browning. Set aside.
2. Slice peppers in very thin strips; slice carrots julienne style. Pour oil onto peppers and carrots, using just enough to coat lightly.
3. Heat frying pan and stir-fry briefly until barely tender. Add mushrooms, pineapple and squash. Toss until well mixed.
4. Pour in soy sauce, stirring constantly. Fold in chicken. Add salt and pepper slowly.
5. Leave on heat just long enough to get piping hot. Serve immediately with a side dish of rice.

Makes 6 servings

SQUASH ABUNDANCE

Preheat oven to 350°F.

4 cups thinly sliced zucchini, scallop, banana, crookneck, or other summer squash
2 tomatoes, sliced
1 onion, thinly sliced and separated into rings
3 tablespoons chopped parsley
1 teaspoon marjoram
½ cup butter
¼ cup tamari soy sauce
1 clove garlic, minced

1. Fill a baking dish with alternate layers of squash and tomato and onion.
   Sprinkle each layer with parsley and marjoram.
2. In a saucepan, melt butter, add soy sauce and garlic.
3. Pour over vegetables.
4. Bake at 350°F. for 20 to 25 minutes, until squash is tender.

Makes 4 servings

Variation: For a heartier dish, bake the casserole in a cheese sauce:
   Melt ¼ cup butter in a saucepan; add 2 cups milk and 1½ cups grated
   cheese. Heat and stir until cheese melts, then add 1 tablespoon cornstarch
   dissolved in water. Cook until sauce thickens a bit. Pour sauce over
   casserole, top with grated Parmesan and bake as directed.

Winter Squash & Pumpkins

Just as asparagus and early peas serve to reawaken winter-deadened taste buds, and tomatoes and cucumbers at their peak answer our summer needs for vegetables to eat raw and chilled, so do the easily stored winter squash with their hearty orange-yellow flesh satisfy our autumnal urges to prepare for the colder months ahead.

Popular varieties include the massive Hubbard, which weighs up to 15 pounds and is often substituted for pumpkin in pie recipes; the deeply-ridged and dark green acorn, which is just the right size for two servings and is a perfect vessel for a variety of stuffings; the turban-shaped and dark green buttercup; and the butternut, dull tan when ripe and formed like an elongated pear. Though pumpkins are a bit more tender than winter squash, do not develop as thick a rind, and therefore will not store for such long periods, they are treated in exactly the same manner as their squash cousins, and have very similar nutritional value.

It's good practice to harvest your winter squash a week or two before the first heavy frost. Take a knife and cut the fruit from the vine with at least an inch of stem attached. If possible, let them sit in the field a week or so to finish ripening and to toughen their skins. If this curing period is cut short by an unexpected cold spell, bring the squash inside to a room where

the temperature is about 70°F. and hold them there for several days before storage.

When well-ripened, winter squash will have a hard shell which is left almost untouched by pressure of the thumbnail. Wash the squashes, taking special care with the side that rested on the ground, and dry thoroughly. Avoid bruising the fruits, and examine them closely for any signs of injury.

Winter squash keeps best when stored in a dry place where the temperature ranges from 40° to 50°F. It will dry out at higher temperatures and will not remain edible for as long a time. For best results, store perfect squashes in single rows on shelves well off the floor. During the storage period they should be examined periodically for the formation of surface molds encouraged by condensed moisture. If mold develops and is not wiped off, it can work its way inside the squash and destroy most of the flesh, without causing extensive surface damage. If stored with care, squash will keep for the entire winter. If the correct storage conditions are not possible, winter squash can also be successfully canned, frozen, or dried.

The easiest way to prepare winter squash is to halve it, scoop out the seeds, and bake the pulp in the rind until tender. Serve with butter, maple syrup, or honey, and a sprinkling of cinnamon or nutmeg. Winter squash can also be steamed and mashed to be served like potatoes, or used as the basis of a pie filling. And don't throw out the seeds scooped out of squash and pumpkins. Instead, roast them for 20 minutes at 350°F. for a tasty, nutritious (and child-pleasing) snack. The hull-less seeds of the Lady Godiva pumpkin are especially good for roasting—they're all ready to eat without the extra effort of removing the tender kernels from fibrous hulls. Three pounds of squash will serve four people.

Winter squash has a very high vitamin A content, and is one of the few vegetables that does not suffer nutritional losses during storage. In fact, its carotene content increases during storage and adds to its vitamin A.

WINTER SQUASH TREAT

Preheat oven to 350°F.

2 acorn squash
½ pound sharp cheese
1 small onion, cut in rings

1. Bake squash at 350°F. until soft (35 to 50 minutes, depending on size), then slice lengthwise into quarters. Remove seeds and strings.
2. Slice cheese and onion and place on meat side of squash.
3. Put under broiler for a few minutes to melt cheese—watch carefully.
4. Serve immediately with seasoned salt.

Makes 8 servings

PUMPKIN BREAD

Preheat oven to 325°F.

4 eggs
1 cup honey
2 cups pumpkin, cooked and mashed
1 cup salad oil
2 teaspoons baking soda
½ cup yogurt or buttermilk
3¾ cups whole wheat flour
½ teaspoon salt
1 teaspoon nutmeg
1 teaspoon ground cloves
1 teaspoon cinnamon

1. Beat eggs and honey together. Add pumpkin and oil.
2. Dissolve soda in yogurt or buttermilk.
3. Sift flour with salt and spices, and add to pumpkin mixture alternately with soda mixture.
4. Pour into two greased bread pans and bake at 325°F. for 1½ hours.
5. Remove from pans, and cool bread on wire rack.

Makes 2 large loaves

Note: One pound of pumpkin in the shell yields about 1 cup of cooked pumpkin. It's not advisable to double a recipe like this, but you can cook the pumpkin in the morning and bake two or three batches. This bread freezes very well.

SQUASH CASSEROLE

Preheat oven to 350°F.

6 cups winter squash, sliced into ¼-inch pieces
   (butternut is preferred)
½ cup chopped onions
1 cup shredded carrots
1 cup chopped celery
½ cup butter
1½ cups whole wheat bread crumbs
1 teaspoon basil
1 teaspoon thyme
   salt and pepper to taste

SAUCE:
   2 cups yogurt
   ¼ cup sesame oil
   ⅓ cup grated mild cheese
   ½ teaspoon salt
   1 egg, beaten
   ¼ cup chopped fresh chives or scallions
   ½ cup toasted sesame seeds

1. Steam the squash until just tender.
2. Sauté the onions, carrots and celery in the butter until tender. Add to the bread crumbs along with the basil, thyme, salt and pepper, making a stuffing.
3. Put a layer of squash in the bottom of a greased 2-quart casserole dish. Place the stuffing on top, then the rest of the squash.
4. To make the sauce:
   Stir the yogurt, sesame oil, grated cheese and salt together. Place over low heat until the cheese melts. Stir a little of the hot sauce into the beaten egg, then add egg to the sauce slowly to prevent curdling. Add the chives.
5. Pour the yogurt sauce over the squash and sprinkle with toasted sesame seeds.
6. Bake at 350°F. for 30 minutes.

Makes 8 servings

SPICY SQUASH "BROWNIES"

Preheat oven to 375°F.

1 cup cooked and mashed winter squash
1¼ cups whole wheat flour
1 cup brown sugar, firmly packed
1 teaspoon baking powder
2 teaspoons cinnamon
1 teaspoon ground ginger
½ teaspoon nutmeg
½ teaspoon salt
½ teaspoon baking soda
¼ cup buttermilk
¼ cup oil
1 teaspoon vanilla
2 eggs, well beaten
½ cup chopped nuts

1. Combine all ingredients and beat well, about 400 strokes.
2. Pour into a greased 13 x 9 pan and bake at 375°F. for 30 to 40 minutes.

Makes about 2 dozen bars

PUMPKIN COOLER

½ cup pumpkin, cooked and mashed
2 cups chilled milk
1 tablespoon honey
1 teaspoon brewer's yeast

1. Combine ingredients in electric blender and mix well.
2. Sprinkle with cinnamon before serving.

Makes 2 8-ounce glasses

Note: This makes a cool, refreshing drink, just right for a crisp autumn day.

PUMPKIN RICOTTA CUSTARD

Preheat oven to 325°F.

2¼ cups raw pumpkin chunks
5 eggs
1 cup ricotta cheese
⅓ cup molasses
⅔ cup brown sugar
½ teaspoon salt
1 teaspoon ground ginger
1¼ teaspoons cinnamon
½ teaspoon nutmeg
1 13-ounce can evaporated milk
½ cup finely chopped nuts, optional

1. Place the pumpkin in a small amount of boiling water in a large pot, and cook on medium-high heat until very tender, about 20 minutes.
2. Drain well and puree in a blender or with a potato masher.
3. In a large bowl, beat the eggs. Add the cheese, pumpkin, molasses, sugar, salt, spices and milk. Beat well.
4. Pour into custard cups, and place the cups in a larger baking dish filled with 1 inch of water. Bake at 325°F. about an hour, or until a knife inserted in the center comes out clean.
5. Sprinkle with chopped nuts if desired. Serve warm or cold.

Makes 8 servings

● *Unlike other vegetables, winter squash must not be picked until it is fully ripe. Immature winter squash at best resembles cardboard.*

MAPLE-BAKED ACORN SQUASH

Preheat oven to 375°F.

2 medium-sized acorn squash
4 tablespoons butter
8 teaspoons maple syrup
salt, and freshly ground pepper, to taste

1. Cut squash lengthwise. Scoop out seeds and stringy filaments. Place squash halves, cut side up, in 2-inch deep baking pan.
2. Sprinkle cut surfaces with salt and a little pepper, and place 1 tablespoon butter and 2 teaspoons maple syrup in each half.
3. Pour boiling water to a depth of 1 inch around squash.
4. Bake at 375°F. 30 to 45 minutes, or until tender.

Makes 4 servings

Note: If you cut up some browned sausage links, and fill the squash centers, you have a main dish.

SAUTÉED BUTTERNUT SQUASH SLICES WITH RAISINS AND WALNUTS

> butternut squash
> vegetable oil
> salt
> cinnamon
> golden raisins
> English walnuts, chopped
> honey

1. Rinse squash. Cut neck into as many quarter-inch slices as desired, no need to pare, allowing 2 or 3 slices per person.
2. In a large, heavy skillet, heat enough vegetable oil to cover bottom of pan and sauté squash at medium heat for a few minutes on each side until lightly browned. Reduce heat, cover, and cook gently until fork-tender, about 7 to 10 minutes.
3. Sprinkle with salt, cinnamon, raisins and walnuts, about ½ tablespoon each of the raisins and walnuts for each slice of squash.
4. Drizzle lightly with honey. Cover and cook another 2 or 3 minutes. Serve at once.

Note: The remaining portions of squash, the hollow seedy parts, may be saved and stuffed for another meal.

PUMPKIN PUDDING

Preheat oven to 400°F.

1½ cups cooked and pureed pumpkin pulp
¾ cup brown sugar
½ teaspoon salt
1 teaspoon ginger
1¼ teaspoons cinnamon
½ teaspoon nutmeg
½ teaspoon ground cloves
3 eggs, beaten
1¼ cups buttermilk
1 6-ounce can evaporated milk
1 cup raisins
½ cup chopped nuts
½ cup coconut
2½ cups cubed whole wheat bread
2 to 4 tablespoons butter, as needed

1. Mix all ingredients except bread and butter together well.
2. In a heavy skillet, brown the bread cubes in the butter.
3. Put the bread into the bottom of a 2-quart baking dish; pour pumpkin mixture over it.
4. Bake at 400°F. for 50 minutes, or until knife inserted in the center comes out clean.

Makes 6 to 8 servings

PUMPKIN PANCAKES

2 cups flour (whole wheat or unbleached)
1 tablespoon brewer's yeast
1 tablespoon wheat germ
3 tablespoons sunflower seeds, finely chopped
2 cups milk

2 eggs, well beaten
1 tablespoon oil
1 tablespoon honey
1½ cups pumpkin, cooked and mashed
½ teaspoon salt
⅛ teaspoon nutmeg

1. Combine dry ingredients. Combine milk, eggs, oil and honey and add to dry mixture.
2. Fold in pumpkin, salt and nutmeg, and mix well. Cook on a hot, oiled griddle.

Makes 16 to 20 pancakes

TANGY ACORN SQUASH

Preheat oven to 350°F.

2 acorn squash
¼ cup finely chopped white onion
1 clove garlic, minced
2 tablespoons butter
½ cup grated sharp cheese
3 tomatoes, chopped
1 tomato, thickly sliced
   grated Parmesan cheese

1. Bake the squash (whole) at 350°F. until soft, about 45 minutes. Then cut in half and scoop out the flesh, being careful not to tear the skins.
2. Sauté onions and garlic in butter.
3. Mix squash, cheese, onion, garlic, and tomatoes while the squash is hot.
4. Put mixture back into squash skin and put a slice or two of tomato on top of each acorn half. Sprinkle with Parmesan cheese and place under broiler for a few minutes.

Makes 4 servings

ARGENTINE BOILED DINNER

1 cup dried chick-peas (2 cups cooked)
2 pounds beef short ribs
1 stewing chicken, cut in serving pieces
3 Spanish sausages (or Italian)
6 carrots, halved
6 white turnips, diced
6 onions, quartered
2 cloves garlic, minced
1 small Hubbard squash, peeled and cubed
6 tomatoes, quartered
1 small cabbage
2 tablespoons parsley, minced
1 green pepper, seeded and chopped
6 leeks
6 potatoes, peeled and cubed

1. Soak the chick-peas overnight and put to boil in a large kettle with 4 quarts of water.
2. When the water boils, add the beef and chicken. Simmer gently for 1½ hours, or until meat is nearly tender.
3. Add sausage, carrots, and turnips, cook for 30 minutes.
4. Add remaining ingredients and cook another 45 minutes. Test potatoes for "doneness."
5. To serve, arrange meat on a large platter and surround with the vegetables. A horseradish sauce will go nicely with this. The broth is served as soup.

Makes 8 to 10 servings

ORANGE-BAKED SQUASH

Preheat oven to 350°F.

1 medium-sized winter squash
1 tablespoon butter
1 to 2 tablespoons honey

2 tablespoons orange juice
1 tablespoon lemon juice
1 teaspoon cinnamon
    pinch of ground ginger
1 teaspoon grated orange rind

1. Peel squash and cut into chunks or fairly thick slices. Arrange in bottom of an oiled casserole.
2. In a small saucepan, melt butter. Add honey and juices, stirring until well blended. Pour over squash pieces.
3. Sprinkle with spices and orange rind, and bake at 350°F. 40 to 45 minutes. Baste occasionally with the juice mixture.

Makes 3 to 4 servings

PUMPKIN-STUFFED CHICKEN

Preheat oven to 350°F.

1 5-pound chicken, cleaned
3 cups pumpkin, cooked and mashed
½ cup pumpkin seeds
½ cup sunflower seeds
½ cup chopped walnuts
¾ cup raisins
1 cup diced apple (unpeeled)
1 cup chopped celery
¼ cup cornmeal
½ teaspoon salt
1 teaspoon celery salt

1. Combine all ingredients except chicken and lightly stuff into chicken cavity.
2. Bake at 350°F. for several hours, or until chicken is tender and nicely browned.

Makes 6 servings

MUSHROOM-NUT-STUFFED BUTTERNUT SQUASH

Preheat oven to 350°F.

2 butternut squashes
¼ cup oil or butter
   scant ¼ teaspoon salt
⅛ teaspoon thyme
1 teaspoon chopped parsley
⅛ teaspoon sage
   pinch of black pepper
1¾ cup chopped fresh mushrooms
½ cup unprocessed bran
¼ cup finely chopped walnuts
1 cup grated medium cheddar cheese, divided into
   ¼ cup and ¾ cup

1. Wash squash, cut in half lengthwise or use hollow ends of squash from which necks have been removed. Remove seeds and stringy portions. Bake with cut side down in shallow, lightly oiled pan until almost tender, about 40 minutes.
2. Meanwhile, blend oil, salt, thyme, parsley, sage and pepper. Add to mushrooms, bran, nuts, and ¼ cup cheese. Mix well.
3. Turn baked squashes shell side down; salt lightly. Place filling in the cavity, pressing lightly to compact the mixture. Bake at 350°F. until tender, about 20 minutes.
4. Sprinkle with remaining ¾ cup of grated cheese, and return to oven a few minutes until the cheese melts.

Makes 2 to 4 servings

Tomatoes

Of all the vegetables grown in home gardens, tomatoes have to be the hands-down favorite. Even people who don't otherwise garden often find space for a few seedlings in their backyard or for a potted cherry tomato plant or two on the patio. And it's no wonder, considering the rich, juicy, incomparable goodness of homegrown, vine-ripened tomatoes and the pale, pulpy, tasteless specimens found in supermarkets.

New varieties appear annually, and today's tomatoes range in color from the traditional bright scarlet to orange, pink, and yellow. Some varieties such as the orange Caro-Red, are noted for their high vitamin content. Today's gardener can also choose among a variety of sizes: cherry-sized for plunking whole in salads or dips or directly into the mouth; mid-sized, pear-shaped, and meaty varieties for pastemaking; and two-pound mammoths for stuffing and slicing.

For the best taste and highest vitamin content, pick tomatoes when they're uniformly red but not soft. Peak ripeness usually comes about six days after the first color shows. To pick, do not pull the tomato from the plant. Instead, gently twist the fruit from its stem, taking care not to tear the branch. During the summer the plants should provide a steady supply of fresh fruit, and should be picked daily to maintain a high yield. Uncut, ripe tomatoes can be refrigerated, uncovered, for several days, though they taste best when eaten

with the warmth of the garden sun still on them. When the crop reaches its peak, extra tomatoes can be frozen for later cooking or canned whole or stewed, or as juice, sauce, catsup, soup, or preserves.

When frost threatens, most people still have unripe tomatoes on the vines. If they've begun to color they can be put on a warm, sunny windowsill to ripen slowly. They will not have quite the same flavor or vitamin content as vine-ripened tomatoes, but the fresh tomato season will be extended. Green fruit of full size can be wrapped individually in newspaper and placed about 3 layers deep in open crates or boxes. Store the boxes in a warm place, and the tomatoes will ripen without light. Some people pull up the entire plant, with unripe tomatoes still attached, and suspend it from the ceiling in the attic or basement to ripen slowly. When either method is used, the fruit should be checked frequently to prevent waste through spoilage. Smaller green tomatoes can be used for pickles or preserves, and can also be included in various kinds of cooked dishes.

When tomatoes are to be served raw, they should be cored and sliced just before the meal to preserve vitamins and juiciness. To use fresh tomatoes in cooking, it is sometimes necessary to peel them and squeeze out excess moisture and seeds. To peel, dip the tomato in boiling water for 1 minute and then immediately immerse it in cold water; drain, and peel. If the tomato is excessively watery or the recipe calls for the removal of seeds, slit the stem end and remove the core. Hold the tomato stem end down above a bowl, and press tightly to eject juice and seeds.

Three medium-sized tomatoes weigh about 1 pound and should serve three people. Ripe, red tomatoes have a high vitamin C content and are a fair to excellent source of vitamin A, depending on the variety. Orangey kinds, like the Caro-Red, are specially bred for high vitamin A content. If eaten when green, tomatoes provide less vitamin A, and more calories and carbohydrates.

BROILED TOMATOES

3 medium tomatoes, sliced
⅔ cup grated cheddar cheese
2 teaspoons wheat germ
1 tablespoon fresh parsley, minced
   grated Parmesan cheese

1. Place tomato slices in a single layer on a greased baking sheet.
2. Combine cheddar cheese, wheat germ, and parsley; sprinkle some of mixture on each tomato slice.
3. Top with Parmesan and broil until cheese is bubbly and brown. Serve immediately.

Makes 4 to 6 servings

HOMEMADE SPAGHETTI SAUCE

2 onions, chopped fine
4 cloves garlic, minced
⅛ cup olive oil or vegetable oil
12-14 medium tomatoes
½ cup minced green onions
1 green pepper, seeded and chopped
2 teaspoons salt
1 teaspoon freshly ground pepper
1 tablespoon oregano
¼ teaspoon rosemary
½ cup dry red wine

1. In a large frying pan, cook onions and garlic in oil until golden.
2. Plunge tomatoes in boiling water for a minute or so, and peel and quarter.
3. Add peeled tomatoes and all remaining ingredients to onion and garlic in frying pan and bring to a boil. Stir frequently and break up tomatoes. Simmer for 1 hour. Reduce mixture to 8 cups. Divide into two 4-cup servings and freeze.

Makes 8 cups

Note: This recipe helps solve the problem of what to do when the tomatoes start getting ahead of you. This makes a light sauce, preferable in many cases to the thicker "tomato sauce" types. Four short Italian sausages can be browned with the onions and garlic for a meaty flavor, or the sauce can be combined at serving time with browned hamburger or sausage that has been simmered and browned.

CHILLED TOMATO BASKETS

6 ripe, firm medium-sized tomatoes
  salt and pepper
2 cups cooked chicken, cubed
⅓ cup celery hearts, finely chopped
2 tablespoons chopped gherkins (sweet and sour)
½ cup mayonnaise
6 hard-boiled eggs, sliced
  small balls scooped from ripe avocado
  shredded lettuce
  watercress

1. Cut off and discard tops of tomatoes. Carefully scoop out pulp and seeds (save to use in a soup or green salad).
2. Rub insides of tomato shells with salt and pepper.
3. Combine chicken, celery, gherkins, mayonnaise, and eggs. Mix well and spoon into shells. Top with additional mayonnaise and a few avocado balls.
4. Chill and serve on a bed of shredded lettuce and watercress.

Makes 6 servings

GAZPACHO

2 large tomatoes
1 onion
1 green pepper
1 large cucumber
24 ounces tomato juice (2 cans)
¼ cup olive oil
⅓ cup red wine vinegar
  tabasco sauce to taste
  salt and freshly ground pepper to taste
1 cup garlic croutons
½ cup minced chives
1 lime, thinly sliced

1. Whirl in the blender 1 tomato, ½ onion, ½ green pepper, ½ cucumber and 1 cup of tomato juice until vegetables are pureed.
2. In a large glass jug, or pitcher with cover, combine the pureed vegetables, olive oil, vinegar, tabasco, salt, and pepper, and the remaining tomato juice. Stir or shake well.
3. Refrigerate at least 4 hours or overnight.
4. Chop separately the remaining vegetables and arrange on a tray with the garlic croutons and minced chives. Pass with a spoon for each person to garnish soup. Serve each bowl of soup with a slice of lime floating on top.

Makes 6 servings

Note: Gazpacho makes a great first course served on patio or porch. It can be served in mugs or large glasses. Omit the croutons and have spoons handy for those that want to scoop up the last bits of vegetables! A peeled garlic clove can be tossed into the blender with the vegetables if you think your guests are up to it.

CALYPSO SAUCE

tomatoes and small white onions, peeled and
chopped enough to fill a quart jar
1 or 2 cloves garlic, minced
1 small hot chili pepper, seeded and minced
2 whole cloves
1 teaspoon salt
3 whole peppercorns
1 tablespoon lime juice
vinegar

1. Combine all ingredients except vinegar, and place in a glass quart jar. Pour in vinegar to fill the jar.
2. Seal, and let stand at least a week before using as a barbecue sauce. Or use the sauce as a relish with broiled chicken or any roasted meat.

Makes 1 quart

BEST-EVER PICCALILI

12 medium-sized green tomatoes, chopped
1 cup chopped onions
3 green peppers, chopped
3 sweet red peppers, chopped
3 cups cider vinegar
¼ cup honey
2 tablespoons salt
1 teaspoon allspice
1 teaspoon cinnamon
2 teaspoons celery seeds
2 tablespoons mustard seeds

1. Wash and chop all vegetables, and place in a large pan. Add 2 cups vinegar and boil for 30 minutes, stirring frequently.
2. Drain and discard liquid, and return vegetables to pan; add remaining 1 cup of vinegar, honey, salt, and spices.
3. Simmer for 3 minutes. Pack into hot, sterilized jars, one at a time. Fill to one-eighth inch below top of jar and seal immediately.
4. Process in boiling water bath (212°F.) for 5 minutes.

Makes 3 pints

● *To keep cream of tomato soup from curdling, heat the milk and tomatoes separately, and add the tomatoes to the milk when both are hot, stirring constantly.*

DICK'S TOMATO JUICE

ripe tomatoes, quartered but not peeled, enough to nearly fill an 8-quart pot (about 8 pounds)
1 large cucumber, peeled and sliced
generous bouquet of parsley
2 medium onions, peeled and chopped
4 stalks celery, chopped
1 teaspoon celery salt
1 tablespoon salt
1 teaspoon pepper
½ teaspoon oregano

1. Place tomatoes in an 8-quart pot, mashing them down as you go. Add remaining ingredients.
2. Simmer over low heat, stirring occasionally, until onions and celery are tender. Put through a food mill, grinding and mashing the vegetables until there is no juice left in the pulp. If you prefer, puree the vegetables in the blender.
3. Pour into glass containers and refrigerate. Or, reheat juice to boiling point, pour into hot mason jars, seal and store.

Makes 4 quarts

Note: The secret of this delicious juice is that no water is added to the vegetables. It's pure juice. It also makes a delicious soup.

CHICKEN À LA GREEN TOMATO

Preheat oven to 350°F.

1 2-pound chicken, cut up
2 cups tomato sauce
4 green tomatoes
2 large onions, sliced
1 hot green pepper, chopped
½ zucchini, sliced
   oregano, salt, pepper, paprika, as desired

1. Take a baking dish and lay the chicken parts in it. Pour the tomato sauce over the chicken.
2. Cut up all vegetables, and add to chicken and sauce. Add the seasonings. Cover and bake at 350°F. for an hour. Uncover and continue baking until chicken is done.

Makes 4 to 6 servings

Note: Serve with a tossed green salad, hot buns. If you like, serve over a bed of brown rice.

SHRIMP CURRY WITH GREEN TOMATOES

Preheat oven to 300°F.

3 green tomatoes
1 medium onion
½ fresh zucchini or ½ yellow squash
¼ pound mushrooms
1 clove garlic (more if desired)
2 tablespoons butter
½ teaspoon salt
½ cup water
1 tablespoon curry
1 pound fresh shrimp, cooked, shelled, and deveined

CHEESE SAUCE:
   3 tablespoons butter
   2 tablespoons flour
   ½ cup milk
   ⅓ cup cheddar cheese, crumbled or diced

1. Slice tomatoes, onion, squash, mushrooms, and garlic. Melt butter in a large skillet over medium heat, and add vegetables and garlic. Add salt and water. Cover and let cook over medium heat, about 20 minutes.
2. Meanwhile, make sauce:
   Melt butter over medium heat. Add flour and blend. Add milk gradually, stirring constantly. Add cheese and stir until smooth.
3. Stir sauce into vegetable mixture. Add curry and shrimp and correct seasonings. Grease a casserole and pour in the mixture. Cover and bake for 20 to 30 minutes, until vegetables are tender.

Makes 4 to 6 servings

Note: Try serving this dish with cottage cheese, fresh sliced cucumbers, and baked potatoes. It's incredibly delicious.

● *Contrary to popular belief, tomatoes have been grown as food since the sixteenth century, though they have in various times and places been regarded as aphrodisiacs, and as both poisonous and decorative plants.*

HEARTY EGGS

3 cups cherry tomatoes
1 cup potato, diced
1 cup carrot, diced
1 clove garlic, minced
1 onion, minced
1 green pepper, diced
3 basil leaves, minced
4 eggs

1. In a heavy casserole combine the vegetables; cover and cook 20 minutes.
2. Stir in basil.
3. Carefully break eggs on top and cook until eggs are set.

Makes 4 servings

● *Slice tomatoes with the core when you want to keep in the juice, as in making sandwiches and salads. Slice against the core when you want to let the juice out, as for making sauces.*

TOMATO BEAN SALAD

3 cloves garlic
1 teaspoon oregano
¾ teaspoon salt
3 tablespoons olive oil
1 tablespoon wine vinegar
2 cups halved cherry tomatoes
2 cups cooked and chilled green beans
　　lettuce

1. Mince garlic and mix with oregano, salt, oil and vinegar.
2. Pour over the tomatoes and beans and chill.
3. Serve on a bed of lettuce.

Makes 4 to 6 servings

BAKED SPINACH-TOPPED TOMATOES

Preheat oven to 350°F.

1 medium onion, minced
1 large clove garlic, minced
¼ cup butter
2 pounds fresh spinach, chopped
1 cup whole wheat bread crumbs (dry)
2 eggs, beaten
2 teaspoons salt
4 large tomatoes, halved

1. In a 10-inch skillet over medium heat, cook onion and garlic in butter until tender (about 5 minutes).
2. Add spinach and cook a few minutes, until tender, separating and stirring occasionally; remove from heat and stir in crumbs, eggs, and salt. Set aside.
3. Place tomato halves, cut side up, in a 13 x 9 baking dish (if necessary, cut a thin slice from the bottom of each tomato so it stands upright).
4. Mound a scant half-cup of the spinach mixture onto each half; cover and refrigerate if done ahead of time, or place immediately in a 350°F. oven. Bake 25 minutes or until heated through.

Makes 8 servings

● *Here's an interesting way to preserve some of your excess tomatoes: Cut tomatoes in half-inch thick slices and dry (in a home dehydrator or in the oven set at lowest possible heat) until really crisp. Put these dried slices through a grain and seed mill, or grind as finely as possible in a food mill. Every 3 dozen tomatoes will make about a pint of the resulting crystals. The crystals can then be used to make an instant tomato soup by simply adding boiling water and seasonings. Use 1 teaspoonful of crystals per cup of boiling water.*

Turnips & Rutabagas

Are turnips anybody's favorite vegetable? A quick survey of cookbooks reveals that this root, despite its nontemperamental growing habits, its value as a storage crop, and its high vitamin C content, is consistently ignored or allotted a few recipes which seem intended more to disguise its flavor than to enhance it. Perhaps part of the problem is the way turnips are presented in supermarkets—oversize and overage, woody and bitter. Homegrown turnips, in contrast, when plucked young and firm from the ground, have a flavor delicate enough to be eaten raw, a flavor resembling a cross between a tart fresh apple and a crisp new radish.

There are several turnip varieties, some of which have been developed specifically for the production of greens. Turnip tops have a higher vitamin content than the roots, and when young and tender, they can be used raw in salads or steamed like spinach. Frost improves the flavor of some foliage varieties, in much the same way that it improves the flavor of kale.

The roots should be pulled when they are two to three inches in diameter. Larger roots are apt to be coarse and bitter. They should be dug before the ground freezes for the best keeping qualities, but if the autumn weather is mild, they can be left in the garden until Thanksgiving. Harvest the roots by pulling at the base of the leaves. For short-term storage, cut off the greens, and place them in a cool, damp place or in the crisper drawer of the refrigerator.

Turnip roots can be frozen, but the easiest way to store them is in an outdoor storage pit or in a root cellar. For this kind of storage they should be topped, but not washed, and packed in straw or moist sand.

Before cooking, turnips should be scrubbed and have their tops and roots removed. Unless the turnips are quite young, the skins tend to be bitter, and the roots should be peeled as thinly as possible. Older turnips can be improved by blanching them for three to five minutes before cooking as directed in the recipe. Turnips can be steamed or baked, cooked whole, sliced, diced, or grated. About 2 pounds of turnips will serve four people. Turnips contain vitamin C, calcium and other assorted minerals.

RUTABAGAS

Rutabagas are a hybrid of turnips and the cabbage family. Though they are also known as winter, yellow, or Swedish turnips, they are actually bigger and hardier than the common globe turnip, and take from four to six weeks longer to mature. Rutabagas can be used as soon as they are mature, but their flavor improves if they are left in the ground until after the first frost. They should not be allowed to freeze, however, or their keeping qualities will be impaired.

Rutabagas can be stored in the same way as turnips; in fact, some gardeners say they keep far better in storage than turnips. As always, only the most perfect rutabagas should be set aside for storage. To test each one's soundness, tap it with the knife handle after trimming off roots and tops. If it makes a solid ringing sound, like the sound made when you tap on your elbow, it should store well. To prevent sprouting during storage, slice about ½ inch into the globe when removing the tops.

Like turnips, rutabagas can be glazed, baked like potatoes, and used in casseroles, stews, soups, and fritters. They are slightly higher in nutritional content than turnips, having a good quantity of vitamin A and C and supplying significant amounts of iron, thiamin, riboflavin, and niacin.

COUNTRY-FRIED TURNIPS

2 tablespoons butter
1 pound turnips, peeled and cut in thick slices
¾ cup chicken or beef stock
1 tablespoon lemon juice

1. Melt butter in a large skillet. Add turnips and cook over low heat until turnips start to soften.
2. Add stock, cover, and simmer until turnips are tender, then remove lid and let some of the liquid cook down to leave a sauce.
3. Sprinkle with lemon juice and serve.

Makes 6 servings

Note: Call these country-fries, and turnip haters will think they're eating potatoes.

MASHED RUTABAGA

1¾ pounds rutabagas, scrubbed and peeled
   salt to taste
1 tablespoon butter
¼ cup milk
   dash of nutmeg, or ½ teaspoon chopped, fresh mint

1. Dice rutabagas and steam 15 to 20 minutes, until tender.
2. Drain, add salt to taste, butter, and enough milk to make a smooth consistency.
3. Mash like potatoes and serve immediately, sprinkled with nutmeg or mint.

Makes 4 servings

● *Some cooks tell us that you can substitute boiled, mashed rutabaga in a pumpkin pie recipe and hardly know the difference.*

273

TURNIPS WITH HOT LEMON DRESSING

1 pound yellow turnips, or rutabagas
2 tablespoons butter or oil
½ tablespoon lemon juice
   salt and pepper to taste
1 tablespoon chopped fresh parsley

1. Pare and cut turnips into 1- to 2-inch pieces. Steam until tender, 15 to 20 minutes.
2. Heat butter, lemon juice, salt and pepper to taste, and parsley, for a minute. Pour over hot turnips in serving dish.

Makes 4 servings

GARDEN SUKIYAKI

1 cup sliced turnips or parsnips
2 cups sliced zucchini or other summer squash
½ cup sliced leeks
1 cup cauliflower slices
2 cups sugar peas
1 cup sliced carrots
3 cups sliced beet greens or other greens
1 pound mung or lentil sprouts
½ pound *tofu*, optional
2 pounds round steak, pork or boned chicken
3 tablespoons oil
3 tablespoons tamari soy sauce
1 tablespoon honey
3 tablespoons cornstarch
3 tablespoons sherry

1. Slice all vegetables into uniform strips, about 2 inches long and 1 inch wide and ⅛ inch thick; cut the zucchini, carrots, and parsnips lengthwise. Keep each variety separate. Sugar peas and sprouts can be left whole. The greens can be chopped in 2- by 2-inch pieces.

2. If the meat is partially frozen, it is easier to slice. Cut it into pieces about the same size as the vegetables.
3. Combine soy sauce, honey, cornstarch, and sherry and set aside.
4. Heat a *wok,* Dutch oven, or very large skillet to medium-hot. Add the oil and sauté the meat, stirring often. When it's almost done, add the turnips, squash, leeks, carrots, and cauliflower, stirring to coat vegetables with oil and meat juices.
5. Cover and cook briefly until vegetables are barely tender. Check and stir often, as it doesn't take long to cook these small pieces.
6. Add the greens, peas, and *tofu* and cook until greens get a bit wilted. Stir often.
7. Add the sprouts last.
8. Pour soy sauce mixture into the juices in the pan (just move aside the vegetables a bit). Cook and stir until the sauce thickens (about a minute).
9. Serve immediately.

Makes 8 servings

Note: The variety of this dish is as endless as the things you like to eat. Green beans, shredded cabbage and broccoli are just some of the other vegetables that can be used in this dish.

TURNIPS WITH APPLES

1 pound turnips or rutabagas, pared and cut into small
    pieces
3 tart apples, pared and thinly sliced
    salt and pepper to taste
    butter
    cinnamon

1. Steam turnips over boiling water until soft, about 20 minutes. Add apple slices and steam a few more minutes until soft. Remove from heat.
2. Mash together turnips and apples, seasoning with salt, pepper, and butter to taste. Sprinkle with cinnamon.

Makes 4 servings

AUNTIE BETTY'S BREW HA-HA

1 cup brown rice
½ cup bulgur
3 tablespoons soy grits
3½ cups water
¼ teaspoon salt
½ pound ground beef
3 to 4 carrots, sliced
2 turnips, sliced
1 pepper, sliced in strips
1 large onion, sliced
½ pound mushrooms, optional
1 to 2 cups tomatoes, fresh or canned
2 teaspoons oregano
1½ teaspoons basil
1 teaspoon marjoram
1 teaspoon dried mint
   salt and cayenne pepper to taste
   tamari soy sauce to taste
   oil as needed

1. Place rice, bulgur and soy grits in a saucepan, along with the water and salt. Cover tightly and bring to a boil, then simmer 40 minutes, or until water is absorbed.
2. Meanwhile, brown the ground beef.
3. Sauté the carrots, turnips, pepper, and onion in *wok* or cast-iron skillet until still somewhat crisp. Add the mushrooms and continue sautéing.
4. When all vegetables are almost tender, add the tomatoes, cooked grains, ground beef, and seasonings. Continue to simmer together for 10 to 15 minutes to allow flavors to blend.
5. Serve with extra soy sauce and gomazio (found on page 290).

Makes 6 servings

Note: Serve this dish with a fresh salad for a complete meal.

- *Don't forget to save your vitamin-rich turnip tops to cook as greens.*

TURNIP CHEESE BAKE

Preheat oven to 350°F.

2 cups boiled diced turnips
1 cup cottage cheese
1 cup yogurt or buttermilk
1 cup grated cheddar cheese
1 tablespoon minced parsley
½ cup chopped onion
2 eggs, beaten
1 clove garlic, minced
1 tablespoon fresh marjoram
½ teaspoon salt

Mix all ingredients together. Pour into buttered baking dish and bake at 350°F. for 40 minutes.

Makes 4 to 6 servings

● *Turnips and rutabagas are a welcome addition to stews and vegetable soups. They also make fine complements to game dishes.*

SWEDISH TURNIPS AND POTATOES

2 cups cooked, mashed rutabagas
1 cup cooked, mashed potatoes
4 tablespoons top milk
2 tablespoons grated onion
⅛ teaspoon nutmeg
   salt and pepper to taste
1 to 2 tablespoons melted butter
1 tablespoon chopped parsley

1. Whip mashed rutabagas and potatoes together with milk, onion, nutmeg, salt and pepper.
2. Top with melted butter and parsley and serve piping hot.

Makes 6 servings

RUTABAGAS AND CARROTS

1½ cups shredded rutabaga
  salt and freshly ground pepper, to taste
½ cup shredded carrot
¼ cup minced onion
3 tablespoons oil

1. Cook rutabaga in a small amount of water until tender. Drain, season with salt and pepper and place in a serving dish.
2. Meanwhile, sauté carrot and onion in oil until tender. Drain.
3. Make a depression in the center of the rutabaga and mound the carrot-onion mixture inside. Serve piping hot.

Makes 3 to 4 servings

● *Be sure to keep the pot tightly covered when cooking turnips to preserve their clean white color.*

● *A pound of raw turnips will make about two cups cooked.*

TURNIPS GLAZED WITH HONEY

6 small whole white turnips, unpared
1 tablespoon honey
1 tablespoon butter or oil
  salt to taste
  cinnamon to taste

1. Steam whole turnips until tender, about ½ hour. Mix together honey, butter or oil, salt, and cinnamon in small saucepan.
2. Heat over low flame for about a minute. Pour immediately over hot turnips and turn turnips gently until well coated. Garnish with fresh parsley.

Makes 3 to 6 servings

Accompaniments

The fine flavors of garden-fresh vegetables should never be smothered under piles of heavy sauces and gloppy gravies. But the right finishing touches, applied with discretion, can really highlight the special goodness of vegetables picked in their prime and prepared to perfection.

This section is devoted to dressings, dips, sauces, pie crusts, and other extras that provide just the right accent to the naturally delicious tastes of your fresh vegetables.

VEGETABLE DIP #1

1 cup oil
½ cup vinegar
1 cup yogurt or sour cream
1 teaspoon dill

Blend all ingredients until smooth, and add one or more of the following:

grated sharp cheese
crumbled blue cheese
chopped olives
chopped white onion
chopped parsley
sunflower seeds
soy nuts

Makes 2½ to 3 cups

VEGETABLE DIP #2

1½ to 2 cups ricotta cheese
¼ cup finely chopped onion
¼ cup finely chopped chili peppers (Fresnos or other
mild ones)
¼ cup finely chopped radish
1 clove garlic, minced
1 teaspoon dill
yogurt to thin

Blend all ingredients and serve with vegetables or whole grain crackers.

Makes 2½ to 3 cups

HORSERADISH DIP

1 cup yogurt
1 tablespoon horseradish (or more, to taste)
½ teaspoon salt
¼ teaspoon paprika

Combine all ingredients and chill.

Makes about 1 cup

YOGURT DRESSING #1

1 cup yogurt
2 tomatoes
1 avocado and/or 1 cup spinach
¼ cup chopped parsley
1 onion
½ cup mayonnaise
    gomazio or tamari soy sauce to taste

Place all ingredients in blender and blend until smooth.

Makes 2 to 2½ cups

YOGURT DRESSING #2

1 cup yogurt
4 tablespoons lemon juice
¼ to ½ teaspoon dry mustard
1 clove garlic, minced
½ teaspoon salt
½ to 1 teaspoon paprika

Combine ingredients and let stand in refrigerator before serving.

Makes about 1¼ cups

OIL AND VINEGAR DRESSING #1

1 tablespoon fresh lemon juice (½ lemon)
4 tablespoons vinegar
⅔ cup oil
   few drops of onion juice
¼ teaspoon salt

Combine all ingredients and shake well.

Makes 1 cup

OIL AND VINEGAR DRESSING #2

1 cup safflower oil
½ cup tarragon vinegar
½ teaspoon salt
1 clove garlic, crushed
1 teaspoon basil
1 teaspoon oregano
1 teaspoon kelp powder

Shake all ingredients together.

Makes 1½ cups

HERB DRESSING

2 cups oil
1 cup apple cider or wine vinegar
1 teaspoon thyme, basil, tarragon, or dill (or a combination of them)
1 to 2 cloves garlic
½ teaspoon salt

Combine all ingredients and blend in blender until smooth.

Makes 3 cups

CELERY SEED DRESSING

¾ cup honey
4 teaspoons dry mustard or 2 teaspoons prepared
   (Dijon) mustard
1 quart corn oil
1⅓ cups apple cider vinegar
1¾ tablespoons celery seed
   juice of one lemon

1. Place honey and mustard in mixing bowl or blender. Slowly add oil, vinegar, celery seed, and lemon juice while first two ingredients are mixing.
2. Beat or blend until creamy—which doesn't take long. Store in glass jars and keep refrigerated. Makes a tasty marinade for cucumbers or baby beets thinly sliced.

Makes about 5½ cups

VINAIGRETTE SAUCE

½ cup olive oil
¼ cup tarragon or wine vinegar
1 tablespoon minced chives or onion
2 tablespoons chopped parsley
½ teaspoon salt
¼ teaspoon paprika
   pepper to taste
1 tablespoon chopped sweet pickle, optional
1 tablespoon chopped pimiento, optional

1. Blend oil and vinegar in blender; add remaining ingredients and blend briefly.
2. Chill before serving.

Makes about 1 cup

NO-OIL SALAD DRESSING

3 tablespoons vinegar
2 hard-boiled eggs
1 teaspoon dried tarragon
1 clove garlic (to taste)
¼ cup yogurt
   fresh basil as desired

Combine all ingredients in blender and blend until smooth.

Makes about ½ cup

BLENDER MAYONNAISE

1 egg
3 tablespoons cider vinegar
1 teaspoon honey
½ teaspoon salt
½ teaspoon dry mustard, optional
1¼ cups oil

1. Place egg, vinegar, honey, salt, and mustard in blender and blend well.
2. Pour in the oil slowly, in a thin stream, while blender is running. Continue to blend until mayonnaise is thick and smooth.
3. Remove mayonnaise with a small rubber spatula and refrigerate in a glass jar. Mayonnaise will thicken as it chills.

Makes 1½ cups

GREEN MAYONNAISE

1 cup mayonnaise
2 tablespoons minced fresh parsley

2 tablespoons minced fresh chives
2 tablespoons minced fresh tarragon or dill
2 tablespoons minced spinach or watercress

Combine all ingredients and chill.

Makes 1¼ cups

Note: A piquant topping for cold vegetable dishes, especially welcome in summer.

MOCK HOLLANDAISE or MAYONNAISE SAUCE

½ cup mayonnaise
2 tablespoons milk or cream
⅛ teaspoon salt
1 tablespoon lemon juice

1. Combine mayonnaise, milk and salt in the top of a double boiler, over hot water.
2. Heat for 3 to 5 minutes, then stir in lemon juice and serve hot.

Makes about ⅔ cup

HOLLANDAISE SAUCE

½ cup oil
2 egg yolks, beaten
juice of half a lemon
½ teaspoon salt
dash of pepper
½ cup boiling water

1. In the top of a double boiler, pour the oil and slowly add the beaten egg yolks. Add lemon juice, salt, and pepper, then boiling water.
2. Cook over boiling water, stirring constantly, until the sauce takes on the consistency of a thin custard. Serve at once.

Makes about 1 cup

MORNAY SAUCE

2 tablespoons butter
2 tablespoons unbleached flour
1½ cups milk
   salt and pepper to taste
¼ cup grated Swiss cheese
¼ cup grated Parmesan cheese

1. Melt butter in a saucepan; blend in flour to make a *roux*. Stir in milk and cook, stirring, until thickened.
2. Add salt and pepper, and stir in cheeses until melted, and sauce is smooth. Serve at once.

Makes about 2 cups

Note: Serve this mellow sauce over mild-tasting vegetables, whose flavors would be overwhelmed by a tangier sauce.

VELOUTÉ SAUCE

2 tablespoons butter
2 tablespoons unbleached flour
2 cups chicken or vegetable stock
   salt and pepper to taste
   pinch of nutmeg

1. Melt butter in a saucepan; blend in flour to make a *roux*. Stir in stock and cook, stirring, until thickened.
2. Add seasonings and serve piping hot.

Makes about 2 cups

SUNRISE SAUCE

2 tablespoons butter
1 bay leaf
1 clove garlic, crushed
2 tablespoons unbleached flour
2 cups chicken or vegetable stock
1 to 2 tablespoons tomato puree or paste
  salt and pepper to taste
  pinch of marjoram

1. Melt butter in a saucepan; add bay leaf and garlic, and sauté gently for a few minutes. Remove bay leaf.
2. Blend in flour to make a *roux*. Stir in stock, add bay leaf, and cook, stirring, until thickened.
3. Stir in tomato puree, salt and pepper, and marjoram. Heat briefly, remove bay leaf, and serve at once.

Makes about 2¼ cups

Note: Try this sauce over your favorite steamed vegetables for a new taste sensation.

QUICK DILL SAUCE

2 tablespoons butter
2 tablespoons unbleached or whole wheat flour
1 cup chicken or vegetable stock
½ cup milk
  salt and pepper to taste
¼ cup chopped fresh dill

1. Melt butter in a saucepan; blend in flour to make a *roux*. Add stock and cook, stirring, until thickened.
2. Add salt, pepper and dill, and stir well.

Makes about 2 cups

BLUSHING BEET SAUCE

¾ cup beet liquid (juice from cooked beets)
1 tablespoon honey
1 tablespoon apple cider vinegar
2 tablespoons flour

1. In a small saucepan bring the beet stock, honey, and vinegar to a boil.
2. Stir in flour and cook until smooth and thickened.

Makes about 1 cup

Note: This sauce is especially good over cooked beet greens. Use it on all cooked greens.

MINTED BUTTER SAUCE

½ cup minced mint leaves
½ cup butter, softened
2 tablespoons fresh lemon juice

1. Rub mint leaves and butter to a paste. Add lemon juice and beat until creamy.
2. Store in refrigerator until needed. Goes appetizingly well with broccoli, carrots, or beets, added just before serving.

Makes enough sauce for 8 servings of vegetables

BLACK BUTTER

¼ cup clarified butter
1 teaspoon lemon juice or vinegar

1. Melt butter in a small pan and cook over low heat until very dark brown in color.

2. Stir in lemon juice and serve at once.

Makes 4 servings

Note: It's important to use clarified butter for this recipe, or else the black butter will taste bitter. To make clarified butter, melt butter in a saucepan; remove from heat and let stand until sediment forms on bottom. Skim the butterfat from the top and strain the liquid. Refrigerate until needed.

LEMON BUTTER

¼ cup butter, softened
2 teaspoons lemon juice
1 teaspoon chopped fresh parsley
  pinch of salt

Whip butter and beat in remaining ingredients. Chill for several hours to blend flavors.

Makes 3 to 4 servings

HERB BUTTER

½ cup butter, softened
1 tablespoon lemon juice
1 tablespoon chopped fresh parsley
1 tablespoon chopped fresh chives

Whip butter and beat in lemon juice and herbs. Chill several hours to blend flavors.

Makes 6 servings

Variation: If you prefer, substitute 2 tablespoons of chopped fresh basil, tarragon, or other herbs of your choice for the parsley and chives.

BASIL PASTE

To those who love the pungent taste of fresh basil during the summer, the dried herb is a real disappointment. Here is a way to store basil for the winter and still preserve much of its zesty flavor for use in your favorite vegetable dishes.

Put leaves and stems of fresh basil into the blender. Slowly add enough olive oil to form a smooth paste. (If you like, some garlic can be added to the paste as well.) Store the paste in small jars, keeping the one you're using in the refrigerator. Use the paste wherever you use fresh basil during the summer.

GOMAZIO OR SESAME SALT

Preheat oven to 250°F.

1 pound sesame seeds, preferably unhulled
¼ cup salt

1. Toast the sesame seeds in a warm oven (250°F.) for 20 minutes, or until lightly browned.
2. Add the salt slowly, to taste.
3. Blend and store in an airtight container. Use as a general seasoning on salads, vegetables, and casseroles.

Makes 2 cups

VERMONT CRACKERS

Preheat oven to 375°F.

2 cups whole wheat flour
½ cup cornmeal
½ teaspoon salt
½ cup butter
¼ cup safflower oil
8 tablespoons milk
 liquid lecithin for oiling pans

1. Measure and sift dry ingredients together.
2. Cut in butter with pastry blender.
3. Add safflower oil and milk to make a stiff dough.
4. Roll out as thin as possible. Cut with cookie cutters or cut with a knife. Liquid lecithin can be used to oil cookie pans.
5. Crackers can be glazed with egg glaze and sprinkled with sesame seeds, poppy seeds, cheese, garlic salt, or any variation desired.
6. Bake at 375°F. for 6 to 7 minutes. Turn crackers over with a spatula and bake for a few more minutes until done.

Makes about 40 crackers

SESAME CRISPS

Preheat oven to 300°F.

1 cup raw short-grain brown rice
  salt to taste
3 tablespoons unhulled sesame seeds
  liquid lecithin for "greasing" the pan

1. Bring 1 cup raw short-grain rice to a boil in 3 cups water. Turn down to a simmer and let cook for 45 minutes. Drain, set aside all but 1 cup for another use.
2. Combine the 1 cup of mushy rice with salt to taste and the sesame seeds. Mash with a potato masher or fork. On a flat surface, pat out rice mixture between two sheets of wax paper the same size as your baking sheet. Roll out as thin as possible with a rolling pin. Gently peel off the top sheet of wax paper. Then turn bottom sheet of paper (with the rice on it) upside down onto the baking sheet which has been coated with lecithin. Gently peel off this paper, using a knife to loosen stubborn spots. Score with knife in desired shapes.
3. Bake in preheated oven at 300°F. for 45 minutes, or until golden in color. Let cool 5 minutes before removing crackers from pan.

Makes about 2 dozen crackers

WHOLE WHEAT-RICE PIE CRUST

Preheat oven to 425°F.

1 cup whole wheat pastry flour, sifted
1 cup brown rice flour
¾ teaspoon salt
4 tablespoons butter
3 tablespoons oil
5 tablespoons ice water

1. Sift flours and salt together.
2. Using pastry cutter, cut in the butter and oil, until mixture resembles coarse crumbs.
3. Add ice water, kneading slightly to form a ball of dough.
4. Roll out half of the dough between sheets of wax paper and press into pie plate (9 inch). Roll out the second half.
5. Bake in preheated oven, 425°F. When used for *quiche* the dough can be baked, before the *quiche* is added, for 15 minutes at 425°F. then add *quiche,* lowering oven to 375°F.

Makes 2 9-inch pie crusts

WHOLE WHEAT PIE CRUST

4 cups whole wheat flour
1½ teaspoons salt
1½ cups butter
2 tablespoons white vinegar
1 egg
¼ cup water

1. Combine whole wheat flour and salt. Cut in butter.
2. Beat vinegar, egg, and water in another bowl.

3. Combine the two mixtures, stirring until moistened. Then work with your hands to form a ball. From this make 4 dough balls for 4 single crusts. These *must* be well chilled before rolling out.
4. Roll each chilled dough ball between pieces of waxed paper and then place in 10-inch pie pan, making a fluted edge on outside.
5. When baking crust without filling, prick bottom with a fork. Bake at 400°F. for 10 to 12 minutes.

Makes 4 single pie crusts

Note: These unbaked dough balls can be kept for about three days in the refrigerator if well wrapped. Or you may freeze the dough balls until you need them.

HARVEST TIMES AND TECHNIQUES AT A GLANCE

Artichokes	Cut stem 1½ inches below base of head, when head is still compact, tightly closed, and bright green in color.
Jerusalem Artichokes	Dig tubers any time after first frost, and throughout winter.
Asparagus	Snap off stalks at ground level when spears are 6 to 8 inches above ground, and tips are still compact. Harvest in third year after planting.
Snap Beans	Snap off pods just below stem end, when 3 to 4 inches long, tips are soft, and beans are still small inside pods.
Lima Beans	Pick when beans are green and tender in pods, before they grow large and fully plump.
Beets	Pull up plants when roots are a few inches in diameter.
Broccoli	Cut head with several inches of stem attached, when heads are firm, and dark green or purplish green in color.
Brussels Sprouts	Twist off individual sprouts when 1 to 2 inches in diameter, firm and bright green.
Cabbage, Red and Green	Cut through stem at base of head, when head is solid and color is good, before head splits.
Celery Cabbage	Pull up plants when stalks have thickened into compact, cylindrical heads.
Carrots	Dig before roots exceed 4 inches in length and 1 inch in diameter.

Cauliflower	Cut stem well below head, when curds are compact and firm, about 1 to 2 weeks after leaves have been tied.
Celery	Cut roots below soil surface any time after plants are half grown.
Celeriac	Dig bulb any time after stem at ground level exceeds 2 inches in thickness, throughout winter if weather is mild.
Swiss Chard	Cut outer leaves when 7 inches high; inner leaves will be ready about a week later.
Corn	Cut ears when silks are dry and brown, ears are full, and kernels pass milk test.
Cucumbers	Cut from vine with some stem attached when finger-sized for pickling, 5 inches long for eating.
Eggplant	Cut stem when fruit is 4 inches in diameter and 6 inches long, skin is firm and glossy.
Beet Greens	Pick individual leaves when young and tender, or cut when roots are harvested.
Collards	Cut whole young plants or tender leaves from top, after a few light frosts.
Dandelions	Dig in early spring, when leaves are small, and before flowers bloom.
Endive and Escarole	Pull up plants in late fall, before a hard frost.
Kale	Cut whole plant or pick larger leaves while still young, after a few frosts.
Turnip Greens	Pick individual leaves while young and still tender.

Watercress	Cut when young and still light green in color.
Kohlrabi	Pull up plants when bulbs are 2 inches in diameter.
Lettuce	Cut heads when full formed; cut loose leaf varieties at ground level, when outer leaves are ready. Harvest early in the day.
Mushrooms	Twist off stem at ground level when cap has broken away from stem.
Okra	Pick pods before they exceed 4 inches in length, when still soft.
Onions and Garlic	Pull and allow to cure a few days after tops shrivelled and fallen to the ground.
Scallions	Pull before bulbs have formed.
Leeks	Dig any time after matured in fall, and throughout winter.
Parsnips	Dig any time after first frost, and throughout winter.
Peas	Hold vine with one hand and pull off pods with the other, when pods are bright green, velvety, and well filled.
Sugar Peas	Pick before pods fill with peas.
Sweet and Hot Peppers	Cut with ½ inch of stem attached, when still solid and green, or after mature and red.
Potatoes	Dig tubers on a dry day, any time up to 6 weeks after vines have withered.
Sweet Potatoes and Yams	Cut vines and carefully dig tubers as soon as first frost has hit the leaves.

Radishes	Pull early and summer varieties as soon as fully grown; winter varieties may be left in ground until frost.
Rhubarb	Grasp stalk near base and twist away from crown, when stalk is 1 inch thick and 10 inches long.
Salsify	Dig any time after first frost, and throughout winter.
Soybeans	To use green, pick pods when rounded and mature, before they start to turn yellow; to use dried, pick pods just as they are dry, while stems are still green.
Spinach	Pull plant when 6 or more of its leaves are 7 inches long, or pick individual outer leaves when ready.
Sprouts	Use sprouts when 1 to 2 inches long.
Summer Squash	Pick when young and skins are soft—patty pan when 1 to 4 inches in diameter, others before they are 8 inches long.
Winter Squash and Pumpkins	Cut from vine with an inch of stem attached, when fully mature and rind is hard, but a week or 2 before first frost.
Tomatoes	Twist fruit from stem when uniformly red, but not soft; pick any unripened tomatoes before first frost.
Turnips	Harvest by pulling at base of leaves, when roots are 2 to 3 inches in diameter, before ground freezes.
Rutabagas	Dig after first frost, but before ground freezes.

COMPLEMENTARY HERBS FOR VEGETABLES

Vegetables	Herbs
Artichokes	parsley, basil, tarragon
Jerusalem Artichokes	parsley, dill, thyme, marjoram, rosemary, celery seed, mustard seed
Asparagus	parsley, chives, tarragon, thyme
Snap Beans	parsley, dill, oregano, thyme, rosemary, savory, basil, chives, marjoram, chervil
Lima Beans	parsley, dill, thyme, rosemary, savory, basil, chives, marjoram
Beets	parsley, basil, dill, chives
Broccoli	sage, parsley, oregano, caraway, chervil, dill, rosemary
Brussels Sprouts	chives
Cabbage, Red and Green	parsley, basil, dill, bay leaf, sage, tarragon, oregano, thyme, caraway seed, poppy seed, celery seed
Celery Cabbage	chives, dill
Carrots	parsley, mint, chives, basil
Cauliflower	parsley, chives, basil, tarragon, basil, thyme, rosemary, savory
Celery	parsley, basil, dill, oregano, chervil
Celeriac	parsley
Swiss Chard	parsley, basil, oregano, marjoram, thyme
Corn	parsley, chives, basil, oregano, celery seed
Cucumbers	celery seed, chives, dill, bay leaf, parsley, mustard seed, celery seed, basil, chervil
Eggplant	parsley, basil, chervil, sage, oregano, thyme, tarragon

Vegetables	Herbs
Greens	basil, dill, parsley, oregano, tarragon, chives
Kohlrabi	dill, basil, parsley
Lettuce	basil, chives, chervil, dill, mint, mustard seed, oregano, parsley, tarragon
Mushrooms	parsley, basil, chives, tarragon, rosemary, thyme, marjoram
Okra	parsley, dill, basil, thyme, bay leaf, chives
Onions	parsley, dill, chives, rosemary, thyme, mint, tarragon
Parsnips	parsley dill, sage
Peas, Sweet and Sugar	parsley, dill, mint, basil, marjoram
Peppers	parsley, sage, thyme, rosemary, chervil, marjoram, savory, basil, oregano, tarragon, chives
Potatoes	parsley, basil, chives, mint, dill, caraway seeds
Sweet Potatoes and Yams	parsley, chives
Radishes	parsley, chives
Salsify or Oyster Plant	parsley, tarragon
Soybeans	parsley, basil, dill, thyme, sage, bay leaf
Spinach	basil, dill, oregano, parsley, tarragon, chives
Sprouts	parsley, thyme, basil, chives
Summer Squash	parsley, basil, thyme, oregano, mint, marjoram, rosemary, chives
Winter Squash and Pumpkins	parsley, basil, chives, thyme
Tomatoes	parsley, oregano, chives, basil, rosemary, bay leaf, dill, mint, thyme
Turnips and Rutabagas	parsley, marjoram, mint, basil, oregano, bay leaf, celery seed

Index